JUNE 4, 2017

TO: CA

Here is a gift for you and your family. I'm very grateful that you gave me much love while raising me in my first couple of years in the church, especially asking me sweetly to shave my moustache.

Thank you for loving and attending True Parents all these years, especially your 42 years of foreign mission work. God bless you!!!

Ken Owens

Memoirs of a Unification Church Photographer

Or

How I became Mr. Smile Please
by Ken Owens

COPYRIGHT PAGE

Copyright © 2016 by Ken Owens

All rights reserved. All photos are copyrighted © by HSA-UWC, HSA-UWC New Future Photo, or by members of HSA-UWC. This book or any portion thereof may not be reproduced or used in any manner whatsoever without the express written permission of the publisher or HSA-UWC except for the use of brief quotations in a book review.

Printed in the United States of America
First Printing
ISBN-13: 978-1533047755
ISBN-10: 1533047758
Printed by Createspace Publishing
4960 La Cross Road
N. Charleston, SC 29706
Cover design by Jonathan Gullery

I dedicate this book to our True Parents, The Rev. and Mrs. Sun Myung Moon; my parents John and Frances Owens; Karrin Louise Westerdale Brady who introduced me to the Unification Church; and to my wife, Meeyung Cho Owens, who gave birth to our three beautiful children.

Explanation of Terminology

There are several terms that I use that may be new to those who are not in the Unification Church.

Rev. Sun Myung Moon was called by Jesus to fulfill his mission on Earth as the Third Adam. Because he fulfilled everything Jesus asked him to do, Rev. Moon is called "True Father."

Mrs. Hak Ja Han Moon was chosen by Rev. Moon to accomplish the mission that "Eve" should have accomplished in her role with Adam. Because of her absolute faith and obedience, Mrs. Moon fulfilled her role and is known as "True Mother."

Together, Rev. and Mrs. Moon are known as the "True Parents."

Table of Contents

Introduction 1

Chapter 1 3
   Early life and San Francisco 3

Chapter 2 11
   True Parents in Hawaii 1974 11

Chapter 3 15
   Barrytown 15
   Forty Hour Street Preaching 15
   True Parents Visit 16
   One Brother's Experience Pioneering 16
   A Vision 17

Chapter 4 19
   Mobile Fundraising Team 19
   Introduction to MFT 19
   Getting Mugged in Boston 20
   Original World Products 21

Chapter 5 22
   Yankee Stadium 22

Chapter 6 25
   Washington Monument 25

Chapter 7 29
   New Future Photo 29
   Talking Out Loud 30

Chapter 8 31
   East Garden 31
   First Visit 31
   True Parents Arrivals 31
   Four Cake Surprise 36
   Waiting at the Stairs 36
   True Father Kissing True Mother 37
   Carpet 38
   Offering Tray 38

- True Mother 39
- Security 39
- Young Children 40
- Hudson River Photo 41
- Singing to True Parents 42
- Birthdays 43
- Surprise Assistant 45
- Mr. Smile Please 46
- Night of Danbury 47
- Tie Signal 47
- True Mother and the Stairs 48
- Cake Candles 48
- Page 1021 48
- Julie's Name 49
- Honeymooners 49
- Rescue 50
- Moon Over East Garden 50

Chapter 9 54
- Belvedere 54
- True Father and the Dog 54
- Won Pil Kim Photo 54
- Heung Jin Nim 55
- Very Early Arrival 57

Chapter 10 58
- Heung Jin Nim and Victory over Communism Tour 1983-84 58

Chapter 11 61
- 1984 Court Decision 61

Chapter 12 63
- True Mother's South America-Asia Tour 63

Chapter 13 64
- Ocean Church – Cape Cod 64

Chapter 14 68
- Holy Days 68
- God's Day and the Elevator 68
- True Mother's Arm 68
- Holding the Microphone 69

Chapter 15 70
Matchings 70
New Yorker Hotel 1979 70
Korea 71
Photo Matching in East Garden 71
Second Generation at East Garden 72
I Guessed Right 73
My Matching 74

Chapter 16 77
Blessings 77

Chapter 17 81
ICUS, AWR, WMA, WFWP, WCSF 81

Chapter 18 84
Kodiak 84
True Father's Snack 84
True Mother and Kwon Jin Nim 85

Chapter 19 86
Kirov Ballet in Russia 86

Chapter 20 89
Gorbachev at Kremlin 89
and 89
The Little Angels 89

Chapter 21 94
North Korea 94

Chapter 22 96
Birth of My Children 96
   Julie Meesun 96
   Leilani Unhye 96
   Douglas Hyo-yung 97

Chapter 23 99
Kwon Jin Nim-Sun Jin Nim's 99
Blessing 99

Chapter 24 100
South American Tour 100

Chapter 25 103
The Pantanal Workshop 103

Chapter 26 106
- Speaking Tours 106
- Flying Over Denver 114

Chapter 27 117
- Qatar 117

Chapter 28 118
- Middle East Peace Initiative 118
- Jerusalem Declaration 122
- Coronation of Jesus 123

The First Visit to Gaza 125
- Native Americans in Israel 125
- Yassar Arafat's Funeral 127
- The Women's Pilgrimage 127
- Martin Luther King III 128
- The Security Checkpoint at Gaza 128
- Special Event in Nazareth 129

Chapter 29 131
- Gratitude for Korean War Veterans 131

Chapter 30 138
- Hyo Jin Nim A Filial Son 138

Chapter 31 142
- DREAMS 142
- Dream of New Son 142
- True Mother and Texas 143
- True Father and Photographs 143

Chapter 32 144
- ARTICLES 144
- Advice to Young People 144
- Does Homosexuality Have a Universal Basis for Existence? 146

Chapter 33 152
- Coronation of God 2001 152

Chapter 34 154
- Cheon Jeong Gung Peace Palace 154

Chapter 35 158
- Fourth World Tour 2006 158

Chapter 36 164
First International Cattle Drive for Peace and Unity 164

Chapter 37 175
My Memories of Two Great Brothers 175
Robert Munce Davis 175
New Future Photo 175
My Brother, Shimo New Future Films 177

Chapter 38 179
Last Times I Saw True Father Las Vegas 179
90th Birthday 181

Chapter 39 182
True Father's Seung Hwa 182

Chapter 40 186
Final Thoughts and Prayers 186
My prayer: 186
God's prayer: 186

Addendum 189
Madison Square Garden 1974 189

Introduction

I have been asked by many of my friends, and my wife in particular, to write a book or memories about my years in the Unification Church, founded by the Rev. Sun Myung Moon, and especially my thirty-three years of experiences photographing True Parents. Somehow, the day I celebrated my 65th birthday, something suddenly urged me to get it done. I had written a few short testimonies, but this will be more in-depth, incorporating experiences, articles that I have written; of dreams, a revelation and a vision I received from God.

There are many hundreds of elders, and brothers and sisters, who had been with True Parents far longer than I have, far more deserving than I, and who have had many more cherished, intimate moments with them. The fact that I was able to have some moments with our True Parents was a great blessing.

I would like to thank True Parents for changing my life and to have the honorable blessing to have so many chances to photograph them during the historic lives. I would also like to thank those in church leadership, such as: President Neil Salonen, Dr. Mose Durst, Dr. Tyler Hendricks, Dr. James Baughman, Rev. Ki Hoon Kim. Most especially, I would like to thank Dr. Chang Shik Yang and Dr. Michael Jenkins, who knew the value of filming and photographing our True Parents, and kept those of us in New Future Photo and New Future Films extremely busy documenting the many activities of our True Parents. I would deeply thank Michael Brownlee, Robert Davis, and Hiromichi Shimoyama who guided me in trying to take the best photographs I could. To Chris Garcia and Stefan Des Lauries for being my assistants in the 1990s. I would especially thank my spiritual mother, Karrin Louise Westerdale, who saw something in me and introduced me to the Unification Church in San Francisco back in 1973. I am very grateful to my wife, Meeyung Cho, who has encouraged and taught me to be a much better person before God. To my wonderful children: Julie, Leilani and Douglas who gave me the title: Appa. Lastly, I would like to thank my parents, John and Frances Owens, who raised me in the US Navy and by their patriotism, to become one who became more centered on the nation and the world, than on more selfish reasons.

My special thanks to Heather Auerbach and Roger Wetherall for making my manuscript perfect.. And to Jonathan Gullery for making a great cover for this book.

There are so many experiences, that it would be impossible to mention them all. So, I will just give the historic ones, those that are too important to forget, some very happy times, and some very sad. I hope that you will understand and love True Parents more after reading this.

Chapter 1

Early life and San Francisco

I was born a Navy brat. For those who do not know, a Navy brat is a child who was born and raised while their parent was serving in the United States Navy. My dad, John Douglas Owens, served on aircraft carriers during World War Two and the Korean War.

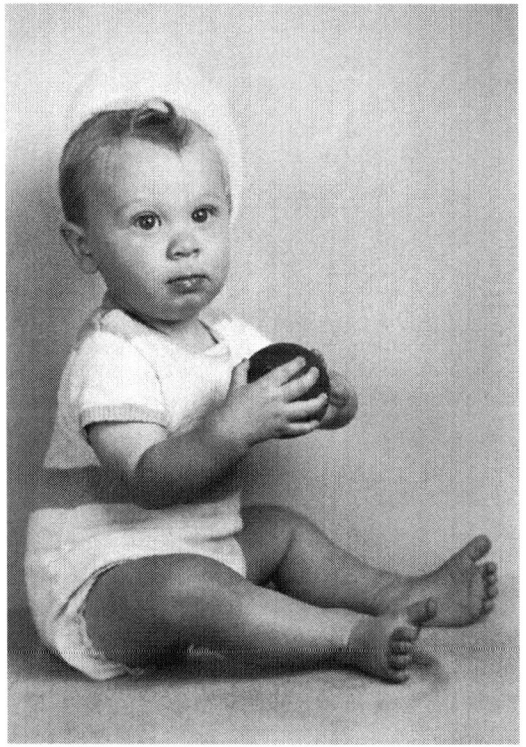

Figure 1 Future sailor at the age of one

I was born on the sixth floor of the Balboa Naval Hospital in San Diego on March 6th, 1950. During the first fourteen years of my life, we traveled to Alameda; Hawaii; Tennessee; Rhode

Island; El Centro, CA, Stockton and finally San Francisco, due to my father's military travels.

I was pretty much a quiet, shy, skinny kid, who played soccer and never went on dates.

Figure 2 Wide-eyed choirboy in the center on US Navy base

My best friend in high school and college was a second generation Japanese named Michael Ozaki. He grew up in the Fillmore district and had to fight his way through his neighborhood. Through our friendship, I began to search more internally about myself and of others.

Figure 3 Age about 17 years

Figure 4 Mike Ozaki and myself in Golden Gate Park

Having graduated from George Washington High School in 1968 and City College of San Francisco, I still didn't know what field I would go into. My favorite subject was history, but there was no future in it, not knowing that years later I would be photographing the most important events in history.

I didn't realize till many years later there were three movies that influenced me a great deal.

The first was "Sergeant York." This was a true story of American born in the hills of Tennessee who was very religious but didn't want to fight during World War I. Through much searching in his heart and in the bible, he realized he could do both, serve God and serve his country. He became America's hero soldier of the war.

The second movie was "Ben-Hur" about a rich Jew who is falsely accused and sentenced to be a galley slave. He survived by seeking revenge, but met a quiet man from Galilee and witnessed his execution. Ben-Hur was transformed by life and death of this man named Jesus.

The third movie was "Inherit the Wind." It was about a real trial in 1925 in Tennessee of a science teacher who taught evolution in a state that made the teaching of evolution illegal. By the end of this movie, I realized that in reality, religion and science are actually working together in explaining God's purpose in creating mankind and the universe as a whole.

Unfortunately, at that time, with the Vietnam War raging in Asia, my draft number was low and instead of waiting to be called to the army, I joined the navy in 1971, which I liked better anyway.

But, I was still searching internally and observing more about what was happening around me. I guess I was an agnostic, meaning I wanted to believe, but needed proof.

Flying to San Diego for naval training, I looked out the window and realized: "Flying high over the clouds, one may see the marriage of Heaven and Earth!" I wrote it down and gave it to one of the flight attendants.

After training, I became a radioman onboard the USS Preble (DLG-15) out of Pearl Harbor.

The last night before going to Vietnam, for the first time, I went to Waikiki Beach to think and feel about what was to come. A Christian came over to me and we talked for a while. The next morning, we shipped out to war. About seven months later, after our ship saw action in Vietnam, and getting hit twice by enemy shellfire, we arrived back in Hawaii, ready for a long rest.

But, I was still wondering and searching, and since my friend, Michael, was now a student at UC Berkeley, I decided to visit him on leave (navy term for vacation) and find some books about religious philosophy, not religion per se, since none had accomplish their goal of world peace.

Figure 5 Radioman on the USS Preble

When I arrived at Berkeley, and before finding Michael, I noticed a group of people talking about world peace based on new principles. I was so intrigued that I took their photo, not knowing I would be associated with their movement within a week.

Figure 6 Unified Principles at UC Berkeley

A few days later, I went to the main library in San Francisco to find more books, but a blue-eyed blond Swedish girl from St. Louis, Karrin Louise Westerdale, blocked my way.

She said she was with a movement that had new principles and asked me to come for lunch. Since, I didn't want to hurt her feelings, I said I would.

When they prayed, I knew it was some kind of a church. She asked me to come that night for a lecture. I said I'd try. After I left, and wondering what to do, a voice came out of nowhere and said: "You better check this out, it's going to change your life!" Well, since I still didn't want to hurt her feelings, I went that night to the Page Street center. A Korean man gave a lecture, Rev. Sang Ik Choi, but I couldn't understand a word he said. So, Karrin took me into the kitchen and gave me the whole lecture again. I agreed with everything she said and I asked what to do now. Before I went back to my ship in Hawaii, I met her a few more times, even helping her do some leafleting on cars. When I left, she said that she would write to me when a new church center would be opened in Honolulu.

Figure 7 Karrin Louise Westerdale

About two months later, she wrote that her spiritual sister and a brother had arrived and were waiting for me to visit. When I had the chance, I visited them one night, had a taco dinner, and moved in the next day. I still had two more years of my enlistment to go, but now I had found what I was looking for. Within the next week or two, both Carmela Acohido and Bruce Brown gave me lectures. The final lecture was very informal. Bruce and I sat on the floor of the brother's room, dressed in our t-shirts and cut-offs, while Bruce told me the lecture with his notes strewn all over the floor. That night, I was looking out the window to the hills behind Honolulu, and realized for the first time: God does exist. That's how I joined, being the first person to join the church in Hawaii.

During the next two years, when I was in port, I would live at the church center as much as possible, helping as much as I could, and once a week, go to the Navy commissary and buy food for the church center. Bruce would drive me there and I would buy ten bags of groceries for $80. When I got outside, I would look in the distance and see Bruce's bare foot hanging outside the car window. It made it very easy to find him.

In the 1970s, the airlines could not fly non-stop from America to Korea. Most of the time, they would stop over in Hawaii for refueling. Since this would take time, the passengers would be free to get off the plane and breathe some fresh Hawaiian air before re-boarding.

True Parents and their entourage would regularly do this when they were either flying to America or returning to Korea, and we, the Hawaiian members, would greet them and keep them company until they had to leave.

Two visits I remember distinctly. One was just after the June 7th Yoido Rally in Korea in 1975 in which over one million people participated. True Father was so excited that his briefcase was full of photos from the event. We gathered around him and he happily showed us all the photographs. It was great to see him so happy.

Figure 8 True Parents and members at Hawaii Airport

The other time was when Kook Jin Nim was with them. He was always a shy one and I suggested that we show him a big pond that had many carp. But, he was very happy to stay with True Parents.

It was here in Hawaii that I first experienced one of the traditions of our church. A few weeks after I was discharged from the Navy in July of 1975 at Pearl Harbor, we had to go fundraising to help the center. With a box of candy bars, we set off to fundraise at the intersections outside the gates of---Pearl Harbor, my old base. It wasn't so much that it was 85 degrees outside, and with candy bars yet, but I was put right outside the gate where I walked away from the Navy. All I kept thinking was: "Don't let my shipmates see me doing this!" "Don't let my captain see me here!" I was nervous all day.

Chapter 2

True Parents in Hawaii 1974

The first time I ever saw True Parents was in Hawaii in 1974. I had just arrived back from my second tour of Vietnam and participated in trying to keep the Yom Kippur War from becoming World War Three. When I arrived back to Honolulu, everything changed from a quiet center in an apartment building to a house behind Waikiki where everything was centered upon True Parents' immediate arrival for a major speech. To top it off, Rev. Ken Sudo was about to arrive with his International One World Crusade team of French and German members to witness to people to come to the banquet.

Figure 9 Bruce Brown and Carmela Acohido

Bruce and Carmela were scrambling everywhere, getting a venue ready, housing for the IOWC members, and a house for True Parents themselves to stay in, which they finally found on Namauu Drive, in a small valley behind Honolulu.

On the day of the banquet, a huge rainstorm hit the island, causing major flooding everywhere, including the house where True Parents stayed. Everyone was worried about the banquet, if the guests would come.

That night, we all gathered at the Hilton Hawaiian Village Hotel. The banquet room was ready, the members were dressed in their finest. For the first time since I was five years old, I wore a suit, with a flowered Hawaiian tie.

Figure 10 Hawaiian tie and lei

I was standing at the top of the escalator, with my new Nikon camera that I bought with my combat pay, when True Parents suddenly appeared. Seeing True Parents for the first time, I saw a bright light shine on them as they passed by me. I was so amazed that I forgot to take a photograph.

Since I had a camera, Bruce asked me to take photos of the event. This was my first official assignment photographing True Parents.

Figure 11 True Parents and Dr. Bo Hi Pak at Hawaiian Reception line

Figure 12 1974 Day of Hope Hawaiian Banquet

True Parents stood in the receiving line, with Dr. Bo Hi Pak and President Neil Salonen, as they greeted the new guests. More and more guests arrived, all in their Hawaiian suits and dresses, with smiles as they greeted our True Parents. Before we knew it, the banquet hall was full. I took one photo of True Parents looking into the hall before they entered, and True Mother had her mouth open in amazement. Despite a terrible storm during the day, our banquet turned out to be the largest of the 32-City tour.

After all these years, I still remember when True Father stood up, introduced himself and then told a joke. Dr. Bo Hi Pak explained it this way:

"Rev Moon is very amazed by the names you have here in Hawaii. As we drove on the highway from the airport, Rev Moon was trying to pronounce the names in Hawaiian. He saw a sign and said "Cayma Cayma Highway" I replied, "Oh no, that is pronounced Kamehameha (kamay-ha-may-ha), you say it like that." "Oh!" replied Rev Moon. As we drove on, he saw another sign and tried to say: "Pepie-leenie, pepie-leenie!" "Oh no!" I replied. "That's a pipeline, pipeline."

By the end of the night, every table was filled, and True Parents were very happy.

Figure 13 True Parents, Mrs. Won Bok Choi and Bruce Brown at the Pali

The following day, True Parents and all the members went around the island of Oahu for a day of sightseeing. At Pali Lookout, between Honolulu and the northern side of the island, True Parents stopped for photos. A gust of wind came and part of Mrs. Won Bok Choi's hair flew away. True Parents laughed when this happened. True Parents were very happy that the 32-City tour was a great victory.

Chapter 3

Barrytown

In October 1975, three months after walking off the ship and leaving the navy, I left for Barrytown Training Center, across the Hudson River from Kingston, New York, to attend the 40-day workshop with Hawaiian-born Joe Tully. This was the first time I was able to completely focus on studying the Divine Principle.

Each day was full of lectures, testimonies, activities, prayer conditions, sometimes all night long outside, and lots of singing and studying.

Forty Hour Street Preaching

One of the most memorable parts of this workshop was when everyone went to New York City for a 40-hour street preaching condition in front of St Patrick's Cathedral and Grand Central Station at 42nd Street. We would be in groups of three or four people taking turns giving a quick lecture while the others talked to people who stopped by. I remember one person in particular who came up and asked me to confirm that it wasn't an apple that Eve ate in the Garden. I pointed out very clearly from scripture that it was illicit sex (Jude 6 and 7). He gave out a big smile and literally danced away.

By the end of the thirty-sixth hour, everyone was so tired and weak from standing, but we supported each other, which gave us strength to finish the fortieth hour. I was not only tired, but getting sick as well, my spine tingling with pain, but I wanted to finish so badly. While we all gave lectures those last three hours, I suddenly had a strong feeling in my heart what it was like for Jesus to be crucified on the cross. It was like a runner giving all his strength just before the finish line, with nothing left, but pain and determination to win.

When the fortieth hour finally finished, we were all smiling and we dragged ourselves back to the buses. Most people slept on the way back to Barrytown, but I kept thinking about those last three hours.

True Parents Visit

The second time I ever took photographs of True Parents was while attending one of Barrytown's 40-day workshops. True Parents had visited the building for a tour and while having lunch, I was asked, since I had a camera already, to take photos. I was given an extra camera to use and to take photos of the luncheon. After I was done, I was told to do a bow on the way out. Standing at the doorway, instead of taking the cameras off, I wore them and made a terrible racket as they hit the floor at the bottom of the bow. Being nervous the whole time, I left as quickly as I could.

One Brother's Experience Pioneering

One of the reports we heard of was about one brother who, after finishing his workshop, was sent to North Dakota for pioneering. He struggled for some time, so he decided to do an all-night prayer vigil. During his prayer, he saw a vision of an Indian brave's face coming straight towards him with a vengeful look. The brother became afraid, but instead of stopping his prayer, he made it stronger, focusing on repenting to the Indian for America's war on his people. As the brave come closer and closer, the brave's face getting angrier and angrier, the brother prayed harder with tears. As the brave finally reached him, the brave suddenly stopped, smiled, and went away, accepting the brother's apology.

As soon as that brave left, another appeared in the distance, and he too, had an angry look and charging at the brother. Again, the brother repented for what America did, and as the brave approached, he too stopped, smiled and left. All night long, one brave after brave charged the brother, he repented, and again each brave smiled and departed.

By the end of the night, the brother was tired, but happy that he was able to relieve each Indian brave of his resentment towards America.

A Vision

One day during my 120-day class, the day began with a special morning service. The staff members came in very quietly with serious faces and carrying pans of water. We all knew then that something special was going to happen. Rev. David Hose read from the Bible of Jesus washing the feet of the Disciples. We were going to re-enact this event and we became very serious.

After Rev. Hose's feet were washed, he washed the other staff members' feet. Then, they passed the ceremony onto each one of us who would then, in turn, wash the next person's feet.

After my feet were washed, I then washed the next person's feet. I looked around the room to see how everyone was doing. Some were looking at others, some were praying and others were crying. I then prayed about this ceremony and that God's heart would be with everyone. I then meditated.

While meditating, I suddenly saw myself kneeling before Heavenly Father. He was sitting on a throne and all I saw were His knees, legs and feet. It was all black around us, yet He was shining brightly. For several seconds, I looked at Him. Then, He reached out His feet to me and I washed God's feet. After I finished, I kneeled back, looking at Him. Then, all of a sudden, the scene shifted and I was now sitting on the throne, looking down at God who was kneeling before me. His face was shining very brightly. He then took my feet and He washed them. I was so surprised that God, who is Almighty, would humble Himself to me, sinful, little me. I was so dumbfounded that I began to cry, cry for the first time in twelve years. I would then keep reliving the vision and I would cry even more. The brother next to me, heard me cry and said, "Alright!"

After the ceremony was over, I told Rev. Hose what I had just experienced. He then asked me to retell it to the whole class. There were "oohs and ahs" and one sister's eyes just lit up with joy. I told them that I understood now that it wasn't just Jesus who washed the Disciple's feet, but God as well. God loves us so much

Chapter 4

Mobile Fundraising Team

True Father always pointed out to members that we all had to go through two main journeys of growth in our lives. The first was externally through fundraising. The second was by witnessing. Mainly during fundraising, we would grow spiritually by overcoming hardships by being in different weather climates: from minus 50 degrees during the 1977 blizzard in Buffalo (my frost-bitten toes always remind me of that time), to over 100 degrees in Southern California. From morning to night, we would be fundraising with different kinds of products doing shop-to-shop, houses or late night blitzing in bars and restaurants. By making conditions of prayer, cold showers, and many other determinations, we tried our best to grow internally towards God while financing the movement and helping people set their own conditions by donating to the church.

Heartistically, we grew by denying ourselves many comforts while giving our time and energy to others. Sometimes, we would be persecuted by those who didn't understand why we were doing this, instead of focusing on making money for ourselves. We just accepted their persecution and said: "Thank you, God bless you!"

I wasn't the best fundraiser, by any means, but I was very grateful that I tried my best and learned how to overcome my shyness and to relate to many different kinds of people.

Introduction to MFT

In April of 1976, all students and some of the staff in Barrytown were formed into teams and sent across the country to fundraise for Barrytown's activities. I was sent on Zola Bokar's team out to Los Angeles. After driving about five days in a van crowded with people, product, and Zola's cooking stove, we arrived around mid-day. The fundraising commander gathered us all together and announced: "Welcome to the National Fundraising Teams; you are all now on MFT!" He then sent us out fundraising, tired as we were, for the rest of the day. Thus, began my four years of fundraising.

Figure 14 Official Unification Church ID Card

Getting Mugged in Boston

There was a serious incident on while I was in Boston. I went with one brother to do an area in Charlestown. A van was supposed to pick us up at a parking lot. When I got into the van, a gang came over. I got out to see what they wanted. They started chasing me around the lot. The van driver drove away quickly. They caught me a couple of times and threatened me. One of them actually took a full swing into my stomach, but God must have protected me, because I didn't feel a thing. I ran into a diner to escape. Meanwhile the driver drove down a one-way street the wrong way, right in front of a police officer, who had just gotten off duty. The driver told the cop and eventually he found me in the diner. I was scared, but thankful things worked out. What I didn't realize until later was that I still had my fundraising money in my shirt pocket.

Original World Products

After two and a half years of actual fundraising, John Hessell wanted me to join Original World Products at the East Sun Building in Queens, New York. The main purpose of the company was to make products like laser prints and mounted butterflies in domes, and ship them to shopping malls throughout the country where we would have booths set up. The Christmas season was our busiest and most profitable. It was very hard work, but we felt we were contributing a lot to the church.

At one point we made scented candles that for the Christmas season. For several weeks we made all kinds of candles that could be sent all over America. One night, it was decided to make lilac scented candles. Well, the only way I can describe it is the old cartoons when the characters smell something they float in the air to where ever the scent is. Well, it was almost the same with lilac. Within minutes, almost all the females throughout the building came floating down to our area, with their noses in the air and sweet smiles on their faces. It was a sight to behold.

Chapter 5

Yankee Stadium

During my time on MFT, two major events occurred in 1976 in which the entire church movement focused on. One was Yankee Stadium and the other was Washington Monument,

Here are excerpts from my diary a few days leading up to the Yankee Stadium event of June 1st, 1976.

May 27th and 28th: Our fundraising team left Kansas City after breakfast and buying shoes. I got car sick, probably too much bouncing: and me, sailing through two typhoons in the Pacific. During the night, we met up with Revie Sorey, right guard for the Chicago Bears. He had a CB radio in his car and we went an average of 80mph all the way to New Jersey. We arrived at 43rd Street Headquarters, right behind Denny Townsend's van. We went to the New Yorker to register and then back to Headquarters for dinner and a meeting. On the way back to the New Yorker, our driver missed a turn and we round up back in New Jersey. Eventually, we got back to the hotel and I saw Mrs. Nanod and her daughters: Sandy, Debbie, Sharon, and Keith Chow. My spiritual mother, Karrin, is somewhere in the hotel: GOOD!

May 29th: We went to Harlem after morning service. I got teamed up with Lynda Marie Voelkel and cleaned Park Avenue between 108th Street to 102nd Street. Earned several blood blisters on my hands, no gloves. Then, we went to 125th Street for a parade and rally where we marched and sang. After lunch at McDonald's, naturally, I went witnessing with Jim West. It's easier to witness in the street than in apartments. At the end of the day, we ate dinner at Headquarters at 43rd Street and went back to the hotel. The day ended spectacularly. I finally met Karrin for the first time since she witnessed to me in San Francisco. We had a lot of catching up to do. She said that she is one of the hostesses to True Parents on the 37th floor.

May 30th: We went early to Belvedere for Pledge and hear True Father's sermon. He was very relaxed. Afterwards, I was assigned to New Future Photographics for the event. We held a meeting and looked at new equipment. Michael Brownlee decided I should be his assistant during the event. I went back to the hotel to sleep, but lo and behold, my sleeping bag was gone. I was able to talk to Karrin for an hour and a half.

May 31: The day before Yankee Stadium. We went to the stadium to prepare for the event. It took a long time to get in, but finally managed it. We put everything in the third base dugout. We found two rooms we could use as a darkroom and meeting room. We took pictures of Won Pil Kim and David Kim, and the New Hope Singers singing to them. We went back to the hotel, but too late to talk to Karrin.

June 1st: We held morning pledge ceremony in the hotel, and then we went to the stadium around Noontime. We prepared the equipment and received last minute instructions and preparations. At about 5pm, while I was still inside, gusts of wind suddenly came with heavy rains. We went outside and saw sheet music from the brass band, all muddy and wet, strewn all over the hallway floor. Outside, debris from the storm littered the playing field around the stage.

Figure 15 Walking behind True Father and Dr. Pak to the stage

People were slow in coming. When the time arrived for the main event, I saw True Parents in the first base dugout. They had very serious expressions on their faces. I became spiritually drained. President Salonen became concerned about True Father's safety and asked that I walk behind True Father and Col. Bo Hi Pak out to the stage. I didn't think I could be much of a shield for True Father, but I tried. Thankfully, Mike McDevitt walked beside us. I felt it was a blessing to be on the field with True Father, but also felt I didn't deserve it. Throughout True Father's talk, I kept circling the stage, helping Mike with his cameras and taking a few photos myself. After True Father finished, I again walked behind them back to the first base dugout. I looked at the members in the stands. There were many different expressions on their faces: happy, serious, sad, and tearful. As for me, I was sad.

After the rally, we collected all the camera gear and film. Mike Lograsso and Doug Wetzstein went with the de-posturing teams who took down all the thousands of posters that were plastered all over the city. Bob, Franz and I went to Headquarters and sorted the equipment and then headed back to Belvedere. We heard that a Japanese brother, Watanabe, died today.

Chapter 6

Washington Monument

These are my diary entries for the last three days leading up to and including the Washington Monument Rally on September 18th.

September 16th: Our fundraising team left Buffalo for Piscataway, New Jersey. On the way, we read the Madison Square Garden and Yankee Stadium speeches and Christianity in Crisis book. We arrived an hour and a half late. We had time to get ourselves physically and spiritually ready for the trip to Washington D.C. One Japanese leader spoke to us. He said that True Father was very angry and sad after Yankee Stadium. We must be very serious now. It's the last chance for America or communism will take over and 600 million lives will perish. We must be completely serious until the last fireworks go off. If the Monument Rally is victorious, True Father will see President Park of Korea. I remember that I went and took some photos of President Park when he came to the Presidio in San Francisco to meet with President Nixon in August of 1969.

September 17th: Left New Jersey early and arrived around 9:30am at the NAACP Center at 10th and "U" streets in Washington D.C. Afterwards, we went to the Ambassador Hotel. I saw Debbie Nanod, Keith Chow, Bill Miho and Lynda Voelkel. I was sent to pass out leaflets around the Monument area. Mostly did cars around the State Department, White House, Department of the Interior and the park area. We were told to watch out for people wearing red carnations who were ex-members trying to stop us. I met Ken Bower, whose parents heard one of our lectures while they were in Hawaii. Mike Brownlee told me he was trying to get me on the photographic team, but hadn't succeeded yet. After having dinner at the NAACP Center, I spoke to Debbie and her sister Sharon about how they were doing and about Hawaii. This was a time to have a serious attitude, deep prayer and deep heart to protect True Parents, both physically and spiritually.

September 18th: I went early to the Monument to be an usher in front of the stage under the direction of Rev. Martin Porter. We all set up chairs in front of the stage. It took Mike Brownlee several hours but he finally got permission for me to be on the photographic team for the day. Rev. Porter is also a good photographer in his own right. During the day, I got familiar with some of the equipment and did some running around to get some permission papers copied on the Lincoln Memorial and for Robert Davis to go in the helicopter for shots above during the event.

Many problems arose as time got near and people began gathering at the Monument. My thoughts at this point were of great excitement, that victory was definitely coming. But then, I flashbacked to Yankee Stadium and I became serious again. The adrenalin was really flowing.

Figure 16 300,000 at Washington Monument

Bill Saunders went up to the top of the Monument with his cameras. Doug Wetzstein and Bob Armstrong climbed up the camera towers, Robert eventually got into a helicopter, Laurie Toker was in the communications center, Mike Lograsso and Howard Stavis roamed around the crowd and Mike Brownlee,

Franz Zurawski and Hitoshi Nagai photographed around the stage area. Ken Weber and I started our long walk to the Lincoln Memorial with our cameras and tripods to photograph the monument and fireworks. When we arrived, we had to wait to get escorted up to the roof of the Memorial where we were going to work. At the steps of the Memorial, there was a group of about twenty black Christian ministers who were protesting our event. I took photos of them for history. Mike Brownlee tried hard to keep us up there, but the Park Rangers said that so many people came that they needed more help at the Monument. So, Ken and I went downstairs and set up on the right side of the front columns. If you ever saw the movie "Mr. Smith Goes To Washington," this was the exact spot that James Stewart sat.

Even though we were so far away, we could hear everything: singing, announcements and True Father's speech. A small film crew, who was working with us, was right next to us filming. Most of our work didn't start until the fireworks began. It was so amazing; it just kept coming, and coming. Planes taking off and landing at National Airport saw everything from above the Monument. Ken and I worked constantly with excited hearts, trying to get the best photos possible. At the end, we were just about jumping, not only from the fireworks, but also knowing that victory was assured.

Figure 17 New Future Photo crew. I'm the only one wearing a tie.

Afterwards, we took back our equipment to the monument and then to the publications department to sort out equipment and get some sleep. It was a long day.

Do you think True Father was happy with the victory at Washington Monument? You bet he was!

Figure 18 Victory hug after Washington Monument

Chapter 7

New Future Photo

On May 30^h, 1980, I was transferred from Original World Products, a part of MFT, to New Future Photo, officially graduating from four years of MFT work. This was my first day of a thirty-three year mission photographing many of our True Parents' activities. Robert Davis, who was in charge of New Future Photo, said I was trainable. I think that he liked my Nikon camera and two lenses as well.

From the very beginning, I helped photograph many of the great events, speaking tours and conferences that True Father organized: from the International Conference on the Unity of the Sciences or ICUS, with scientific scholars centered on Absolute Values; to religious conferences, such as the Assembly of the World's Religions and American Christian Leadership Conference, bringing together not only religious scholars, but leaders from many of the world's religions to discuss the unity of religious harmony, something that no other man has been unable to do on such a world-wide level. On the political level, True Father invited presidents, vice-presidents and prime ministers from dozens of the world's nations to the Summit Council, discussing the solutions to world problems centering on God. When he would speak to the world's educators and professors, such as the participants at ICUS and the Professors World Peace Academy, True Father would guide them into ideas they had never thought of before, systematically and undeniable. True Father guided the Middle East Peace Initiative trips to Rome, Israel and Jordan, bringing the world together to help bring the Israeli/Palestinian conflict to a peaceful resolution. And, very historically, achieving the ceremony that crowned Jesus as the King of Kings.

At each of these events, True Father would speak to all the participants as if he were speaking to each one of them personally, inspiring them centering on his revelation of the Divine Principle. Sometimes, he would look at a small piece of paper containing the important points he wanted to share with his guests. All the participants, no matter how educated, powerful or well known, they would sit there quietly, spell-bound, listening and understanding every word True Father said. No matter how many times I photograph these events, my admiration and awe towards True Father would continue to deepen my heart towards him.

When True Father spoke to members, he would be very serious in conveying God's heart and the Divine Principle to help members understand. Sometimes he even scolded them, so they can become better people. And many times, he would tell many jokes to see them happy. But, his love for us never changed. He wanted all of us to do our best.

Talking Out Loud

One side note! After many years, I've noticed that while taking photographs, I would realize that I was talking to myself. During an event, whether it was True Father speaking, a birthday, special celebration or a conference, I would really be focusing on the next two or three shots. And then, I find myself talking out loud. I guess I could concentrate more while doing that.

So, if you hear someone talking to himself: he's either crazy, or a photographer.

Chapter 8

East Garden

First Visit

The First time I visited East Garden actually came by accident. It was at a Sunday Service at Belvedere and it was Young Jin Nim's birthday. True Mother had gone back to East Garden to make sure all the arrangements were made for the birthday celebration. Ye Jin Nim stayed behind till True Father finished his speech. At the end, True Father said, "Oh, today is my son's birthday…you are ALL invited!" Ye Jin Nim's mouth opened in shock. She immediately called True Mother basically saying "Omma, guess what Appa did! He just invited all the members to East Garden for the birthday!" What did True Mother do? She had McDonald's make lunches for all who came.

Even though True Parents used East Garden as their residence while in America, they held many daily public events there: from meetings with various church and business leaders; banquets and speeches with special VIP guests from around the world including Heads of State, political leaders and leaders from many religions; celebrations of our special Holy Days; birthdays for their children and grandchildren; and Sunday services with True Father giving his long and exciting sermons.

Here are some of the events that took place at East Garden.

True Parents Arrivals

True Parents traveled all over the world and the times they would arrive back to East Garden were joyous occasions.

Figure 19 True Parents arriving with grandchildren offering flowers. My son Douglas is in the white shirt.

Leaders and members would line up in front of the building, brothers on one side and the sisters on the other. When True Parents' car arrived, everyone would give a bow and cheer. True Parents would come out of the car and the cheers would get louder. True Parents would approach the steps and their grandchildren would give them flowers and a hug.

True Parents would enter the main hall, sit in their chairs and the True Family would give a bow. Then, the grandchildren would all gather and give their grandparents kisses, which was called "po-po time."

Figure 20 "Po-po" time

Then, the leaders and members would come in would do their bow. True Parents would cut the welcoming cake and all would sit for prayer and a meal.

Figure 21 Leaders and members greet True Parents

Figure 22 True Parents blowing out the kissing candles

Figure 23 Members watching True Parents cutting the cake

Figure 24 True Parents singing to members

Afterwards, True Mother would go upstairs and talk with the True Children and grandchildren, while True Father would speak and hear reports.

Figure 25 Dr. Bo Hi Pak giving a report

Figure 26 True Father giving joy to the Second Generation

One arrival was very memorable. True Mother was coming back from a speaking tour and all the members were given flowers to throw onto True Mother's car as she arrived. The moment came and the car started down toward the main house, and with True Father looking on, all the members started throwing flowers. By the time the car reached the house, it was totally covered in flowers of all different colors. It was a beautiful sight.

Figure 27 True Mother's car covered in flowers

Four Cake Surprise

This is an example of how important communication is. One time, everyone was supposed to gather at East Garden for Sunday Service with True Parents. Usually, I didn't use more than two rolls of film. But, when I entered the main hall, there were four birthday cakes all in a row. I naturally freaked out. I quickly went to the kitchen to ask anyone on the staff if they had any film with them. I was able to get two more rolls of amateur film, but it was a lot better than only two. I made Headquarters promise to let me know ahead of time from then on.

Waiting at the Stairs

For many years, there had been several hundred ceremonies and meetings that took place at East Garden. We would be downstairs, anxiously waiting for True Parents arrival from the second floor. At the new house, I would wait at the bottom of the stairs, waiting to see True Father start his way down. One day, I went half way up the stairs, and peeked around to the top and wait for True Father shoes to appear. Then, I would run down, motioning the members at the bottom foyer to rise, then run around the dish washing corridor, letting the security team and Dominic Barber the sound man, who was holding True Father's lapel microphone, in mere seconds of the appending arrival, make a left turn to the entrance of the ballroom, announce for everyone to stand up. After a while, Colonel Han told me to say the word "attention" in Korean, which sounds like "Chariot", and to do it militarily. Well, I did that and when I did, not only did the members have big smiles on their faces, I heard True Father give out a big laugh behind me. It sure was one way to make True Parents entrance a happy one! From then on, I continued to wait half way up the stairs for True Father's appearance.

True Father Kissing True Mother

I have taken at least several hundred thousand photos of True Parents during my thirty-three years. But, during the last ten years, True Father became more affectionate with True Mother and at times would kiss her on her cheek.

Most of the time, he would do this while he was singing a song, and he moved closer and closer to her. I would then try to get set and press the camera shutter at the right moment. There were times he would stop just short and move away, but there were a few times, he did kiss her.

I would click away and get the great moment. Then, I would say to myself: "Yes!"

Figure 28 True Father giving the perfect kiss

I may have gotten about eight to ten of these beautiful moments, but they were well worth the joy of getting them.

Figure 29 Great reason True Mother is smiling

Carpet

During special ceremonies, such as Holy Days or Ahn Shi Ils, a special weekly ceremony, True Parents would bow on a special carpet to Heavenly Father. Then, they would sit down and wait for the True Family to line up for their bows. True Mother didn't want that carpet to remain there, so she motioned me to come next to her, gather and fold the carpet and remove it as quickly as possible and give it to Paul Fontaine before the True Children had finished lining up for their bow. This became one of my responsibilities during each ceremony.

Offering Tray

One time, during a Holy Day, one of the staff had put the offering tray right in front of the Offering Table. True Parents came in and before bowing; True Father immediately put the tray to the side. From then on, I would move the tray to the side, so True Father didn't have to bow down to money.

True Mother

There is one thing I've truly noticed about True Mother: she is a very beautiful woman. She was extremely supportive of True Father. She was always there when he needed her, making sure everything was ready for him, and guided him in many ways. Having fourteen children has taken its toll on her.

Figure 30 True Mother still beautiful after 14 children

But, even though she may be tired, she was always there for him. She would always make sure her children and grandchildren did their best. She's very calm, but very serious at times, very collected of herself and really cares and loves the members. She doesn't show anger, but just her eyes tell the whole story if she is. She just says very quietly: "You're late!" That's all you need to know. All you can say is you're very sorry in Korean, in a voice that you will do better next time.

We all need to pray and to attend to her more than ever.

Security

I would like to step aside a moment and mention a special group of brothers with whom I have the greatest respect for. Photographing True Parents for so many years, I had to work with the East Garden Security team. These brothers dedicated themselves night and day safeguarding our True Parents, even to the point of sacrificing their lives if need be. Usually, they would stay in the background; watching and safe guarding our True Parents, making sure no one in the audience had any strange ideas or plans. I realized early on that since I could move around, I could add my two eyes as well, seeing people in the audience more closely. The security team was very grateful for that. I felt the seriousness of their mission and wanted to be of any help I could. Sometimes, even though I would be photographing, if one of the security brothers told me to move a little to the side, I would obey. True Parents' safety always came first before getting a good photograph.

One incident did occur in Oakland, California during one of True Father speaking tours. Security knew that some deprogrammers were in the area, so they were on extra alert. Already, the deprogrammers had attacked one of our elders in the lobby, but Security thought there might be more. Near the end of True Father's speech, I suddenly had an inclination that something was going to happen, and I tried to get Mike Chapman to move to the center of the stage. But, before he could act, True Father finished his speech; the audience rose in applause and three men charged the stage. While security stopped two of them, I dropped my camera and flash and tackled the third, though a bit late, but got him to the floor. It was all caught on video. Even though I landed on my left side, the comb I had on my right back pocked broke in half. I wish I had done more to help, even though I had a limp for a few days. But, that's what our security brothers had to look for and react quickly against every day for so many years.

So, for these great brothers who stayed up and watched, in the heat of day and freezing cold of night, and events with several thousand people in attendance, we must be eternally grateful to these sacrificial brothers who protected our True Parents.

Young Children

On one Saturday around 1994, True Mother invited all the young children in the New York area to come to East Garden. They all dressed up in their best clothes and gathered in the main hall. I brought my daughters, Julie and Leilani. Julie was dressed in her black evening dress and white sash. When they all gathered, True Mother came out and all the children did a bow to her. She then gave a small talk with her beautiful smile, for about ten minutes, because children that age can't sit still longer that than. Then, before she gave them lots of snacks, she had them all line up and gave each a money gift. They would come up to True Mother, greet and accept her gift. When Julie came up, True Mother stopped and asked her who her parents were. Julie stood quietly, with her finger to her cheek, and I waited for her to answer, all the while taking photos.

Then, Charles Paterson said: "Ken Owens!" True Mother and everyone around her looked at me. True Mother then looked back at Julie and pinched her cheek. That was a very fond moment for Julie.

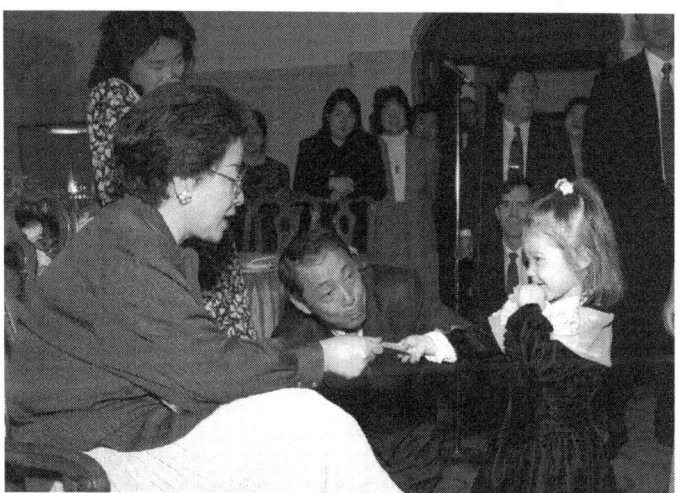

Figure 31 Julie Meesun receiving a gift from True Mother

Hudson River Photo

Many leaders were asked to come to East Garden to celebrate True Parents' wedding anniversary. I had a two-fold mission that day, not only to document the anniversary and the leaders conference afterwards, but also to take passport photos of True Parents, True Children and staff. During a lunch-break, I went upstairs to True Parents' room. When I entered, True Mother had just given True Father a brand new suit jacket. They were in such a happy mood, that she wanted to have a portrait. We went out onto the balcony, which overlooks the Hudson River, and took a few photos, with the river behind them.

Figure 32 True Parents with the Hudson River

They were so happy together. Afterwards, before I took their passports, they asked me to sit with them for a little snack. Hyung Jin Nim and Jeung Jin Nim were also there. It was very special moment to be the only person sitting with them on this special occasion.

Singing to True Parents

Even though I had my responsibility to photograph special occasions, I was able to have the blessing of singing in front of True Parents. Twice I sang at East Garden and two more times during True Mother speaking tours during the after speech celebrations with the Internet connection to True Father at East Garden. I sang only two songs: one was the Hawaiian Lullaby, which I learned in Hawaii, and the other was "Oh, Shenandoah" which I've always loved.

The first time I sang "Oh, Shenandoah" at East Garden was during a special celebration. The room became very quiet, with True Parents and most of the True Family at the head table, and leaders and members seated throughout the room, all looking at me. I became very nervous that the room had become so quiet. The only thing I could do was to look at the wall behind True Parents, so I could still focus on singing without making a mistake. After I finished, True Father remarked that I had the "voice of a flowing river." I was always grateful to know that I made True Parents' happy.

Figure 33 Singing to True Father during True Mother's speaking tour

Birthdays

Figure 34 True Parents giving birthday prayer

Through the years, True Parents would invite members to come and celebrate their children's birthdays. As the years passed, more children would be born, while their brothers and sisters grew older. Then, the grandchildren would be born from the True Children and True Parents would celebrate their birthdays as well. Year after year, the True Family grew larger, the birthdays more numerous, and the family portraits grew wider and wider.

Now, all the True Children are grown. Some have departed earlier than they should have, but the True Grandchildren are growing and True Parents' lineage grows forever more.

Figure 35 True Parents and Shin Joon Nim blowing candles

Figure 36 True Family in True Parents room

Surprise Assistant

One of the most fun times in photographing at East Garden was when a new grandchild is born. First, they go through the 8-day ceremony, the important 100-day ceremony, and finally their first year birthday, where the child is dressed in their finest Korean outfit and pick out from the offering table what their life would be like: by picking up a pencil, paint brush, string, food, Divine Principle book, or money.

Figure 37 True Father getting his grandson's attention

On one occasion, True Parents was celebrating Shin Won Nim's 100th day. At this stage of their lives, babies at this age can't quite sit up straight yet, so when it was time for the portrait session, Shin Won Nim was propped up between some pillows, and with clothes perfectly in place, the portraits would begin.

Now, the hard part was trying to get him to look at the camera so I can take his photo. I learned by this time that if I said "Bananananana" several times, he could look at my direction. But, this time, I discovered that I had an assistant who had a better way to get the baby's attention. When I realized someone was next to me, I slowly turned my head just a little and, lo and behold, True Father was leaning and clapping with a huge smile on his face to get his grandson to look up. It worked.

There were many times that True Mother would also be by my side. To be a grandparent must truly be a wonderful experience. There were a few occasions where I became an assistant.

Figure 38 Helping grandchildren on their photography skills

Mr. Smile Please

In 1997, I joined my wife and four-year-old son, Douglas, in Jardim to attend the 40-day workshop. It was True Parents desire that all members should attend at least one of the workshops in this special place. After graduating six weeks later, I returned and received news that True Father had missed me.

There was a celebration at East Garden while I was gone, and when True Father came into the room, he asked: "Where is Mr. Smile Please! Where is Mr. Smile Please?"

Since I photographed many celebrations at East Garden and special events, I would take photos of True Parents and True

Family and to make it more enjoyable for them, I learned to say the phrase "Smile please" in Korean. Of course, my accent may have something to do with it, but True Parents would always smile when I said this.

Night of Danbury

The day leading up to when True Father had to go to Danbury was difficult one. During the day, True Father met with leaders to give last minute instructions. Everyone was very serious and repented for not doing more for True Parents.

During True Father's last meal before leaving, I'm not sure whose idea it was, but the leaders started posing behind True Father as he was eating. He wasn't looking up at all, just eating. One by one, and some in groups, they kept posing behind True Father. I felt very awkward that they were doing it, and I felt very sorry for True Father about it, but I had to keep photographing them.

Then, the most difficult part of the evening took place up in True Parents room. They asked all the children to come up where they were given final advice and did a prayer together as a family. Then, I was asked to come in to take a family portrait. Because the entire family was there, I had to back up all the way into True Parents bathroom in order to get everyone in to photo. Most of the daughters had swollen eyes because of their tears. True Mother was trying her best, but I knew it was very difficult for her. It was very difficult for me to photograph them. It never is in this kind of situation.

Afterwards, I went outside across the pool where many members were waiting. True Father wanted to give a serious talk, but one that would inspire them during this time. True Father had hope, because every time he went to prison, God would work miracles and advance the providence faster. When he finished, we all did three manseis, and then he waved farewell as he went to Danbury. It was a very difficult day!

Tie Signal

It was during this time that True Father and I had a silent signal between us. Since he was at hundreds of public functions, and there were always photographers and video cameras to record him, sometimes his tie would be crooked. I didn't want future generations to see his photos and videos wearing a crooked tie. So, I would catch his eye, and motion with my hand up and down signaling him that his tie was crooked. He would give a small smile, and straighten his tie.

True Mother and the Stairs

One day, I was called to East Garden because True Mother wanted to see me. This was at the old Stone house. I was motioned to go to the top of the stairs and wait there. When True Mother came, we sat down on the top of the stairs to discuss some photographs she wanted. I don't exactly remember what the photographs were, but sitting casually on top of the stairs, with True Mother, was something I never forgot.

Cake Candles

True Parents had to cut thousands of cakes during their lifetime. At East Garden, there easily were hundreds presented to them, from their arrivals, birthday celebrations and church holy days. One day, True Parents stood in front of the cake, and I positioned myself near True Mother so I could get clear shot of both of their smiling faces. Then, True Father suddenly put the tops of the two candles together and, with a big smile, said they were "kissing." Everyone laughed. True Father would then take True Mother's hands around the cake knife and would cut first from the right side on down and then from the left side. Then, they would go to the front of the cake and do the same thing, while all the members would applaud loudly. From that time forward, all cakes would have two candles kissing each other.

During one special ceremony, True Father decided to pray with the new Cheon Seong Gyeong book. Standing next to True Mother, he opened it randomly in the middle and started to pray. After he finished, he put the book down, still opened, and ended the ceremony. After they departed, I looked at the page he opened randomly to and it turned out to be page 1021…two very providential numbers.

Figure 39 True Parents special prayer with Cheon Seong Gyeong

Julie's Name

My wife really wanted True Parents to name our first daughter. The chances were not good, but she pushed me. She had already decided "Julie" as a middle name, but she wanted True Father to give a Korean first name. When the opportunity finally came, I went to True Mother at the breakfast table, showed her a photo of our new daughter and asked if it was possible. She asked me what middle name we gave. I said "Julie." True Father then quickly said: "That's a good name!" And that's what he wrote.

Honeymooners

One nice memory happened during True Parents' wedding anniversary. During the ceremony, I would take a portrait of True Parents. Just before I took their picture, I said: "Ah, beautiful honeymooners!" And True Father answered quickly and in a loud voice: "YES, honeymoonerrrrrs!" Everyone laughed. True Parents were so happy.

Rescue

During a holy day pledge service in the main room, True Father was in the middle of his opening prayer. I was photographing them and the members who were nearby. Then, I saw someone moving from behind True Family. It was Yun Ah Nim, Hyung Jin Nim's wife. She was trying to move across the room, but moving very unsteadily. She was pregnant at the time and she got hit with morning sickness at that moment. I went over to her, took her hands and guided her to the side door. There, I motioned to one of the Japanese staff sisters to come and help and we brought her carefully up the stairs to one of the children's rooms. Then, I went back downstairs to continue photographing the event. I was told later that she rested a bit and was feeling better.

A few weeks later, True Father was speaking at Belvedere and when Yun Ah Nim saw me, she thanked me very much for helping her. I replied: "You're most welcome."

Moon Over East Garden

Several times during the year, True Parents would invite special guests for a banquet at East Garden. Each time, True Parents would stand at the entrance and greet each guest personally with a smile and handshake. Then, after everyone was seated, Peter Kim would introduce everyone, give a small introduction about the history of East Garden, and then give an opening prayer.

After the banquet, entertainment would begin with several singers, then the children of the East Garden staff would sing and dance, which made the guests very happy. After the children of the staff sang, one or two of the guests would be invited to sing as well. Next, several of the True Family would sing a song or two, usually

Country Roads by John Denver. Then, with great applause, True Parents would sing at least three songs, much to the delight of the guests.

After all the singing and even dancing were over, True Father would begin talking to the guests. (One time, he had a yellow slip of paper to guide his thoughts. It was all centered on the Principle of Creation lecture.

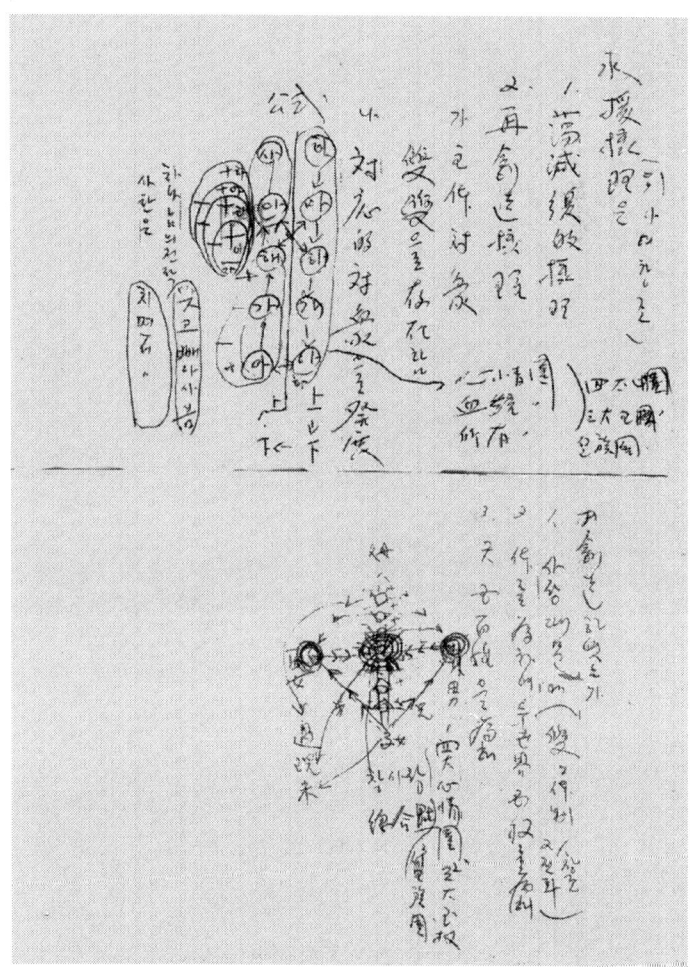

Figure 40 True Father's notes to Korean ministers

After an hour or two, True Parents would exchange gifts with the guests, say goodbye and see them to their buses. As the buses departed, they would stand by the road and wave and smile as each one past.

Figure 41 True Parents and Hyo Jin NIm waving to Korean Ministers

After one of these events, in which the guests were religious leaders from Korea, True Father didn't want to retire until he was sure they had arrived safely back to the New Yorker Hotel. So, he invited all the members up to the roof of the house where we would sing and listen to True Father. As soon as we got up to the roof, he noticed the full moon over the Stone House and told me to quickly take photos. So, with my Hasselblad medium camera, and bracing the camera against the railing and holding my breath for the longest time, I took a series of long exposure photos, up to 45 seconds, guessing and hoping I got a good photograph.

Figure 42 Moon over East Garden

Several weeks later, True Mother liked the photo and ordered two large prints. One was hung upstairs in their room and one sent to Han Nam Dong, their residence in Seoul. Pleasing True Parents is always our greatest pleasure.

Chapter 9

Belvedere

True Parents lived in Belvedere in the 1970s and early 1980s before moving to East Garden. During that time, they would have members come for Sunday Services, workshops, Holy Day celebrations, sports events, and special guests from around the world would be taught and entertained by True Parents.

True Father and the Dog

Before I went to Belvedere for the first time, Bruce Brown told me a story that happened while he was attending a workshop. Some of the brothers were watching out of the second floor window, looking at True Father at the Holy Ground, near the big rock. Off in the distance, they noticed a dog come out of the bushes. They realized that the dog had foam around its mouth and it was looking straight at True Father. Then, in an instant, the dog started to run at full speed toward True Father. The brothers tried to yell, warning him about the dog. Well, True Father just looked at the dog. As the dog got nearer and nearer, True Father didn't move. Then, within a few yards of him, the dog suddenly stopped in its tracks, crawled on all fours towards True Father, and when it reached his feet, the dog rolled over on his back, with its paws in the air, and smiled at True Father. The brothers who witnessed this were in total shock and amazement.

Won Pil Kim Photo

Long before I joined New Future Photo, I was asked by Robert Davis to photograph Rev. Won Pil Kim, who was giving a testimony of True Father's life during a Children's Day event. I remember that Rev. Kim was very easy to photograph because he hardly ever moved. I did the best I could and gave the film to Robert.

Since I was at the Barrytown workshops and later very busy fundraising on MFT, I had forgotten about the photos I took of Rev. Kim.

Figure 43 Rev. Won Pil Kim giving True Father's Course

Years later, I saw the book by Rev. Kim called "Father's Course and Our Life of Faith." The front cover was one of the photos I took of Rev Kim on that day at Belvedere. It became my first published photo for the church.

Heung Jin Nim

One Sunday, when True Father was giving his Sunday sermon, I would do my usual round of taking photos from different angles of the training center room. I had a Nikon camera with a very long lens and an oversized flash. All three pieces became very heavy to hold. The best place to be was at the side door, near the kitchen area to photograph True Father when facing the audience of brothers. Since the equipment was so heavy, I would lean my left shoulder against the doorway to balance myself and be as steady as possible.

Figure 44. True Father and Col. Han near True Family

When I was looking through the camera lens, something touched my right shoulder. I turned my head a bit and noticed that it was Heung Jin Nim, resting his chin on my shoulder. Being a budding photographer himself, he was looking to see how True Father would look like through the lens from where I was. I never forgot that moment.

Figure 45 True Father addressing the brothers

Very Early Arrival

Due to my military training, I've always hated being late. Every Sunday, I would try to arrive by 4:15am, so I could be totally ready before True Parents arrived. One morning, I arrived on time, with only three or four members who had arrived just before me. Some of the staff was already finishing preparations, when suddenly the big doors opened and in walked True Father, at about 4:25am. He wanted to see how many members would arrive early. He was not very happy to find so few members. Since, none of the leaders had not yet arrived, True Father sat down in his chair and waited. Meanwhile, the staff was desperately calling the leaders to get to the Training Center as quickly as possible. Few of the leaders were staying at the Belvedere house, so they were running as fast as they could down the hill from the main house. From then on, the leaders and members arrived earlier for Sunday Service.

Chapter 10

Heung Jin Nim and Victory over Communism Tour 1983-84

In early December of 1983, True Parents were preparing to return to Korea for a ten-city Victory Over Communism tour. The day they were to leave, I was given an envelope from Headquarters to give to Rev. Kwak at JFK airport. I arrived at the Delta terminal just in time to catch True Parents and Rev. Kwak about to board their plane. After I delivered the envelope, I saw Hyo Nin Nim and Heung Jin Nim were there to see True Parents off to Korea.

After they said their goodbyes, both Hyo Jin Nim and Heung Jin Nim walked back out of the terminal talking to each. Little did I know that that would be the last time I would see Heung Jin Nim.

Figure 46 Hyo Jin Nim and Heung Jin Nim

The following day, I was told that Hiro Shimoyama and I were to also go to Korea to document some of the events. We were able to photograph the events in Seoul, Taegu, Masan, Cheungju, one or two others, and the last would be Kwangju, in the southern part of Korea.

Shimo and I arrived in Kwangju the day before the event. We had heard that there was a special museum for one of True Father's ancestors, the one who introduced cotton to Korea, just outside the city. We decided to go there to document it. Just as were trying to leave after documenting everything, our van got stuck in the mud and we tried to get it out. This delay actually was a blessing, because we suddenly saw many headlights coming in our direction. It turned out that True Parents and some elders decided to visit this special museum, because True Mother had never been here and True Father wanted her to see it. So, Shimo and I got our cameras and we went to several of the buildings that True Parents visited. There was also a large boulder size rock that was dedicated to True Father's ancestor, which was at least ten feet tall. Before leaving, True Father prayed in one of the small buildings with True Mother by his side. Then, we all departed for Kwangju to prepare for the event the next morning.

The next morning turned out to be extremely cold. Just before the event started, I went outside to get some exterior photos. There were many people outside who couldn't get in, and they were standing around some pickup trucks with television monitors showing the event inside. After taking some photos, I went inside, and realized that fog had developed on the lens, so I couldn't take any photos for several minutes, until it cleared up.

The event went smoothly with entertainment, guest speakers, especially from the Western PWPA (Professors World Peace Academy) guests that True Father invited to attend, and then True Father spoke. All of us did not realize at that time, but Heung Jin Nim would have his accident at this moment. We learned later that an assassin was trying to get into the arena but couldn't, and it was Heung Jin Nim's sacrifice that prevented the killer from getting inside.

After the event, we all joined in a caravan and drove back to Seoul to prepare for a victory celebration and for Un Jin Nim's birthday the next morning at Han Nam Dong.

The next morning, just as the ceremony began, True Father started to speak very softly and seriously. Dr. Bo Hi Pak went over to Un Jin Nim and spoke in her ear. They had gotten word of Heung Jin Nim's accident. Un Jin Nim ran off crying. Everyone was very somber and tearful.

Even though True Parents wanted to go back to America that day, they still had an important event at the Little Angel School, which I believe was for the Moon Clan representatives of Korea. Just before this time, the Moon Clans elected True Parents to be the leader of the entire Moon Clan in Korea. Immediately, after that event, True Parents rushed back to America.

After Shimoyama and I returned to New York, preparations were already being made for January 1st God's Day, but Heung Jin Nim's situation was on everyone's hearts.

A few days after Heung Jin Nim ascended, Robert photographed the ceremony for Heung Jin Nim at Belvedere, where True Parents and True Family formally said goodbye, before Heung Jin Nim's body went to Korea for burial.

Robert and I thought that True Parents had also gone to Korea as well. A ceremony that would take place at Belvedere at the same moment as in Korea was being held for members. Robert said he was busy, so he told me to go. I barely made it there before the ceremony started and much to my shock, True Parents and many of the True Family were there, sitting on the floor in front of a small offering table. Only Hyo Jin Nim and Ye Jin Nim went to escort Heung Jin Nim to Korea.

This turned out to be one of the most difficult and emotional events I ever had to photograph. Photographing them was very difficult, especially when I used a telephoto lens and see tears in their eyes. True Mother was the most difficult for me to photograph. But, True Father had made a determination that he would not shed a tear until the ceremony in Korea was completed. But, I remember very well that one time when I looked through the lens to True Father, I saw a small glimmer of tear deep inside his eye. It was a very difficult time for him. I had to record the event, but it was very painful see them so sad. It was very difficult to see through the lens with my own tears in my eyes.

There would be two more Seung Hwas I would photograph that were difficult. The first was Young Jin Nim's in Korea. The most dramatic part was that True Parents hadn't seen Young Jin Nim's body until he arrived at the Wonjon. True Parents asked that the casket be opened, so they could say goodbye to their son. The second was True Father's Seung Hwa in 2012, which I will describe later.

Chapter 11

1984 Court Decision

One of the most traumatic times in our church history in America was the court trial of our True Father. Many accounts have been written about the trial; especially our True Father's own words and by a reporter named Charlton Sherwood in his book "Inquisition". He was sent to write a scathing report on True Parents and our church, but as he dug deeper, he realized that it was the government and its prosecutors who really did criminal things to our church.

During this time, we at New Future Photo would take turns to attend the trial, taking photos outside the court, and to keep up with events there. One time I was able to be in the small room where True Parents and leaders were during the time the jury was deliberating. True Father was totally focused on how the church was expanding.

On the day of the final verdict, I had just arrived to the courthouse and to call Robert if anything happened. Shortly after I arrived, the jury came in. I sat in the back row, listening and praying intently. When the guilty verdict was announced, it was a big shock. I saw True Father stand up, and with a smile, walk over to the prosecutors who were congratulating each other. True Father wanted to shake their hands, but they brushed him away, gloating their victory.

I immediately called Robert to tell him the news. It was definitely a sad day for our church. But, True Father was hopeful because he was confident something great would come from it. It did.

Finally, the Christian ministers of America, including some very famous names, came out openly to support our True Parents and for religious freedom. The birth of American Clergy Leadership Conference came from that time.

Chapter 12

True Mother's South America-Asia Tour

In the 1990s, True Mother did her first world speaking tour. I was selected to photograph the last half of the tour, starting in South America and ending in Asia. After True Mother spoke in Brazil, Argentina, Uruguay, Peru, New Zealand (I loved New Zealand, reminded me of Hawaii), Australia, Malaysia and Taiwan, we arrived back in Korea. True Parents wanted to take the whole staff to Che Ju Island for a rest, but she told me to go to Japan first and make an photo album from the tour. I went to Tokyo and the photographers from Japanese Headquarters, especially Yusuke Ogawa, worked hard making the album. When I arrived back in Korea, I went straight to Han Nam Dong where True Parents lived. When I arrived, True Mother met me in the living room, and as I stood holding the album to her, she flipped through all the pages of photographs. Then, we went to the dining room where True Father was sitting and she showed the album to him, explaining all the photos. Both True Parents were happy.

One incident on the tour I couldn't photograph was when we had to change planes in Singapore. Our plane was late arriving and we were nervous as anything that we would miss our flight. Unfortunately, when we arrived at the arrivals gate, we found out we were at the end of a long, narrow airport and our departing plane was at the extreme other end. As soon as we got off the plane, all of us, including True Mother, who was very determined to get on that plane, and we carrying all of our carry-on luggage and very heavy camera and video camera bags, began running what seemed like a half-mile of zig-zagging from one end of the airport to the other. As we finally arrived at the gate, totally out of breath and no strength in our bodies, the attendant smiled and said: " Welcome, we've been waiting for you!" They had delayed the departure just for us. We were so happy, exhausted, but happy.

Chapter 13

Ocean Church – Cape Cod

True Father created Ocean Challenge in the early 1980s, a fishing contest open to the public on Cape Cod. The main focus of the event was to catch giant tuna. The people of Gloucester didn't like us there, especially the fishermen. But, when they saw True Father bringing in giant tuna almost every day, they started following him out to the area and fishing near him. What confused them was that he would keep catching tuna while they couldn't. So, wherever the New Hope boat was, the fishermen of Gloucester were close by.

Figure 47 True Father with giant tuna

One summer, True Father had seminary students, and even his own children, go on the Master Marine boats to catch tuna. True Father's schedule was to leave by 4am on the New Hope boat and stay out until he caught a tuna.

We of New Future Films and New Future Photo had to go and document the fishing, going out also on the boats. When the sun was out and the seas calm, it was great. When it got stormy, we went out anyway.

Figure 48 Master Marine boat heading for the giant tuna

One day, I went out with True Father on the New Hope boat. The boat crew asked me to catch some dog sharks that could be used as bait. Before my hook hit the bottom, they would strike and I would start hauling them up. They were very easy to hook, but they didn't come up easily. They would do fast circles all the way up in order to dislodge the hook. They usually lost. I caught several within fifteen to twenty minutes. True Father didn't hook a tuna that day, but it was great just to be on his boat.

When I was on the small boats, and not much was going on, they would ask me to do the chumming. For those who haven't experienced it, chumming is cutting small bait into pieces and mixing it with liquid blood, and throwing it behind the boat, which would leave a trail of goodies for the fish to follow up to the hooks. Those who had strong stomachs, they may not get sick, but for all the others, it was like a tradition, adding our own chum overboard.

One boat had only sisters on it. They not only knew what they were doing, but that day they hooked a tuna that was almost 1000 pounds. When they finally tied it to the boat, they celebrated. One sister had a shirt that said it all: "It's Miller time!" Then, with their boat weighed down on one side, they limped back to port with their big prize.

Figure 49 Pulling in a giant tuna by hand

Being on the boats, whether at Cape Cod or in Alaska, always brought me back to my days in the Navy, sailing from one end of the Pacific to the far reaches of the Indian Ocean, and back again. Being on land, with only the sky and the land, one experience's many beautiful things in nature, but you can hide when the weather gets stormy. Out in the ocean, however, with the beauty of the colors of sunrises and sunsets from horizon to horizon, the swaying of the mast with its lonely red light above trying to catch the countless millions of stars that one can only see at night with no other lights for hundreds of miles; the rolling of the waves from a mirror-like calm with flying fish landing on the deck, gently rocking you back and forth as if you were still in your mother's arms, to a raging typhoon with swells twenty to thirty feet above your head and waves beating you from all sides, and the salt spray hitting your face like thousands of needles; and knowing above all else that there are miles of water underneath the ship, waiting to engulf you. One feels the beauty, serenity and the anger of being at the total mercy of nature's elements surrounding you. You are always in awe with its wondrous beauty, but you give it tremendous respect and admiration.

It is truly the best place to pray and mediate. True Father loved the ocean deeply, because out there, evil does not exist, and praying becomes a natural feeling. I miss it dearly.

Chapter 14

Holy Days

True Parents initiated many church holy days in which we celebrate each year. I helped photographed many of them from 1980 to 2013. Most were in America, especially in the New Yorker Hotel, Manhattan Center, East Garden and Belvedere, and a few I covered in Korea and one in Uruguay. Three instances I recall vividly at the New Yorker.

God's Day and the Elevator

Robert Davis and I had spent several hours in the evening of December 31st setting up for the Midnight ceremony and the beginning of God's Day. After we had finished, we had about three hours, so we went into one of the New Yorker elevators to head upstairs to change into our suits. Just as the elevator began to rise, it suddenly stopped. Crowded as we were, we thought it would start up again quickly, But, it didn't. Before long, we realized that we were really stuck and the thought entered our minds that we might not make it to the Midnight Prayer. After two and a half hours of anxious moments, and praying that True Parents might delay until we got there, we were able to slide into another elevator next to us. With only thirty minutes to spare, we changed and made it in the nick of time to photograph the entire ceremony.

True Mother's Arm

Up until the 1990s, True Parents, during Pledge ceremonies, birthdays and prayers for Holy Days, would raise their arms while they prayed. After many years, True Mother started to have difficulty keeping her left arm in the air. It would slowly drop to below her waist during the prayer. One solution was that I would offer my monopod, which would be covered in white and padded so that True Mother could rest on it until True Father finished the prayer. It wasn't long after this that they no longer held their arms up, but would eventually face each other holding hands.

Holding the Microphone

At a Holy Day at the New Yorker Ballroom, during the special prayer by True Parents, True Father's lapel microphone stopped working. Even though I was trying to photograph, I knew that his prayer was important for recording. Since, I was near there anyway, I was given a regular microphone and squatting in front of True Parents, I held the microphone up to where True Father's voice was heard. My arm ached after a while, but I felt it was worth it.

Chapter 15

Matchings

I photographed many matchings and blessings that True Parents performed. Whatever nationality the participants were from, I could see True Father matching people truly from God's eyes and heart, whether directly in person or by photograph! True Father had said one time that he could see seven generations of our ancestors and also seven generations of our descendants. So, True Father was matching us so we could give birth to great children. At the blessing ceremonies, you can see the sparkle of love in each of the couple's eyes! Only True Father can see and feel true love in each person and what great people their children would become.

New Yorker Hotel 1979

I have been to many matchings, photographing most of them from the New Yorker Hotel, East Garden and Korea. The most fun one was held at the New Yorker Hotel in 1979. Most of the members up to that time had not been matched, and since we knew almost everyone from being on Mobile Fundraising Teams or other missions, it was great fun and sometimes shocking when someone we knew got matched to someone we knew. There were lots of comments like: "Wow, you got match to my MFT captain!" or "You're matched to my spiritual mother!" or even "You got matched to him???"

Figure 50 True Father picking a new matching couple

Korea

One really exciting matching happened in Korea at the Little Angels School in 1982, before the 6,000 couple blessing. True Father was getting upset with the Koreans who had their own ideas about who they wanted to get matched with. They would take a long time to decide, mostly declining, and coming back to try another one. True Father got so angry with them, that he ordered them to all sit down and watch. He then asked all the Japanese to stand, and within one hour, he matched over 300 couples. That's how True Father spanked the Koreans for being so stubborn.

Photo Matching in East Garden

Most matchings took place just before a blessing. One time at East Garden, Paul Fontaine and the staff built special easels, about seven feet long and six feet high and lined in rows of aisles filling the entire main hall, so that matching photos could be placed on them. Then, True Father would go up and down the aisles selecting and matching new couples. Several leaders would assist him, following him up and down the aisles of easels. One or two assistants would stand by next to True Father and when he matched a couple, the assistant would take the photos and staple them together. Then, another assistant would take them to a table where the names would be recorded into a database and the photos kept together. This would take place most of the day until there was no more candidates that True Father could match together. Then, the word would be sent to either the states or other countries to inform the couples of their matching.

Second Generation at East Garden

In December of 2004, True Parents asked that Second Generation candidates come to East Garden to be matched and blessed. Two days before the matching took place, several candidates were asked to stay at East Garden as representatives. One of them was Hiromichi Shimoyama's daughter, Karin.

On the day of the matching, many of the candidates who had arrived, were summoned to the main hall where True Parents could meet them and give a talk. Most of the candidates were told it was just to meet True Parents and hear True Father's words. So, they didn't dress formally for the occasion.

True Father spoke for several hours, and then, said: "Well, since you are here already, we might as well start the matching!" All the candidates went into shock and nervous mode.

First, he matched some Korean candidates, and then some by photographs. Then, he focused more on those who were present.

Figure 51 True Father choosing new Second Generation couple

One by one, couples were being matched. Then, True Father saw one couple sitting together, and quickly matched them. They were in shock. All the other candidates looked to see who was sitting next them. True Father did match another couple more like that, but he continued looking around as he did before. By the time he finished, there were only a few left, but True Father said that their matches were not there.

The following day or so, the blessing occurred in the main hall of East Garden. It was very emotional, especially for the parents because there was no room in the hall for them to see.

Figure 52 True Parents with newly blessed Second Generation at East Garden

After the final group photo was taken, the parents finally entered and it became very noisy with lots of tears of joy and hugs.

I Guessed Right

At one matching in the New Yorker Hotel, I was in the balcony, and I saw Bill Miho from Hawaii. True Father was looking straight at him and I started to look at the sisters and guess which one he would pick. I saw one sister with short, auburn hair and stared at her. True Father looked, he pointed, and she stood up. I was shocked.

My Matching

During the early part of 1987, word came that True Parents were going to bless Hyun Jin Nim at the New Yorker Hotel. Two weeks before the event, Koreans were told that there was going to be a matching and to get ready for it. Several Koreans came to get their matching photos done. One of them was my future wife, even though I didn't know it yet. I knew her somewhat because she would come in sometimes to buy photographs for the Koreans. Well, a few days later, the word of the matching was announced and a workshop was going to be held to prepare that weekend. One part of the workshop was for everyone to divide up into groups lead by a blessed couple. I picked Mrs. Nora Spurgin because I knew her very well. My future bride-to-be was also in the group. We had to share our brief testimonies to each other. Well, I was touched by her testimony and thought about her.

One week later, the matching took place in the ballroom of the New Yorker Hotel. True Parents only wanted those who never went to the matchings to go in first and hear directly the importance of the blessing before the matchings took place. Robert Davis was in the Terrace Room for the portraits of the new couples when they came down stairs. I was in the ballroom all morning, photographing the speech and matchings. When True Parents went for lunch, I went to the lobby and saw my future wife sitting in the area where the new security desk is located now. I went to her to make sure that she was okay. She said "yes!"

After lunch, all candidates were allowed in, and the matchings continued. True Mother and a few Korean leaders sat on the stage watching True Father matching more and more couples. After an hour or two, True Father wanted all westerners who wanted Asian wives to line up. Well, I put my camera on my shoulder and stood in line, about a quarter of the way from the back of the room. Most of the Asian sisters were Japanese, but when one Korean was matched, True Father wanted the other Korean sisters to stand. The brother standing next to me was immediately matched to the

Korean standing in front of us. (A note here: this couple would have a son who would someday be blessed to our second daughter. Small world, yes!) Then, True Father asked me how old I was, and I said 37. Then, he yelled several times toward the stage where one certain Korean was standing, asking her how old she was.

Figure 53 After bowing to True Mother

When she said 34, True Father gestured with his arms that we were matched. During this time, she didn't know that True Father was talking to me, so when I stepped forward, that's when she knew. I bowed to True Father and walked down to her. Then, we stopped in front of True Mother to bow.

President David Kim of the Unification Theological Seminary asked for my camera. Rev. Byung Ho Kim reached for my camera and took our photo. True Mother was smiling.

Figure 54 Our first official portraits by Rev. Kim

We then did our bows of acceptance, and went to Applebee's for small snack and talk. My wife said later that she wanted to be blessed to someone who was close to True Parents, but not a leader. Then, she went to see her friends about me and I went back into the ballroom to continue photographing the rest of the matching.

Chapter 16

Blessings

Figure 55 True Parents and newly blessed couples at the Manhattan Center

I have photographed many of our True Parents blessings, from several of the True Children's blessings, to the Olympic Stadium size blessing of over 30,000 couples. If you were part of a team, it would be easy to photograph. But, if there are only one or two of you, it becomes extremely challenging to photograph.

Figure 56a Blessing Ceremony at Madison Square Garden 1998

In order to tell the whole story of the blessing, the event has to be photographed from all angles: from the activities on the stage where True Parents, True Family and dignitaries are. Then, the couples have to be photographed, either as couples, in small groups or all the couples in one overall photo. Next, the little things as well must be documented.

Figure 57b True Parents and newly blessing couples at Hammerstein Ballroom

All the activities on the stage must be photographed; from the entrance of the attendants, the entrance of True Parents, the prayers, speeches, the Holy Water ceremony, the ring ceremony, True Parents reading the vows and marriage declaration, the VIPs giving their congratulatory remarks, the couples bowing to True Parents, and the three cheers of mansei.

By the end of the ceremony, the photographer is very tired, yet happy, because he was able to see so many new couples blessed, even some he knew.

But, he is not done. True Parents would have entertainment for the new couples with artists singing and dancing. Then, the True Family would sing, and lastly True Parents would sing three or four songs and hopefully True Father would kiss True Mother on the cheek.

Figure 57c Holy Blessing in Korea at Seoul Olympic Stadium

And finally, to end the day, True Parents would have a large banquet for the dignitaries and leaders who attended the blessing, with more entertainment and True Father's farewell speech.

By the end of the day, the photographer has no energy left. But, since the leaders and publications people need photos immediately, the photographer must process the photos in his computer, choose the best ones, correct them and send them before the next morning.

The only blessing he doesn't have to worry about photographing is…his own.

Every aspect of the matching, wine ceremony and blessing is photographed, except one. There is no record of the 3-Day Ceremony. I can't figure it out. It's a ceremony that everyone longs to perform, yet we have no photographic record of it. Oh well, maybe someday in the future.

True Parents held many blessings since 1960. No matter how many times one witnesses a blessing, it was always amazing that True Parents would bless not only the First Generation members of our church, our Second Generation children, but those of all other faiths as well: including Christians and their clergy, Jews and their rabbis, Muslims and their imams, and many other religious followers and their leaders. True Parents are truly the only ones who can bring unity among the religions of the world.

Chapter 17

ICUS, AWR, WMA, WFWP, WCSF

There had been many large events created by True Parents. One was World Cultural and Sports Festival in Seoul. The WCSF took the place of the International Conference for the Unity of the Sciences (ICUS), World Media Association (WMA) and Assembly of World's Religions, and a blessing, combining all the events into several days. I remember that working by myself, I had to make sure I got photographs from all angles of the arena. Several times, while onstage, I would be totally soaked in sweat, I could hardly see and I had to wipe my eyes with a small washcloth if I remembered to bring one. Dr. Frank Kaufmann sat nearby and watched in amazement as I went through my paces during this event.

After True Parents opened the Festival, all of the conferences, the matching and blessing, and the closing banquet had to be photographed. By the time the week was up, all of the photographers and video crew who photographed and filmed the events were totally wiped out.

Figure 58 5th ICUS conference Washington DC 1978

Figure 59 True Parents with ICUS chairmen

Figure 60 True Parents with major religious leaders

Figure 61 True Mother, founder of WFWP

Chapter 18

Kodiak

In the late 1980s, True Parents began staying in Alaska from July and August. True Father always loved the Creation, but Alaska was very special to him and through the many times he visited, he always prayed and set conditions by spending the entire daylight hours fishing, either on the ocean or on the many rivers in Kodiak.

True Father's Snack

Figure 62 On a boat Kodiak, Alaska

The first time I went to Alaska was after one of True Mother's speaking tours, she invited the staff up to Kodiak to see True Father and do some fishing.

The day after we arrived, I was on one of the boats, camera at the ready, and I caught a small halibut. Then, the radio from

Father's boat called out that Father was hungry for a snack and asking for halibut. Well, we moved over to his boat, gave them my fish and that's what Father had for his snack!

True Mother and Kwon Jin Nim

Figure 63 Fishing at Olds River

One day I went with True Mother and Kwon Jin Nim and other members to the Olds River. I was able to do some fishing while waiting for True Mother to catch her fish. The river current was flowing out to sea while the salmon were trying to swim upstream.

Most people were casting straight across the river, with not much luck, but I casted upstream and let the bait flow down in front of the fish. True Mother caught two fish that day, while I caught eight. Kwon Jin Nim didn't fish, but used his fingers to shoot any fish getting caught. True Mother had to calm him down since he got a little wild with it. That night, True Mother told True Father about my fish; he was amazed.

I went several more times to Kodiak, but that first visit was the most memorable.

Chapter 19

Kirov Ballet in Russia

 Dr. Bo Hi Pak invited me to fly with him, Mrs. Pak and Hoon Sook Nim to Leningrad (St. Petersburg), where she was invited to perform as a guest soloist at the Kirov Ballet Theater. Leningrad is a very old city, which went through a terrible siege during World War Two. Being a communist city, it was a very unhappy one. The spirit was very heavy. Hoon Sook Nim said every time she went out for a walk, she felt someone was watching her. Even Dr. Pak felt very insecure. One night, some North Koreans came knocking on the door around 2 a.m. or 3 a.m., inviting him to a party. Dr. Pak knew it was very dangerous to open the door. Satan always works best at night. Even though the North Koreans insisted, the door stayed closed.

 At the night of the performance, the small Kirov Ballet Theater was completely full. I was told later that even though Hoon Sook Nim was nervous, the audience loved her.

 I realized that night, something magical had happened. I realized the difference between a good dancer and a great one. Watching the Kirov dancers, I saw that they were perfectionists in their dancing. They would dance with pinpoint accuracy, in their steps and their leaps. But, there was no emotion coming from them. When Hoon Sook Nim started to dance, the audience saw something they had never seen before. They looked at her face, and saw so much emotion coming from it. The expressions from each move showed how much emotion and heart she was showing them. She literally brought out the heart of the character she was portraying, and it captivated the audience. As soon as she finished, they all stood and wanted her for many encores, showering her with flowers that covered the stage. To me, that's the sign of a great performer.

On a side note, the entire audience was very quiet, listening to the orchestra and focusing on the performers, especially Hoon Sook Nim. The only funny part about it was the theater photographer was doing her job very well, but her camera was so loud that when she took a photograph, people on the other side of the theater could hear the noise of the shutter. It was a horrendous sound.

The president of the Kirov Ballet, who later opened the Kirov Ballet Academy in Washington DC at True Parents invitation, helped organize our trip to Moscow by train, because Dr. Pak was very nervous about the Russian airline. We didn't board a regular train, but one in which only Party officials were allowed to ride. Hoon Sook Nim and her mother had one compartment; Andrew Kessler, who was our translator, was in another compartment and I shared a compartment with Dr Pak.

Figure 64 Hoon Sook Nim with her parents Dr. and Mrs. Pak

For the first two hours of our journey, we all were in Hoon Sook Nim's compartment, drinking Russian tea and talking on a wide range of subjects, especially ballet. It was a very relaxing and cozy time we had together. It is a great memory. Afterwards, we retired. As everyone knows, Dr. Pak is very famous in our movement and has been at True Father's side for many years. Before going to bed, Dr. Pak got onto his bed, curled up into a ball, with his hands and head on the pillow and very humbly and with filial piety, said his goodnight prayers. He is a very great and humble man.

The next morning before arriving in Moscow, I saw Hoon Sook Nim in the passageway using the handrail to do her stretching exercises. She said if she missed one day, she had to work two days to catch up.

One final note about Hoon Sook Nim: She brought her Universal Ballet Academy to New York and was having a casting call for two young girls to play a small part in the ballet, called The Blind Man's Daughter, to be performed at Lincoln Center. Out of about 100 applicants, my daughter Leilani was chosen.

Her role was to dance onto the stage as the young daughter of a blind man, get picked up high in the air a couple of times and then smilingly dance off stage. She performed perfectly. The only thing she worried about was the dancer who picked her up held her so tight that she couldn't breathe. She smiled anyway and lived through it.

What made it extra special was that just before the performance began, True Parents arrived from Korea, and straight from the airport, they sat in the audience with hundreds of people, including dignitaries. It was a grand night for our daughter.

Figure 65 Leilani before performing at Lincoln Center

Chapter 20

Gorbachev at Kremlin

and

The Little Angels

In 1990, True Parents fulfilled their 1976 goal after Washington Monument of going to Moscow. The motto was "Must go to Moscow!" When they arrived at the airport, members of the Soviet media, who helped Dr. Bo Hi Pak set up the World Media Conference, welcomed True Parents with smiles and hope.

The Media Conference was a very important event with representatives of the media from many nations attending, but True Parents number one goal was to go to the Kremlin and meet with President Mikhail Gorbachev directly.

For True Parents, it was more than just a social visit to make friends with President Gorbachev, but to tell him directly that his nation was in grave danger of collapsing into chaos if he didn't abandon the ideology of Marx and Lenin. So, for True Parents, it was a most serious and important visit to the Soviet Union.

Figure 66 True Parents and Dr. Pak with Russian media

Figure 67 True Parents shaking hands with Russian policeman

After we arrived at the hotel, we gathered in True Parents suite and quickly went out to the balcony that overlooked the city. True Parents, Hyo Jin Nim, Ye Jin Nim and Dr. Pak were able to gaze at the city. With my long arms, I was able to get some photos of them smiling.

Figure 68 True Parents and Hyo Jin Nim looking at the city of Moscow

During the conference, True Parents were asked to come to the Kremlin to meet with President Gorbachev. We were escorted into the Kremlin, and then into the main conference room where the country's president always welcomed special guests. Mr. Kwon, the Korean photographer, and myself were grouped with the other photographers and video people near the back and for ten minutes or so, were able to take all the photos we wanted. Then, Mr. Kwon and I were escorted out and had to wait outside. But, they would let one of us stay for the end. Since Mr. Kwon was senior, I gave him a magazine of film so that he could take photos for me, and he stayed. I had to be escorted out of the Kremlin and wait outside the gate. History shows that the conference was historic. But, Mr. Kwon never gave me the film back.

Figure 69 True Parents and True Children in Red Square

It was a great, historic event that ended a few months later when President Gorbachev resigned and the Soviet Union collapsed.

The last night of our stay ended when President and Mrs. Gorbachev, as guests of True Parents, watched the Little Angels sing and danced for them. Mrs. Gorbachev totally fell in love with them. We took photos of them with True Parents, Dr. Pak and the Little Angels on the stage afterwards. It was a complete victory for True Parents. Next stop was North Korea.

Figure 70 True Parents with President and Mrs. Gorbachev with the Little Angels

Chapter 21

North Korea

There were times that I was nervous for our True Parents safety. The most nervous time was when a group of us were going to go with True Parents into North Korea to visit Kim Il Sung. When we arrived in Beijing, we were told that the North Koreans only wanted the Korean contingent to enter the country with True Parents. Only Kim IL Sung and a few of his top advisors knew of True Parents arrival and they were concerned what the rest of the leadership would think. True Father told us that he didn't know what to expect, and that he may not be coming back, ever. Before they left, I gave Peter Kim, True Parents main assistant, ten rolls of film so he can record wherever True Parents. The rest of us who stayed behind in Beijing were very worried for them.

As we learned later, everything went very well. They were greeted with great fanfare at the airport. When they met Kim IL Sung, True Father purposely hug him with a big smile. They had a serious meeting in which True Father told Kim IL Sung directly that his atheistic ideology was wrong. That night, a lavish banquet was held with much singing and toasting.

With a special escort, True Parents and their entourage were driven to True Father's home in the north. They prayed at his parents' graves, met his two sisters and aunt who raised him and took many photos.

Figure 71a Praying at True Father's parents' graves

When they did return a week later, they were so happy that as they were leaving the plane, a slight snowfall sprinkled upon them.

**Figure 71b True Parents with Dr. Pak and Peter Kim
returning to Beijing from North Korea**

That night, we all sat on the floor of the hotel room and True Parents, with a great big smiles, and with photographs scattered everywhere on the floor, told us everything that happened on their victorious journey.

Chapter 22

Birth of My Children

It's every married couple's desire to have children. To experience all levels of love, one must also become a parent. I understood from early on that I needed to be present at our children's births, no matter how many we were blessed to have.

Julie Meesun

In the case of our first child, Julie, it was one of extreme excitement and anxiety. My wife had decided that since drinking ginseng was extremely healthy and nourishing, she drank a cup a day during the first months of her pregnancy. When the doctor told her that it was actually making the baby grow faster, and since my wife was only five foot tall, it would be best to stop. When the day finally came for our child's birth, the doctors became concerned that the baby was too big. After many hours, the time had finally come and the doctors decided it was best that I not be in the delivery room. They said I could watch through a small window where the doctors washed up. So, here I was, looking through this small pane of glass as two doctors on the delivery end and an anesthesiologist, with huge forearms, standing over my wife's head, pushing the baby down with his arm toward the other doctors. My wife, being Korean, believed it would not be good to scream. So, while she was being pushed, she hardly made a sound, but endured through it all, to deliver our first child. When the doctors held up our new daughter, I started to tear up, feeling a deeper love for my wife than I had ever had before.

Leilani Unhye

Our next child, Leilani, was born in a different hospital. This time, the labor and birth were a bit quicker. The only hard part was hearing another would-be-mother screaming in the next room. This time, I was able to be in the delivery room and be my wife's cheerleader. There were three reasons for me being there. First, she needed me. Since we created this child together, she felt comforted and encouraged during the birth. Second, the doctors wanted me there so that by supporting my wife and helping her, they could focus on the birth of our child. And third, I needed to be there. The only connection I had with the baby as nine months before, and by being there at her delivery, I could have a connection of heart to her. When, the doctors carried out our daughter, she wasn't even breathing yet. So, for a few seconds, I was able to see her start her first breaths and my heartistic connection to my daughter began.

The only concern I had was that hurricane Bob was hitting New York the same day. So, when I had to take Leilani to the car the next day to go home, I had to hold her like a football due to the high winds that were hitting the city.

Douglas Hyo-yung

We decided that our son Douglas should be born in the same hospital as Julie. As like his sisters, Douglas wanted to be born on weekend morning. Everything was going according to plan. When we got to the hospital; the doctor said it would be a few hours at least before the birth. Well, as luck would have it, I forgot my camera. Since the doctor said there was no hurry, I drove back to the New Yorker Hotel to get what a photographer should never forget. A thought then came to me that since there was no hurry, I could wait at home a little bit. But, my conscience said: "Nope, get back there!" So, I went straight back. As soon as I got into the room, my wife was only about five minutes away from delivery. With great gusto, I quickly became her cheerleader and encouraged her. Our son was born a few minutes later. Now, after having two daughters, and the doctor having promised it was a son; it was only natural to take a quick glance to make sure. Having confirmed the doctor's promise was fulfilled, I returned quickly to attend my wife.

Having seen the births of our children, my love and admiration for my wife has been deepened to a level I had never imagined. I cannot image how a husband, after watching his wife give birth to his children, could have any idea of divorcing her. To me, it's inconceivable.

Actually, because of my wife, I envy women. Why? Because women are able to experience a deeper understanding of God's heart than a man could. By carrying a child for nine months and go through the pain of giving birth, the woman has a clearer and deeper understanding of what God went through to create the world and through Adam and Eve, create a family. She also has as deeper love for her child, something a man can never understand. Even Jesus could never understand. That is why the woman should teach her husband what she is going through her pregnancy, and then he needs to be actually present at the birth. It is only until the child is born in front of him, can he begin to have a connection of heart with his child.

There is a story soon after the birth of one of their children, True Father asked True Mother to go somewhere with him. She slumped back in the chair and told him: "You don't know how difficult it is to give birth to a child!" True Father thought and said: "Yes, I don't know. Please rest!"

When their next child was born, True Father was in the operating room, watching his new child being born. His love True Mother deepened through that experience. True Father was so happy that he took this photo of True Mother and their new child.

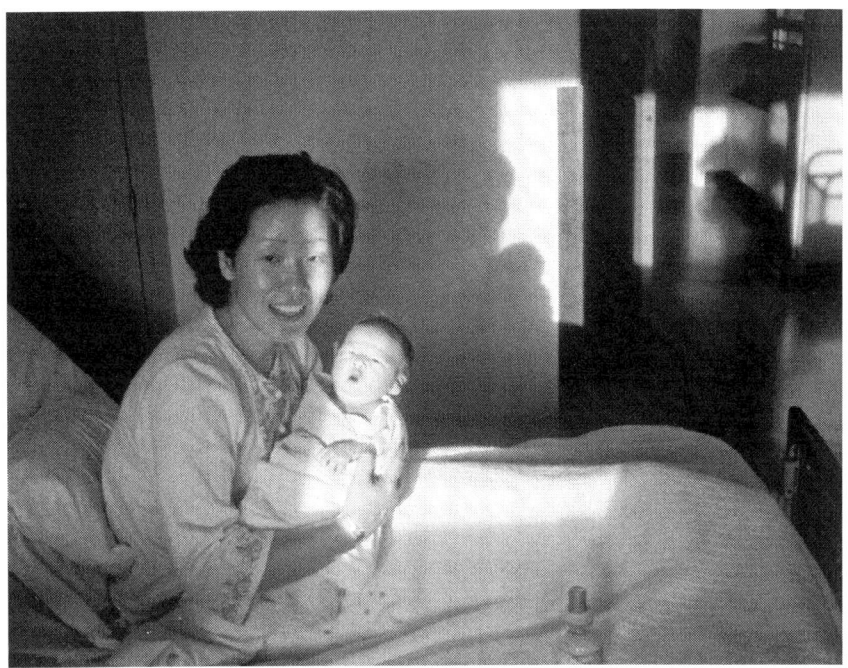

Figure 72 Photo by Rev. Sun Myung Moon

Chapter 23

Kwon Jin Nim-Sun Jin Nim's Blessing

During Kwon Jin Nim and Sun Jin Nim's Holy Blessing in 1995, after the main ceremony, I had to do the various portraits of the brides and grooms with True Parents and the In-laws. Manhattan Center arranged that instead of a ladder, I would climb up a shaky scaffolding to get a better angle for the photos. Even with four strong Second Generation brothers holding it, the scaffolding was still wobbly. True Father wanted to make it a joyous experience, and seeing me on top of this scary place, he yelled: "Dance!" Well, carrying my camera and with hundreds of people in attendance, I began shaking and dancing on top of this moving object. Everyone was laughing and clapping and True Parents had big smiles on their faces. No one knew that even though I had a big smile, how scared I was dancing for True Parents at that moment.

Chapter 24

South American Tour

In the 1990s, True Parents went to South America to visit several countries and try to meet the leaders of those countries. We stayed in Brazil for several days, and traveled to many places, including the great Iguazu Falls, but we couldn't see the president of the country.

Figure 73 True Parents and entourage at Iguazu Falls

While visiting Rio de Janeiro with True Parents and In Jin Nim, we stopped at a beach. True Father saw a fisherman, who was wearing a very small, almost visible bathing suit, casting into the ocean. Father went to him, and through a translator, was able to cast a few times into the ocean. So, there was True Father, with his pants rolled up to his knees and his bare feet in the ocean, standing with a big smile alongside a scantily-clad fisherman, fishing on the beach in sunny Rio!

Figure 74 True Father on the beach at Rio de Janeiro

True Parents were able to see the President of Uruguay, who was very happy to greet True Parents. But shortly after, True Father became very ill and we had to cut the tour short.

Figure 75 True Father with Pres. Luis Lacalle

Chapter 25

The Pantanal Workshop

In the late 1990s, True Parents opened a special workshop place in the Pantanal region of Brazil. They directed that all members should someday attend a 40-day workshop with their families. My wife really wanted to bring our three children to the workshop, but our daughters couldn't get out of school. So, we decided that she would take our four-year old son, Douglas, and I would join them later.

After two very long plane rides and a winding van ride, I arrived at the workshop site. My wife and son had been there three weeks already, so I had some catching up to do. I brought my camera gear in case True Parents visited the workshop. I took a few photos here and there, but mainly focused on studying and being with my family.

For the first week or so, my family and I stayed in our own room. But eventually, we had to separate to the usual brothers-sisters dorms.

The daily routines were like other workshops. But, being in Brazil, it was amazingly hot. The only challenging part of the day was at dinner time. It was usually around sun down, when the sky was pretty. But, it was also the time for the gigantic mosquitoes to come out and swarm all over us while we tried to eat. We ate very quickly.

One amazing brother decided to enlarge one of the fields and make a baseball diamond for anyone who wanted to place baseball. Tom Iversen wanted to leave something for all members to enjoy. So, with the help of many brothers and sisters, it was completed just before he returned to America. He named the field: Field of Dreams.

Three major things I remember do stand out from this workshop. The first was a day-long boat trip, up the winding river through the

Pantanal region, with small farm shacks on the river banks, small alligators, called Yacare caiman, basking in the sun and birds of all kinds everywhere above us. The first stop was at the Americano Hotel, which is more like a small motel on stilts. This is where True Parents stayed many times and declared a major victory for God. The other stop was on the banks in Paraguay where many Korean and Japanese elders were attending a special workshop, personally trained by True Parents, especially in catching many fish per day. It was extremely hot there and mosquitoes were everywhere. Everyone tried to keep the mosquitoes away, but True Father would just sit there and have them enjoy themselves.

    The second thing I remember is that during their visits, True Parents would pose for special portraits for each couple. Since, I had my camera, I was asked to photograph many couples when True Parents did visit. It wasn't easy for our True Parents to sit there for several hundred portraits. Sometimes, they would close their eyes for a few seconds, because it was not easy. I would say my usual "One, two, kimchi!" in different languages so they would know when I would take the photograph. If the portraits were taken outside, it was even more difficult because of the sun. It was extra hard on True Mother, because her eyes were very sensitive. But, True Parents did it because they loved the members very much.But, my wife's main desire was for our portrait to be taken as well. Unfortunately, her plane was leaving the day that True Parents were to arrive. She actually had to leave, with tears, because she couldn't stay a minute longer. But, on the way to the airport, somehow she got word that the portraits were taking place, and she and several others turned around and with great luck, made it back in time for our portraits to be taken. With that accomplished, she was able to go back to America with our son with joy.

Figure 76 Official portrait with True Parents

The third thing was my son, Douglas. It seems he enjoyed him himself immensely while there. Being four years old, he felt very free. He would go to the little store by himself and come back with a snack. He loved the animals that were there, especially the horses and small ostriches. One time, we heard that a large anaconda snake had been killed and skinned. He seemed rather small compared to the twenty-four foot long snake. But, the thing I remember most was Doug's feet. The soil there had something so smelly mixed in that it made the shoes and feet smell terribly bad. It was so pungent that we had to leave Doug's shoes behind. It took almost a year to get the smell out of his feet.

It was a very wonderful experience.

Chapter 26

Speaking Tours

In the 1990s to the 2000s, True Parents became very busy going all over Korea, United States and well over forty countries giving speeches that educated people of the providence. True Father would keep traveling and speaking until it became difficult for him physically. The role of True Mother became more important and she began traveling and speaking as much as True Father. It seems that True Father became more desperate than ever to teach Divine Principle to as many people as possible while he was still able.

Figure 77 True Mother speaking at Manhattan Center

I was able to photograph many of the speaking tours, but their schedules kept them traveling more to more countries. When I was able to fly with them, I would always see True Father read his speech over and over. He was most serious when he was on tour.

Figure 78 True Father again studying his speech

The schedule for these tours became a day-to-day routine, only the names kept changing.

We would do HoonDokHae with members in the morning. Then, some staff would go to the airport with the luggage while True Parents had breakfast and signed programs from the night before. Then, we would rush to the plane, fly to the next city, which we had to remember which one. After landing, I would get out first with the video crew and film True Parents coming out of the plane. Then, we would rush into the first car; get to the hotel just ahead of True Parents. We would then squeeze into the elevator with them, with me next to the door. As soon as the doors opened, I would rush out, hopefully in the right direction, to the suite where children were waiting with flowers and other members standing in line clapping. Then, we would gather in the room, the members would greet True Parents with a bow and leave except the leaders. They would stay and give reports about the event for the night and give them the programs. If there was time, True Parents would have lunch with some of the local leaders and where there would be more reports. Then, True Parents would retire to prepare for the evening event.

After the event, there would be a celebration cake and singing and reports. True Parents would meet with leaders for a short time to end the day.

The next morning would be a complete copy of the day before, except the cities were different. If the tour was only seven or even twelve cities, it wouldn't be so bad, but when we did two 50-city tours, they were rough. True Parents had super human strength to complete those tours.

Figure 79 True Mother's smile

Figure 80 True Father enjoying True Mother's smile

Figure 81 True Father in a quiet moment

Figure 82 Dr. Yang and Rev. Jenkins showing True Father news articles

Figure 83 True Father's great smile

Figure 84 True Father at the podium

Figure 85 True Mother smiling

Figure 86 True Parent receiving award from veterans

Figure 87 True Mother receiving flowers

Figure 88 True Father with Pastor and Mrs. Norman Keanaaina

Figure 89 True Father waves to the audience

Figure 90 True Parents with Dr. and Mrs. Morton Kaplan

Figure 91 True Parents waving goodbye

Figure 92 True Mother singing

Figure 93 True Father loves True Mother's singing

Figure 94 True Parents lighting special candles

Figure 95 True Parents dancing

Figure 96 True Parents giving joy to all

Figure 97 True Parents waving to members before leaving for next city

Figure 98 True Parents with Dr. Yang and Bruce Brown

Flying Over Denver

During the 50-state tour in 2001, we were in True Parents plane flying to Denver from the west coast. True Parents were sitting in the front seat, as usual, I was sitting behind True Mother because there was a table where I can work on photos on my computer from the last city and Dr. Yang was sitting opposite me, facing forward.

Flying over the Rocky Mountains toward Denver is very nerve whacking because of the turbulence before landing. Dr. Yang, who was always working, thinking and preparing for the next city, decided he needed another cup of coffee just before landing, but the cup was so full that when we hit turbulence, he was doing a balancing act to keep from spilling it on his computer.

Just when it seemed he was going to get through it all unscathed, we hit a huge one that sent us down, and Dr. Yang's coffee went straight up to the left of me, hitting the ceiling, onto my left shoulder and barely missing True Father. Our flight attendant was not happy.

The next morning, while we were putting on our seat belts to take off for the next city, True Mother quietly asked Dr. Yang; "Do you have your coffee?" Everyone on the plane laughed, including Dr. Yang.

Victory Celebration

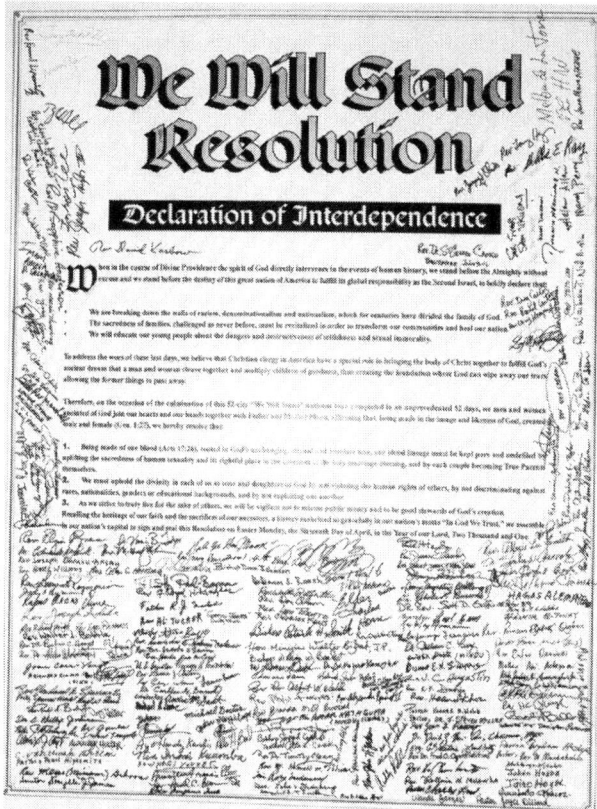

Figure 99 We Will Stand Resolution 2001

At the victory celebration at East Garden at the end of the 2001 50-State tour, True Parents invited many of the ministers they saw on the tour to celebrate with them the great victory. After many reports and testimonies, Dr. Yang and Rev. Jenkins showed True Parents the "We Will Stand Resolution" in which many ministers signed. With smiling faces, True Parents happily signed their names and all the ministers applauded. This has become a very historical document in our church history and one of the great victories in the long history of our True Parents.

The Scariest Moment: the Ukraine

The scariest time during any speaking tour was when True Mother was going to speak in Kiev, in the Ukraine. It was late December and it was frightfully cold. I think we had just arrived from Belarus, where the president and his wife joyfully welcomed True Mother and attended her speech in their beautiful opera house. It was a great success.

But, when we arrived in Kiev, the situation was just the opposite. The government didn't want True Mother to give her speech and we had to change the venue at the last minute. Even though the Soviet Union had fallen two or three years before, many of the KGB agents had relocated to the Ukraine. So, throughout the evening, we were afraid the KGB would find us, break down the doors and stop True Mother.

Luckily, through God's protection, and the Ukrainian members and their prayers and efforts, True Mother was able to complete her speech with great success.

The next morning, it was decided that we would leave as early as possible. So several of us went from the building where we stayed and at about six o'clock in the morning, we walked in the freezing cold with our luggage and gear many blocks to the place where the cars were waiting. We had a feeling that we were being watched the entire time, but we were able to get to our destination and left for the airport without any more difficulty.

This definitely reminded me of the time in Leningrad with Dr. and Mrs. Bo Hi Pak and Hoon Sook Nim when the North Koreans tried to kidnap Dr. Pak.

Chapter 27

Qatar

In the late 1990s, my wife and I went to a 40-day workshop at Cheong Pyeong. After the workshop ended, there was a lottery to pick National Messiahs. We prayed if we get a country, it would be one that we could handle. That country turned out to be Qatar, in the Middle East. I had only one chance to go to that country because of my other responsibilities. Before I left, I had a dream in which I was near the beach area, and suddenly another country decided to invade Qatar. People began running away. But, I didn't want them to. So, I picked up the maroon and white national flag of Qatar and started waving it so people can be inspired and go back and defend the beach.

A few days after I went to Qatar, I was walking near the end of the runway of the national airport, which not only served the airlines, but also military jets. I suddenly heard one jet come in too close while landing, and the wind from the jet broke off one of the flags nearby. I went over, but there was no way to put the flag back up, so I started walking with the flag. I thought a good place to put it was at a nearby museum, but they didn't want it. Then, the police stopped me and I told them what should I do with it. They just said place it nearby. So, I took it back to the original place, propped it up above some bushes so it wouldn't fall down, and walked away.

One day, I visited the Minister of the Interior and talked to him about True Father and Family Federation for World Peace. I mentioned to him that one of my friends was from Sudan. When I mentioned Taj Hamad's name, the minister replied; "Oh, Taj, everyone knows Taj!

Chapter 28

Middle East Peace Initiative

In 2003, Dr. Yang and Rev. Jenkins were inspired to send the clergy from ACLC to Rome and Israel. When True Parents got the reports from the first pilgrimage, they too were inspired and encouraged Dr. Yang and Rev. Jenkins to enlarge it, to bring unity between the Abrahamic faiths throughout Israel and the region. What emerged became truly historical in nature and achieved goals that weren't even imagined before then.

Each pilgrimage became larger and larger, more international in scope that would center totally on the religions of Judaism, Christianity and Islam in Israel.

The main events of each tour would be talks from representatives of the three faiths in Israel, a peace walk through the narrow streets of Old Jerusalem, tours of major religious sites such as: Bethlehem, Nazareth, Mount of Olives, Garden of Gethsemane, Church of the Holy Sepulchre,

Herod's Palace where Jesus was tortured and questioned by Herod, and the streets where Jesus carried the cross to his crucifixion. We also visited Jericho and the West Bank, and bathed in the Dead Sea. We participated in conferences in Jerusalem, Al Aqsa Mosque, Tel Aviv, Dimona, Gaza and Ramallah. Several times we journeyed to Jordan, where we were welcomed by the King's Imam.

Figure 100 ACLC ministers burying the cross in Potters Field

Figure 101 ACLC ministers about to enter Old Jerusalem

Figure 102 ACLC ministers begin Peace walk

Figure 103 ACLC ministers at the Western Wall

Figure 104 ACLC at the Dome of the Rock

Figure 105 Rabbi, Imam and Clergy together

Figure 106 ACLC at Dome of the Rock

Figure 107 Giving a testimony

Figure 108 Photographing main event

I was able to go to Israel twenty-three times, thanks to Dr. Yang and Rev. Jenkins.

Several events do stand out that are worth mentioning:

Jerusalem Declaration

The closing banquet at the first visit to Israel became an historical event. True Parents wanted a declaration to be made by the three Abrahamic faiths showing their unity in bring peace to the Middle East. Dr. Yang and Rev. Jenkins were very nervous about this, but they had absolute faith in fulfilling True Parents desire. With the help of Rev Abe,

Hod Bens-Vee and the ACLC ministers, religious and civic leaders came to witness this great event.

At the climatic moment, Archbishop George Augustas Stallings, Jr. read the Declaration to the entire audience. Then, he and two main representatives of the Abrahamic faiths came forward and with great humility, signed the declaration, with photographs and video recording their signings. In fact, at one point the Jewish rabbi gestured that the Islamic imam could sign ahead of him, which inspired many in the room. Afterwards, everyone in the room came forward and signed the declaration as well. A small space was left open in the center so when the declaration was taken back to America, True Parents signed their names as well, completing a great, historical document.

Fig. 109 Archbishop George Stallings reading the Jerusalem Declaration

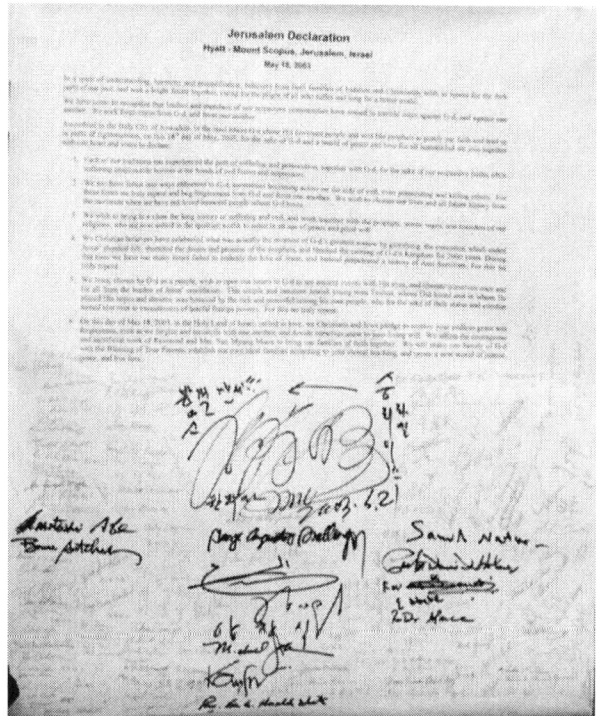

Figure 110 The Jerusalem Declaration

Coronation of Jesus

Figure 111 Rally for Peace and Coronation for Jesus

True Father believed that it was time that a ceremony should take place giving Jesus the crown that he richly deserved in life. At the urging of True Parents, a large rally was held at Independence Park in Jerusalem, with several thousand people of all the major religions participating, and if my memory serves me right, it was broadcasted throughout the country. After the main event, where the leaders of the three Abrahamic Faiths exchanged gifts, the ceremony for the Coronation of Jesus took place, where a chair representing Jesus' throne was on the stage and a crown placed on the chair, proclaiming Jesus King of Israel. Representatives of Judaism, Christianity and Islam were represented on the stage. This was a historic event True Father wanted to give to Jesus.

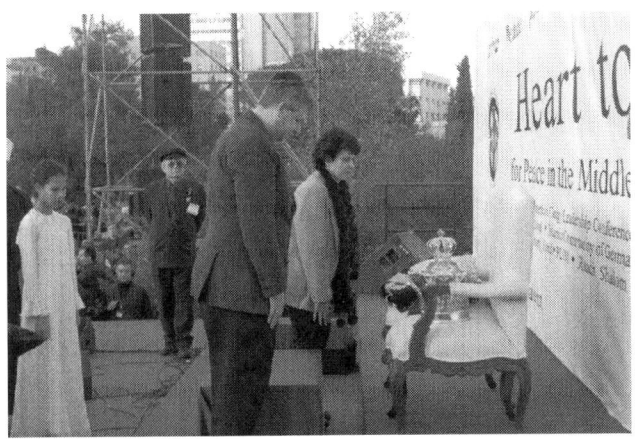

Figure 112 Coronation of Jesus as King of Israel

The First Visit to Gaza

The first time we visited Gaza was exciting, yet very scary. The Palestinians invited many of us, including members of the clergy, for a conference. The dialogue was very informative and future meetings were planned. Then, before heading back to Jerusalem, we stopped off at a small village, I think the name was Rafa, at the western edge of Gaza, bordering Egypt. The entire area was cleared of hundreds of homes to make a DMZ area. The houses at the very edge were covered with bullet and artillery holes. Families were still living there, even small children. We all walked to the edge to see the border. When some of the ministers started to take flash photos, bullets started flying our way, some of them ricocheting off the walls. We quickly ran for cover and went straight to the buses. My friend, Gayokla Nichi Ayala, was sure they were shooting at him, because he was the furthest one out with his arms raised, giving a Native American prayer.

Native Americans in Israel

Figure 113 Native American playing drums for peace

One group of participants totally captivated not only the Jewish people, but the Palestinians as well. During several of our trips, Native American leaders would dress up in their regalia of buckskins and head bonnets. Chief George Akeen and his wife of

Oklahoma would dress up so beautifully that the citizens of Israel would gaze at them and take photographs with them.

Figure 114 Native Americans praying at Jewish Memorial

Our brother, Gayokla Nichi Ayala, would dress up during special occasions and sometimes dance in front of the local people. Even when we went to Gaza and Ramallah, everyone wanted to take a photo with him. Gayokla is a great ambassador for our True Parents.

Figure 115 Gayokla Nichi Ayala dancing at
Jesus' Coronation

Yassar Arafat's Funeral

Another event was when Yassar Arafat died in France and we were invited to attend his funeral in Ramallah. When we arrived, there were already thousands of people trying to get in, even climbing the walls. Many dignitaries from difference nations and organizations were also present. The plan was for the casket to be carried from the helicopter to the main hall where the dignitaries could give their respects. We realized that something was wrong when many of the mourners broke down the doors to the hall and barged in. They wanted to be the ones to be near Arafat's body, not the dignitaries. Later, we found out that with thousands of people were in the compound, it was impossible for the casket to leave the area of the helicopter. So, he was buried right there. On a later visit, we visited his grave, which now had a small, elaborate building on top. We had visited Mr. Arafat several times and he welcomed us warmly. Even though Israel didn't like him, one of the pins he had on his vest was of the flags of Israel and Palestine.

The Women's Pilgrimage

Figure 116 Hundreds of Women for Peace at Dome of the Rock

One very interesting pilgrimage was the sixth one. It was centered only on women. Lead by Alexa Ward, several hundred women journeyed to Israel. Dr. Yang, Rev. Jenkins, myself, a video crew were the only males present. The women held a conference, walked through Old Jerusalem on a peace walk, visited historic sites, and unique to them, held a sister-hood bridge ceremony in which women from the different religions became sisters, including Jews and Palestinians. What amazed me, is that when women are basically by themselves with no men around, they act almost as if they were still in high school; talking, laughing, and just free without any men around. It was most interesting to see.

Martin Luther King III

One of the last times I went Israel was with Martin Luther King III. He was very enlightened with the conferences we held and visiting some of the historic sites. We also took him to Al Aqsa Mosque. He was very grateful for our work there and wanted to help in the future.

The Security Checkpoint at Gaza

One small event happened in Gaza. Rev. Jenkins, Archbishop George Stallings and myself were leaving Gaza and going through the Israeli checkpoint. We had already registered our names and passports to them on the way in, so they knew who we were. But, for some reason, they decided to keep us locked in a holding area for almost two hours, even though it was just the three of us. Archbishop Stallings was always smiling and talking to the guards, who also talked back. But, we still couldn't go on through. Then, I noticed that a Palestinian mother and child were coming through the gate as well. She was carrying many things. The guards gave her permission go to through, but she was having trouble with all her belongings. So, I put down my camera bag and helped her son go through and when she joined him, I passed all her belongings to her. She was very grateful. Rev. Jenkins remarked it was a special moment.

Special Event in Nazareth

Several times, we would visit Nazareth, the city southwest of the Sea of Galilee where Jesus grew up. Usually, we would visit the Church of the Annunciation, which is on the traditional site of the house where, Joseph, Mary and Jesus lived; and Mount Precipice, where Jesus had to escape from the angry crowd because of his teachings.

During one of our visits, we held a special Holy Wine ceremony for some special guests from the city. During the ceremony, I noticed five tourists from Indonesia looking into the room, fascinated of what was happening. I told them that the ceremony was created by Rev. Moon to change our blood lineage back to God's lineage. They understood very quickly and they all wanted to participate. So, I got five cups of the Holy Wine and after they drank, I said a special prayer for them. They thanked me for giving them this special gift and feeling very blessed, they promised to visit our church went they arrived back home.

Figure 117a Giving Holy Wine prayer in Nazareth

Figure 117b At Holy Ground in Jerusalem

Every time I visited Israel, even since my first visit as part of the Youth Seminar on World Religions in 1982, understanding God's heart and the heart of Jesus became more real. Every member of our church should visit Israel, at least once, to have that heartistic connection in their life of faith.

Chapter 29

Gratitude for Korean War Veterans

In the summers of 2005 and 2007, True Parents invited many Korean War Veterans from the sixteen nations that helped stop the North Korean invasion of the south to go to Korea as their guests. The main purpose was to show these aging veterans how much True Parents and the people of Korea were grateful to these men who sacrificed so much of their youth in liberating them from communist aggression.

The morning after the opening banquet, the veterans, some dressed with their medals proudly displayed, went to the Korean War Memorial to dedicate those who sacrificed themselves in the war.

Figure 118 UPKMF Banner

Figure 119 American Korean War Veterans

Figure 120 Veterans of the Sixteen Nations at Korean War Memorial

Figure 121 Korean War Veterans group photo

Afterwards, all the veterans were driven up to the DMZ area, dividing the North and South Korea, to view the tunnels dug by the North for future invasions and visited the lookout areas where they could see North Korea itself. Many of these old veterans had not been to this area since the war.

Figure 122 Veterans looking towards North Korea

They were driven to one of the Korean army camps based near the DMZ. The responsibility of these soldiers is to patrol the DMZ border as first line defense against the North. The veterans of all the sixteen nations were warmly received by these grateful soldiers.

The veterans were truly amazed by how much these men patrolled the border day and night during their two-year enlistment.

Figure 123 Korean War Veterans with DMZ soldiers

After the soldiers showed their skills in marching and hand to hand combat, the young soldiers would help the veterans receive food from the chow lines and would gratefully sit next to these veterans who helped liberate not only their nation, but their great-grandparents, grandparents and their parents from captivity or even death. All of the veterans were truly touched by these young men and it brought back many memories of their youth, and some of their friends who never made it back home.

The next day was a long train ride to the southern part of the country to visit the seaport of Pusan, where at one time during the Korean War, was the only place that the North Koreans didn't capture. The purpose of this trip was to visit the United Nations Cemetery that holds many of the soldiers of the sixteen nations who died in the Korean War.

Even though it was a very hot day, the old soldiers were dressed in their finest and would march into the cemetery in groups behind their nation's flags. To their astonishment, lining up inside the cemetery were their comrades, soldiers of the South Korean Army who fought next to them in the war. There were many smiles and tears as they saw each other for the first time in almost sixty years.

All the nations would then line up for a special ceremony where each nation would lay flowers at each of their nations flags.

Figure 124 Veterans from Sixteen Nations at Pusan's United Nations Cemetery

Afterwards, they would pose in groups and visit the graves, hoping to find at least one of their buddies, who still lie in peace.

Figure 125 American Korean War Veterans

Sometimes, they would find one

Figure 126 British veteran finds his comrade who was killed next to him

The highlight of the last day was the banquet at the Peace Palace hosted by True Parents. True Parents wanted to personally thank each of the veterans for what they had done. True Father would explain how he was interned in a death camp in Han Nam and was freed by the Allies just hours before he was to be executed. True Mother was also grateful because for a time, as a small girl, she and her mother was also captured by the North Koreans and held for a time.

Figure 127 True Parents receiving gifts from veterans

After True Father read one of his important speeches about God's providence and the Pacific Rim, there was entertainment and the sharing of gifts.

Being the son of a veteran, and a veteran myself, photographing these two events, with these old men in the twilight of their lives, watching them go back in time of their youth, I would understand what was going on in their minds and their hearts. And, I would have a deeper love for my dad, who flew in such dangers out in the Pacific during World War Two and the Korean War.

But, most importantly, watching True Parents give all of their heart to these men, who truly gave their lives for a people, a nation, during the prime of their lives.

Chapter 30

Hyo Jin Nim
A Filial Son

True Parents' first son, Hyo Jin Nim, was a great inspiration for all of us, especially to the Second Generation who looked up to him. Even though he had gone through many struggles growing up in Korea and especially here in America, Hyo Jin Nim always loved True Parents and wanted to give them all the joy he could.

He greatest love was music. He wrote so many songs, many of which he recorded and dedicated to True Parents. His songs reflected his love for True Parents and how he wanted to be a son of filial piety to them. Many of his songs were fast, loud, and the compositions complicated, but everyone could feel his heart being expressed through them.

**Figure 128 Hyo Jin Nim and his band
with Joe Longo and Roy Clark**

He spent many years not only composing and recording music, but he was determined to remodel the Manhattan Center and turn it into a world class media and recording center, and where major events could be held in the Hammerstein and Grand Ballrooms. Through his guidance, Manhattan Center is now a reality.

Even though he would work all day, then write and record music till the early morning hours, he wanted to keep the tradition of the Belvedere Sunday Service alive when True Parents were not in the country. He would not speak very long, but he was very focused on what he wanted to give to the members.

Fig. 129 True Father   **Fig. 130a Hyo Jin Nim**

During True Father's incarceration in Danbury in 1985, Hyo Jin Nim did at least one forty-day prayer condition where he and other members would pray for several hours from midnight at the Holy Ground at East Garden so that God could protect True Father during his stay in prison.

On the final night, I was requested to photograph the last prayer for history. It was pitch black, with no moon at all and no lamp posts anywhere near by, and the entire group huddled and prayed with Hyo Jin Nim those final hours. It wasn't easy to photograph considering we were near a small cliff, and I had to tip-toe along the edge in order to be in front of them.

All the members who joined Hyo Jin Nim during the entire forty days including several of the True Family, Second Generation, wives of church elders and East Garden staff, were glad to join Hyo Jin Nim in completing this historic prayer condition.

At the end of the prayer, they wanted a group photo to celebrate this victory. I made many copies and True Mother signed every one for each member. True Parents were very happy for Hyo Jin Nim's determination to help True Father during that time.

Figure 130b 40-Day victory group photo

For all of us who watched him grow up, overcome his struggles and brought so much inspiration to True Parents and to all of us, Hyo Jin Nim is a shining example of a filial son, and a guiding force for all of us to be sons and daughters of our True Parents as well. We all miss him dearly.

Figure 130c Hyo Jin Nim

Figure 130d Hyo Jin Nim great smile

Thank you, Hyo Jin Nim

Chapter 31

DREAMS

As like other members, I had many dreams of True Parents. In most of the dreams I received, I usually had a camera: either I was setting up to do photography or actually photographing True Parents doing something. These are only a few of the dreams I received.

Dream of New Son

In the late 1970s, I heard that our True Mother was expecting again. I asked a Japanese sister what I could do to support her! She said the best thing was to pray for her every night!

So, I prayed that True Mother would be able to give birth to a healthy baby and that she and her child would be fine!

One night, I had a dream in which True Father was sitting on the right side of a covered porch, facing to the left. Behind him, there were thousands of members, as far as the eye could see. And there, seated on his lap was a baby, dressed in blue clothes. True Father, with a great big smile, was bouncing the baby on his lap. And, every time he lifted the baby high above him, the crowd behind them would give a tremendously loud and glorious cheer and applause. True Father would keep doing this over and over again, bouncing his new son and then, lifting him up in the air, his smile getting bigger and bigger. And each time, the crowd of members would give a greater cheer and applause. Father was so happy and proud.

A few hours after I had this wonderful dream, I heard that True Mother had given birth to a son, Hyung Jin Nim.

True Mother and Texas

I was photographing somewhere, maybe Texas, with fields, a flood and cows that were in a field and jumping over the water to where I was standing, and other Texas-like things. I stumbled upon a tycoon's office building (JC Penny in the long name, but the tycoon looked like H. Ross Perot, the billionaire) and it looked like they had special guests visiting. They had coffee and snacks in the lobby area (which one lady dropped the two-level coffee pot…twice), and a new silver helicopter with a large pink ribbon in the middle (billionaires can have helicopters in their lobbies if they want).

I met a couple of members who worked there, including one who asked me about joining as a photographer. I told him I'd have to ask my wife, since I would have to move to this Texas-like place. Then, I realized sitting next to him was True Mother. She was talking to someone. Then, she had to leave to go to True Father. But, her leg was not very well, so I put her left arm over my shoulder and I helped walk her through the hallway and lobby.

We reached a staircase with a very low ceiling, in which it was difficult to stand. I knew True Mother couldn't go down the normal way, so I sat down like a sled and she sat on top of me, and we started sliding down the stairs, bumping all the steps all the way. She was smiling. Just as we got to the bottom, True Father and many people were standing, smiling…just then I woke up.

True Father and Photographs

After True Father ascended to Spirit World in 2012, I received a dream that I was sitting at a large table with True Father looking at many photographs. After a while, True Father looked up at me and said: "Thank you!"

I was so pleased to make him happy.

Chapter 32

ARTICLES

During the years, I was inspired enough to write a couple of articles that were eventually published. The first article "Advice to Young People", I wrote while visiting Japan. I went to a MacDonald's to get some breakfast, and I noticed about five or six young people sleeping in the corner. It seems that they were out very late and decided to bed down for the evening at the all-night MacDonald's. I felt sorry for them and began to think how to give them some advice. The following article is the result of my thinking at that time.

Advice to Young People

If there is one piece of serious advice I can give you, it's this: Keep your purity (virginity). If there is one precious possession that you have, it is your purity. No one else has it. Everyone is born pure (a virgin). But, very few people know how precious it is. Because of their ignorance, they give it away without knowing its true value.

Young people are no longer children and are looking more like adults. But, they do not understand the full responsibility of adulthood. Therefore, they do things on a whim without understanding the full weight (consequences) of their actions, and they spend the rest of their lives suffering because of it.

Your purity is something that only you possess. Once you give it away, you can never get it back. It's gone forever. So, to whom do you want to possess your virginity? Do you want to give it to a complete stranger who would add you as a conquest to his long list and never see you again? Or do you want to give it to a relative whom you think you can trust and wants to start you off right?

No, you want to give your purity to the person to whom you most cherish and love and whom you know would carry your precious treasure always, never letting it go, even for an instant? Who is this special person? This person is none other than your spouse. Before you marry, you always want to keep your most precious things hidden. But, after you marry, you happily give your treasure to this most precious person, for you know your spouse is the one who most appreciates and values your treasure and will guard it well.

When my wife and I were married, we were both virgins. I was 39, she 35. Why did we wait so long? Because we didn't meet each other until we were in our thirties. It is not easy for people to wait for marriage, because it is natural to want to give and receive love. For man, who is the one who initiates love, he is looking for beauty to give his love to. Woman is the one who is ready to receive love by giving her beauty. When man and woman meet, they instantly want to give and receive each other's love and beauty.

But, young people don't understand the preciousness of this, of what happens in a marriage between a husband and wife. By not fully realizing this point, they only count on the physical aspect of a relationship. By concentrating only on physical love, they lose the value of their purity, and can easily give it away. So many young people have regretted it afterwards, having realized how precious their virginity was and that they should have waited.

So, please understand that your virginity is priceless. You cannot exchange it for anything. Once it is gone, it's gone forever. I gave my virginity to my wife. She possesses it and values it deeply. My wife gave her virginity to me. I treasure it in the deepest recesses of my heart. We are very happy because we know who possesses each other's purity. It is our most beloved spouse.

So, please wait. If my wife and I could wait till our late thirties, you can wait a little longer.

True Father spoke a lot about the dangers of homosexuality, so I collected some of his thoughts and from my experiences and wrote down this piece.

Does Homosexuality Have a Universal Basis for Existence?

For thousands of years, debates have occurred on whether or not homosexuality should be a bona-fide way of life in human civilization. In order to answer this question, we must make a final decision on whether homosexuality has a universal basis for existence.

Throughout history, homosexuals and lesbians have said that they have the civil, freedom and equal right, like heterosexuals, to do whatever they want to express themselves with their minds, bodies and actions, even more so in today's free society.

But there has been, throughout human history, great resistance against homosexuality and lesbianism.

Let's discuss this from six points of view.

Let us first investigate this on the basis of religion. There are many arguments based on religious beliefs, especially in the major religions of Judaism, Christianity and Islam. The three main examples, of course, are the fact God put Adam and Eve in the Garden of Eden, one of each, not two Adams and not two Eves. There, they were to grow up and be blessed in marriage from God and have a family.

Matthew 19:4-6: Have you not read that he who made them from the beginning made them male and female, and said "For this reason a man shall leave his father and mother and be joined to his wife, and the two shall become one flesh? So they are no longer two but one. What therefore God has joined together, let no man put asunder."

Leviticus 21:13: He shall take a wife in her virginity.

Ephesians 5:33: Let each one of you love his wife as himself and let the wife see that she respects her husband.

Genesis 1:28: Be fruitful, multiply and fill the earth and have dominion

Qur'an 2.35: O' Adam! Dwell you and your wife in the garden and from it a plenteous food wherever you wish and do not approach this tree, for then you will be of the unjust.

1st Corinthians 7:4: The wife hath not power of her own body, but the husband, and likewise also, the husband hath not power over his body, but the wife.

Another example is when God smote Sodom and Gomorrah for unnatural lust, especially when the men of the city want to "know" the two angels.

Genesis 13-13: Now the men of Sodom were wicked, great sinners against the Lord

Genesis 19:3-5: But he urged them strongly, so they turned aside to him and entered his house, and he made them a feast, and baked unleavened bread, and they at. But before they lay down, the men of the city, the men of Sodom, both young and old, all the people to the last man, surrounded the house, and they called to Lot "Where are the men who came to you tonight" Bring them out to us, that we may know them"

Genesis 18:20: Then the Lord said, "Because the outcry against Sodom and Gomorrah is great and their sin is very grave."

Leviticus 20:13: If there is a man who lies with a male as those who lie with a woman, both of them have committed a detestable act…

Romans 1:26-27: For this reason God gave them up to vile passions. For even their women exchanged the natural use of what is against nature. Likewise also the men, leaving the natural use of the woman, burned in their lust for one another, men with men committing what is shameful, and receiving in themselves the penalty of their error which was due.

1 Corinthians 6:9-10: Do you not know that the unrighteous will not inherit the kingdom of God? Do not be deceived. Neither fornicator, nor idolaters, nor adulterers nor homosexuals… will inherit the kingdom of God.

Jude 7: as Sodom and Gomorrah, and the cities around them in a similar manner to these, having given themselves over to sexual immorality and gone after strange flesh, are set forth as an example, suffering the vengeance of eternal fire.

In the Qur'an:

Surah 7, verses 80-81: do ye commit lewdness such as no people in creation committed before you? For ye practice your lusts on men in preference to women, ye are indeed a people transgressing beyond bounds.

Surah 26, verse 165: What! Of all creatures do ye come unto the males, and leave the wives your Lord created for you? Nay, but ye are forward folk.

Throughout history, Governments, empires, and ideologies quickly came and vanished, but these 1,400 to 4,000 year old religions and the absolute truths they were founded on, whether one likes it or not, these three religions cannot be ignored.

Next, let's examine this issue from the basis of science and nature.

Throughout the universe, there are two fundamental laws that govern all relationships: the relationship of subject and object, and give and take action.

In science and nature, everything exists in a subject-object relationship. There are no exceptions. According to natural and scientific laws, opposites have a specific purpose: they are attracted to each other in a common interest, thus forming counterparts. The relationship of subject and object is found in all relationships throughout the universe. In the case of an atom, the proton, which is subject, and the electron, which is the object, must both be present in order for interaction to begin. Then, when this interaction begins, energy, through give and take action of the subject and object, begins to flow, resulting after these two become one in harmony, thus progressing into a greater form with the direction and objective of higher dimension. Then the atom, through mutual attraction, unites with other atoms to form molecules. Likewise, stamen and pistol form to make plants. Male and female animals unite to make baby animals, and man and woman come together creating children, thus creating families.

Through this process, we come to realize that one cannot exist without its counterpart. Therefore, the purpose for each being is to exist for the sake of the other. A subject cannot exist without its object. A teacher cannot exist without its students, man cannot exist without woman, woman cannot exist without man, parents cannot exist without children, grandparents need grandchildren, the mind cannot exist without its body, the Solar System cannot exist without the sun. Through this, we can conclude that nowhere in the universe, can subject/subject and object/object relationships exist.

"The formation of this vast universe is the common purpose shared by all subject and object pairs. Thus, the universe protects itself and at the same time, it protects and promotes those beings that have attained oneness. Furthermore, it causes repulsion in those beings that lack harmony and repels those that try to invade the existences that have attained oneness. This is how perpetuity becomes possible." (Rev Sun Myung Moon, 5th ICUS 1976)

Two magnets can show this to be true. The North Pole of a magnet cannot unite with the North Pole of another magnet. They, following the law of nature and science, repel each other. But, when the North Pole of one magnet comes closer the South Pole of another magnet, a force draws them together creating give and take action with each other into one united body so tightly that it makes it difficult to pull them apart. This follows the law that counterparts attract. The more the force that binds these counterparts together, the tighter the bond will be. Without this bond of give and take that creates these unified bodies, nothing can exist, not even the universe.

In the natural world, one never finds two male animals or two female animals uniting with each other. Two male animals usually fight each other, knowing that only one subject can exist in a herd.

Another viewpoint that can be examined is an anatomical study of the human body. If we look at the male body, the central point of the male is the sexual organ or reproductive organ. With its definite convex shape and the ability to manufacture, store and send seed, we can know that the main purpose is to impregnate the female's egg. By this viewpoint, we can see that it was designed not for another male, but for its counterpart, the female.

When looking at the female anatomy, there are several areas that we can analyze. The first area is the female breast. The main function of this area is to manufacture and give milk to her child. The second area, the sexual organ (concave shape), is designed for two main functions. One is for the male to enter and impregnate her and the second is to deliver her baby to the outside world. The third area is the reproductive system, which sends the eggs to a position to be impregnated by the male's seed and the womb, which develops the fetus, for its eventual delivery to the outside world. From this viewpoint, we can see that all of these areas were not designed for another female, but for its counterpart, the male. Therefore, only through the union between a man and woman's reproductive organ can children be created, thus fulfilling its purpose for existence. Always remember, the man (husband) has the key that unlocks the woman's (his wife's) love and happiness.

Another viewpoint would be the relationship each member has in the family. All human beings are, whether they like it or not, born into a Heterosexual family, where there is a father and a mother. Only in the family, can true love be found. The four main levels of true love can only be experienced with the family. They are; children's love, which is experienced by the child to its parents; mutual love which is experienced through the relationship between brothers and sisters; conjugal love, which is the highest level of mutual love, is experienced between a husband and wife; and the greatest love found in the family is parental love, the love between parent to its child. Through these relationships, love can be formed. Then, through this love comes life, through bearing children, which continues the lineage of the family from one generation to the next. Therefore, through love, life and lineage, the family can sustain its existence, thus connecting the present to the past and continuing on to the future.

Another point worth mentioning is that only through a true family can one resemble God. God's characteristics are masculine and feminine. Since we resemble God as either male or female, the only way we can resemble God completely is when we are united in marriage with one who resembles the other half of God's image. Thus, when a man and woman unite in marriage with one who resembles the other half of God's image. When a man and woman unite, only then can they resemble God's true image. Can a man uniting with another man or a woman joining with another woman resemble God's complete image? The answer is absolutely no!

Homosexuality, which denies the love relationship between a man and a woman, prevents the love in the couple to create life, thus ending the lineage of that family which has existed for hundreds or even thousands of generations. In other words, the purpose of homosexuality is the destruction of the family.

Lastly, we may theorize the future of homosexuality by statistical hypothesis (controlled scientific experiment.) Let's assume that we have three islands, called A, B and C. Each of these islands are perfectly suited for sustaining human beings for an indefinite period of time, with perfect weather, food, housing and even a hospital. On Island A, we will put 100 21-year old heterosexual couples. On Island B, we will put 100 21-year old homosexual couples. And on Island C, we put 100 21-year old lesbian couples. All the couples of the three islands must follow only two rules: first is that all couples are limited to having only two children; and second, they will all be isolated on their islands, no one enters, no one leave. Other than that, they are allowed to do whatever they please.

The question will thus be: At the end of 100 years, what will the populations of each of the islands be?

Through simple mathematics, one would easily discover that the population of Island A, with its population of heterosexual couples, flourished while populations of Islands B and C, with their homosexual and lesbian couples, ceased to exist due to the fact that, as stated in the anatomical study of the human body, it was impossible for the couples on those islands to create life without their corresponding counterparts. Thus, the conclusion being that only through heterosexual families can civilization continue to exist? If homosexuality is allowed to continue, the obvious result is the end of civilization.

In conclusion, anything that goes against these religious, natural, scientific and family laws is destructive to the existence of the family, which is the cornerstone of civilization and the universe. Homosexuality is a case in point. It proposes that two males or two females can exist in harmony with each other. But, as stated in the examples above, this is not true. Homosexuals, in essence, deny their basic purpose in life. Only when a male and female come together can harmony be established. Two males or two females naturally, scientifically and automatically repel each other. Thus, homosexuality has no natural, scientific, anatomical or religious basis for existence, and should be and must be abandoned for the sake of civilization and the universe.

Chapter 33

Coronation of God 2001

On January 13, 2001, the greatest event in human history, according to True Parents, took place at Cheong Pyeong in Korea; the day that True Parents liberated God's heart.

The ceremony took place in the main hall and everyone, including the video and photographers had to wear holy robes. I always set my gear on the right side of the stage, since the Koreans and Japanese usually stayed on the left side. On the stage was the offering table, but this time there were two sets of thrones, the ones for True Parents in the front. And behind their thrones, was another offering table and another set of thrones, these being white, and in a higher position. These were God's thrones.

All members wore white robes while elders lined up in white robes and pink coverings. As True Parents slowly came down their aisle in their white robes and beautiful crowns, they stopped part way down, bowing.

Figure 131 True Parents procession

Hoon Sook Nim, along with Yun Ah Nim, carrying the crowns and robes for God, came a little too far forward. True Father told Hoon Sook Nim to came back, but she didn't hear because of the music. So, since I was near the stage, I approached her and told her True Father wanted her to go back. As they approached as a group, I photographed more seriously, especially when God's crowns and robes were placed on the white thrones.

Figure 132 True Parents prayer for God's Coronation

Then, it became very busy with True Parents prayer and tea offerings to God. It was during this time that I realized I was the only Westerner on the stage with True Parents. I was hoping I didn't fall or bump into something. Then, True Parents took their positions and special representatives came for their respective bows.

After the final prayer, cake cutting and manseis, True Father went to the front and gave a long speech explaining the importance of the ceremony.

It was a physically draining event to photograph, but spiritually rewarding.

True Parents said this was the most important event in the history of God's Providence. For someone who loved history, I was truly blessed to not only witness it, but to help photograph it for future generations as well.

Chapter 34

Cheon Jeong Gung Peace Palace

Figure 133 Cheon Jeong Gung Peace Palace

The grand opening of the Peace Palace in Cheong Pyung took place on June 13, 2006. It was one of the great accomplishments by True Parents for Heavenly Father.

Graeme Carmichael and I arrived very early, about 5:30am to make sure we would be able to prepare ourselves for the event. Since it was our first time there, we needed to make a plan of how we would photograph it.

After taking some photos of the Palace and garden walls, I took portraits of some of the leaders who had arrived.

We learned that the day's events would be in four parts: two separate ceremonies with True Father giving the main speech. Then, a luncheon for VIPs would be held inside one of the dining rooms. Then, the afternoon would conclude with an entertainment program of singing and dancing.

Always, one of my main concerns was to figure out how to get to a very high place for the overall photographs. The only place possible was one of the side buildings. I planned to go to the top of the building and then with a ladder climb to the roof, which was at a steep angle. Before the end of the day, I climbed that roof twice, but it was worth it.

Figure 134 Overview of Cheon Jeong Gung Peace Palace

Figure 135 Heavenly Parents Thrones designed by Dae Mo Nim

True Parents made two different entrances for the morning events. I noticed in one of their entrances that Hiromichi Shimoyama's daughter, Karin, was one of the attendants. When

True Parents walked by her, I took a photograph. She was very happy.

Figure 136 True Parents passing Karin Shimoyama during their entrance

During the second ceremony, dignitaries from different nations offered crowns to True Parents. I saw my friend, Rev. Dairo Ferribolli, who was the National Messiah to St. Kitts, carrying a crown with his VIP guest. He was smiling.

Figure 137 Rev. Dairo Ferriboli and his VIP guest

Figure 138 True Parents waving to the audience of thousands

The last part of the entertainment was challenging in that while Hyun Jin Nim was singing, he invited some Korean ladies, who were dressed in their Korean dresses, to come on stage. There were no steps for them to climb, so I volunteered to help push them up onto the stage. I helped about six ladies get up there. I thought since they were small, it shouldn't be any trouble. But, I didn't count on the fact their weight was densely packed. By the time I pushed the last lady up onto the stage, I was completely tired.

When the events finally finished, and the long day was getting dark, I barely dragged myself back to the bus to head back to Seoul. It was one of the most exhausting days I ever spent, but I felt very blessed to have been there.

Chapter 35

Fourth World Tour 2006

Being asked to photograph this historic and unique tour, in which religious leaders would go around the world giving True Parents message, was very exciting to me, even though it would not be easy on my family to be away for two months.

I had, in 1982, joined the first Youth Seminar World Tour with 150 college students from many nations who toured nine religious countries in six weeks. But, having no family then, it was very exciting and no responsibility on the family level. With this tour, I am grateful to my wife, Meeyung, and our three children: Julie, Leilani and Douglas, two of whom would have birthdays while I was away, because they understand completely the importance of this tour and are united in that it is important for me to be here.

The ministers began this tour experiencing more than just a chance to visit many countries. In Japan, they understand the love and nurturing of a mother's heart when they were cared for and supported in every way. In Korea, they saw more of the masculine side and realized deeply about True Parents' heart and the reality of the tensions between North (which doesn't believe in God) and South Korea (which does).

On the final day in Korea, Dr Yang approached me and said that I may be giving speeches in Europe, as well as doing photography. I felt very inspired because recording this historic event is a great honor and blessing, but to be able to give the words of our True Parents is the greatest blessing of all because I am now able to partake in making history with these great men and women of God.

Figure 139 ACLC clergy after meeting True Parents

In Europe, the ministers were able to experience a variety of peoples, cultures and religious views by traveling day by day to each country. Throughout Europe, they realized for the first time that it is not easy to live in this area of many nations and that the spirit of religious faith is ebbing away.

In England, they experienced the heart of a people who had dominated a major part of history in the last 400 years.

In Holland, I personally was able to return to my ancestral homeland, to the very small town of Leeuwarden in Friesland, and give True Father's speech there. One lady told me later that she became spiritually opened and saw over two hundred of my Royal House of Orange ancestors appear and listen to the speech.

Everyone then heard of the minister who had gone to Sweden who couldn't make it to his event due to a snowstorm and then, through desperation, read the message from Heaven on the train platform, with hundreds of people coming to listen.

Then, going to Croatia, I was able to see how much growth there is in terms of Ambassadors for Peace, especially after being suffocated by Communism. Many high level people attended the event because they have hope for their nation now.

Going to Hamburg, Germany, a nation finally united after the Cold War, I was able to see how difficult it is to live there because of very high taxes (70%), and learning that Germany is still divided on the religious level, with Lutherans in the north and Catholics in the south. Even though it is the nation's policy for religious freedom, underneath it is very difficult (almost considered as a crime) for any one to create a religious organization or center that is not Lutheran or Catholic.

Continuing on to Paris, where Catholicism is supposed to be the religion of the country, very few attend church and where the government frowns on it, even suggesting that the European Community disavow God. Yet, to have a very large event in Paris where many religious people gathered truly gave hope for the country.

And then, continuing that religious hope by visiting Fatima, Portugal, where three children were given miracles by the Virgin Mary in 1917, I was able to speak at an event where there were three generations: grandparents, parents and children in attendance and be able to emphasize the importance of lineage in the family, where the past, present and the future are connected in one family.

Figure 140 Portuguese Blessed families

The final stop on the European tour is Milan, Italy. The same minister, who poured out his heart in Sweden snowstorm, gave even more here, trying to have the audience clearly understand the message from Rev Moon. By the end of his talk, the minister (Andre Jackson) had the people standing and cheering.

My overall impression for Europe is that the ministers, especially the American Clergy Leadership Conference, should begin having conferences with other leaders of faith here in Europe, having a dialogue with the American ministers so that the European religious leaders can understand how important Rev Moon is to the future of the European nations.

After Europe, I joined team number five and traveled to West Africa. Our team of ministers experienced many different feelings here. One is to see the vast difference between the few in power and the vastness in poverty. In each of the four countries we visited (Ivory Coast and Sierra Leone which had just completed long, bloody civil wars and Guinea and Mali), poverty still dominates one's eyes and heart. The ministers found it to be very difficult to understand why food, money, education and basic services to relieve poverty have not been filtering down to the mass population that desperately needs them. In one country, the president believes that all of the country's resources belong to his people and won't let any other nation have them. The problem is that economy can never grow without trade from one nation to another. The people of that nation are still very poor, because the vast resources stay buried in the ground.

But, the ministers were able to have hope here as well, for the people have deep religious faith in Christianity and Islam. In Mali and Sierra Leone, over 3,000 Muslims gathered in each of these nations to receive God's message and they felt hope in their families and nation, especially in taking of the Holy Wine Ceremony. In fact, the vice-president of Sierra Leone attended and understood Rev Moon's message very well. The ten imams who attended that event eagerly wanted to become Ambassadors for Peace, feeling heaven's call for peace and unity. The Christian spirit is very much alive here and so uplifting in their services that one of our ministers felt how pure the spiritual atmosphere was.

Our ministers left Africa with a since of deep concern for the people of Africa, but had high hopes that the religious leaders and the Ambassadors for Peace of Africa can turn the tide of poverty and inspire the politicians to take the right steps to improving the lives of their people, finally bring peace and love to the continent of Africa.

Traveling eastward again, we made our final stop on the tour to the Philippines. Having traveled here many times during my tour in the Navy, I felt like I was coming home. After visiting the historic 1942 battleground of Corregidor Island, at the mouth of Manila Bay, we were guests at the Presidential Palace and the Speaker of the House of Representatives. We felt very honored to attend these events for we wanted to really share the hope that we have in Rev Moon's words and accomplishments to the people of the Philippines.

On Sunday, we all visited different churches and their services. One church had as many children as there were adults. It was very inspiring to see three generations joining together in song and fellowship. Families coming together in faith give great hope for the future of this nation.

Afterward, we met with seven imams of Islamic faith who wanted to hear more about the Ambassadors for Peace and how to create unity with Christianity in the Philippines. Lastly, Rev Oyamada and myself visited the Apostolic Catholic Church, whose members dress in white robes instead of the traditional black. Their leader is an Ambassador for Peace and a great supporter in our great work for peace. Rev Oyamada gave a great testimonial and I read the words of Rev Moon. The members felt very inspired, especially after receiving the Holy Wine and Blessing as Blessed Couples. They felt they were living the words of Rev Moon.

The next day, Dr Yang and Archbishop Stallings were the main speakers for the large event in Quezon City. Dr Yang gave deep words and Archbishop Stallings poured out his heart in reaching the hearts of the guests, many of whom were of the Apostolic Catholic Church I had spoken to earlier.

In conclusion, one deep impression I have is how much the ministers have changed on this tour. Many had supported us in the past, especially going to the Middle East Pilgrimages and the many inter-religious activities in their hometowns. But, I am recognizing that these historic people are going to be even more valuable in the future, because they have a worldwide view that very few have. By understanding the many different situations and the hope they see in the religious faith and the faith in peace on all six continents, the ministers are truly Universal Ambassadors for Peace. Everywhere they go, whether they are talking to Heads-of-State, religious leaders, Speakers of the Parliaments, majors, or just those whom they meet on planes and trains, they are testifying sincerely and with deep love for Rev and Mrs. Sun Myung Moon. The hope that True Parents had for religious leaders is now blossoming on the worldwide level.

Chapter 36

First International Cattle Drive for Peace and Unity

In February of the year 2008, Hyun Jin Nim and several leaders visited Leda, a land situated next to the Paraguay River in the Chaco region of Paraguay in which eight years ago Japanese brothers, directed by True Parents and headed by Rev. Kamiyama, pioneered and built a tremendous foundation with their own hands from sweat and blood, in temperatures ranging from 40 degrees in the winter to 120 degrees in the summer.

While practicing riding on some of the horses near the corrals, Hyun Jin Nim saw some of our cattle being herded to another part of our pastureland. He and several others joined in to help. During this short ride, Hyun Jin Nim began formulating the idea of a major cattle drive from one part of the Chaco to Leda. But, not just to enjoy ourselves, or to actualize a dream when we were children being cowboys. He would bring the young leaders from Paraguay, who never even saw this part of their country, to participate and educate for the future peace and unity of their nation and the region of South America as a whole.

Figure 141 Hyun Jin Nim and Larry Moffitt in Leda

Some of those young leaders he had met a few days before were so excited when they heard about the cattle drive that they instantly put aside their schedules and wanted to come. One of those leaders is a soccer legend in Paraguay who was very eager to participate. Another young leader, whose wife was expecting their first child any day, realized this event was so important that he came as well.

On June 18th, we all arrived at Fort Olimpo, the same town where True Parents stayed over 10 years ago, educating many of the National Messiahs for over 40 days. With the hot sun blazing down, the town was so excited about the cattle drive they closed the schools and many of the town's people came out for the opening ceremony that would launch the drive. After several VIPs spoke and the priest gave the cattle drive his blessing, Hyun Jin Nim spoke, giving the people his inspiration for the cattle drive and the hope for the future it would bring.

With the conclusion of the ceremony, the participants mounted their horses, and with Hyun Jin Nim and the soccer player carrying the national flag, rode through the streets of the town and onto the dirt rode that would take two days of riding to reach where the herd of cattle would be met.

Figure 142 Hyun Jin Nim begins the cattle drive

For many of the riders, this was their first time not just riding all day on horseback, but even just being on a horse at all. So, throughout the day, with the sun beaming on them and the trees, brush and water holes going past them, the muscles in their bodies began sending many small and then urgent messages to their brains about their sitting conditions on these wide Paraguayan saddles. Some riders already began to realize they would be walking kind of funny at the end of the day.

Finally, near 3pm or 4pm the riders arrived at their first camp of the trip. Mr Sano from Leda, who did much of the preparation work for the drive, met every one at the camp, which was now full of tents and dinner cooking. With the sun setting on one end of the camp and the full moon rising on the other end, all the riders received their dinner, served directly by Hyun Jin Nim and sat into the night hours around the camp fire, talking about the day's ride and listening to Hyun Jin Nim who gave much advice, about True Parents vision for Paraguay, about riding horses, and the cattle drive.

Figure 143 The first night

Figure 144 Thumbs up before heading out

The next morning, we started at 7am, with the sun already up, and began our ride of almost 40 kilometers. By car, it doesn't take long to drive, but on horseback, under the hot sun and our brains still receiving even more urgent messages from certain areas of our bodies, we would reach our newly placed camp mid-afternoon.

Figure 145 On the trail

Again, after being served dinner by Hyun Jin Nim, he and some of the young leaders continued to share their thoughts and visions that were shaping this cattle drive into a history making event. Hyun Jin Nim especially spoke about the histories of North and South America, especially why America grew so rapidly and flourished. He told them that America was founded by those of the Protestant Christian ethic and principles, began a nation with a single unified vision and who's goal was to worship God and live a Christian life with their families.

The next morning, right after breakfast, the gauchos and the herd of cattle they had brought from another part of the Chaco, arrived at our camp. Together, with overcast clouds and a cold wind now covering us on the new morning, we started the cattle drive in earnest, with Hyun Jin Nim still giving us guidance and leading the way on how to drive cattle properly on horseback. The drive was now at a slow pace, for the cattle and horses would graze along the road as we went at their own speed.

Figure 146 Watching the herd for strays

After many kilometers and at least two rest stops, we arrived at our next campsite. With the gauchos putting the herd in an area of pastureland for grazing, we again stretched our legs and prepared our tents for the night. Hyun Jin Nim, always trying to improve himself, practiced throwing the lasso. He did several twirls of the lasso over his head before unleashing it at "yours truly," all the while taking photos. After the last photo, his lasso had wrapped itself over my wrists and pulling, tied my wrists together. He was so happy with this achievement.

Around the campfire, Hyun Jin Nim still gave us, both young and a bit older, even more guidance, especially about the Global Peace Festival centered on True Parents on July 5th, telling the participants that the festival would be a major turning point for the nation of Paraguay.

During the next few days we continued the drive toward Leda, still under the cover of clouds and cold wind. Around lunchtime, we came upon a very small group of houses. The women and children asked us to read a letter asking for help in improving their school for their children. Hyun Jin Nim, seeing their faces, especially the children, some of whom had no shoes, took out his lunch from his saddlebags and, telling all the other riders as well, gave their lunches to the children.

Figure 147 Hyun Jin Nim giving lunches to villagers

Now, Hyun Jin Nim, who wanted to taste a real Paraguayan meal, asked, almost jokingly, if the women could cook a lunch for us. To his amazement, the women spent the next two hours preparing a lunch of fresh chicken for almost twenty of us. After visiting their small two-room schoolhouse, where there were few desks and no books, we all enjoyed the best meal we had had in several days.

After a group photo was taken, we all said our goodbyes.

Figure 148 Thumbs up with villagers

Larry Moffitt had to leave Maxine, telling her: "Well, I hate to leave, but I got cattle to move. I'll be back when I can!" She is still waiting.

Figure 149 Larry Moffitt saying goodbye to Maxine

On the morning of the last day of the drive, the participant whose wife was expecting, called him on his cell phone and told him that she would be having a C-section operation (the umbilical cord was loosely wrapped around the baby's neck) that night to deliver their first child. Still convinced that this cattle drive as a great moment in the history of Paraguay, he still wanted to finished the drive before going back to see his child. He spent the rest of the day with a big smile.

Figure 150 Following the herd

Figure 151 Always watching the herd

We arrived around midday of the last day at the entrance to the property at Leda, where some of the Japanese brothers met us. With five kilometers to go, the cattle drive began its last leg to the finish line.

At one point, Hyun Jin Nim wanted everyone to go at a gallop. It was a great opportunity for photos.

Finally, driving through a nest of mosquitoes and a drizzling rain, Hyun Jin Nim lead the herd and it's riders across the finish line, with Japanese members and workers from the nearby villages cheering.

Figure 152 Galloping home

At noon the next day, a celebration was held, with several VIPs in attendance. After an opening prayer, the celebration cake was cut, and testimonies were several participants.

One testimony was by the person whose wife was giving birth. He was so emotional, he was almost on the verge of tears. Hyun Jin Nim had told him because he participated in this event and that he protected God on this drive, that God would give protection and blessing to him. This came true. During the night, the doctors realized that a miracle was taking place. The umbilical cord unloosened around the neck of the baby and his wife was able to give birth naturally the next morning. At 8:30 in the morning, he became a proud father of a baby boy. He and his wife gave life to their son. Their son gave them in return the title of "parents." His wife and son were doing well. He was smiling and tearful at the same time. Hyun Jin Nim told him now he will see the world and his life much differently.

Hyun Jin Nim spoke, giving his reasons for the cattle drive, True Parents' vision for Paraguay and telling the participants to take ownership of the vision as well. Then, Hyun Jin Nim gave each participant a special gift and a memorial portrait.

Afterwards, everyone went to the corral area, where ten cows were brought. Hyun Jin Nim donated these cows to the mayor of the nearest Indian village to enrich their village with future generations of cattle for the needs of the people of the village. The mayor was extremely grateful.

With a final group photo, the 1st International Cattle Drive for Peace and Unity was completed. For Hyun Jin Nim, God's blessings for Paraguay and the region could truly begin with the victories of the cattle drive and next week's Global Peace Festival. For the participants, their lives have been changed for they are inspired by True Parents' and Hyun Jin Nim's vision for their country. For those of us older folks, we were rejuvenated to dream big again as we had when we first joined the movement many years ago. We may have taken longer to get on our horses than the younger folks, and literally felt every inch of the way, but our hearts and minds are younger now and energized for the work ahead.

Chapter 37

My Memories of Two Great Brothers

Figure 153 Robert Davis, Sydelle and Robert Enyeart, Donna Davis and Hiromichi Shimoyama

Robert Munce Davis

New Future Photo

As my memory fades, my hair thins (yes, it's slowly thinning), how can I ever forget the precious gift that Robert Davis gave to me on May 30, 1980, when he assigned me to join New Future Photo.

The first time I met Robert was in 1976, just before Yankee Stadium. I was on MFT and since I had a Nikon camera and two lenses, I offered my services to help photograph the event. Robert and Michael Brownlee agreed, not only needing more help, but they also liked my Nikon camera and two lenses. For two weeks I was able to help New Future Photo for the event. Three and a half years later, Robert was able to formerly transfer me from MFT/OWP to New Future Photo. His main reason for having me was simple: because I was "trainable," and he still liked my Nikon camera and lenses.

Since that time, Robert, and those who were already there: Franz Zurawski, David Hill, Robert Armstrong, Ken Webber and Hitoshi Nagai, guided me in all the aspects of photography and dark room work.

It was Robert, though, who guided me the most. More than just mastering the technical aspects of photography, of which I'm still learning new things, but most importantly making sure that my heart towards being in front of True Parents was right and humble. If one's heart is not, then there is no way that True Parents and the True Family can trust you, that you can make them happy, because that is our number one goal in life: Making our True Parents happy!

Because Robert believed in me, I was able to experience and record some of the most historical events in history, all centering on True Parents, and traveling to 48 states and 53 countries on six continents. Whew, that's a lot of airplane food.

But the greatest and most precious gift he gave me was the opportunity to be close to True Parents and True Family, sometimes on a daily basis. Seeing them very close up: being happy, serious, angry, a few times very, very sorrowful (which was very hard to experience and photograph), being strong and forceful, but always, always loving. Even though some of the work was long, stressful and extremely tiring to the point I couldn't walk, having those experiences are unforgettable and dear to my heart. And it was all due to Robert for his trust in me.

My family: my wife Meeyung and our children, Julie, Leilani, Douglas and I, our hearts go to Robert's family at this time.

I have known his wife, Donna, since 1976 when she tried to make me a better fundraiser in Los Angeles. I succeeded... for one afternoon. There were many times when she also gave me advice that made me a better son to True Parents. And, how surprised I was when she and Robert were blessed together. Most interesting!! As you can see, they are a great couple.

And then, seeing Joleigh growing up! I feel she is my real niece! How proud Robert and Donna are!! I am!!!

Hiromichi Shimoyama of New Future Films, and I were stuck at San Francisco Airport last week after an event in Las Vegas, on the last day before Robert's passing. Both of us felt very strongly that it was God's hand that was putting us there, so we can be near Robert.

Thanks to True Parents, we know that we will be separated only for a very short time, before we are united for eternity in the spirit world, where True Love really is! True Father said last week in Las Vegas that it is better for the husband to go first to the spirit world.

Thank you, Robert, for sharing your life, your family and your love of True Parents with us.

My Brother, Shimo
New Future Films

For over 35 years, I've known my brother Hiromichi Shimoyama. Having worked together documenting our True Parents activities all over the world, Shimo (as I always called him), is truly my brother. It's hard to realize that with Robert Davis, Ken Weber, Joan Haley and now Shimoyama, those who were New Future Films and New Future Photo, are departing at such a surprising rate.

There are just too many stories and experiences to recall, having worked together recording most of the historical events that our True Parents have done. But, one thing is for sure: he loved our True Parents tremendously, and knew them from very public events to very private ones.

Having grown up in Japan, he wanted to be a cinematographer, eventually making movies for the big screen. But, like other members who were career-minded, he met the Unification Church, and gave up his dreams to serve God and True Parents. Yet, his dream was given back to him after much hard work, fundraising and witnessing, and he was given a chance to film True Parents activities in America. Arriving in 1976, he recorded many historic events and became a leading member of New Future Films.

    I joined New Future Photo in May of 1980, and since then worked side by side with Shimo at countless events around the world. We always arrived early at an event to help set up. I didn't need to, being a photographer, I didn't have that much preparation, but the video gang had to set up lights, sound, cables, tripods and every thing else to document the event from several different angles. In later years, when it was just the two of us documenting events, I would help Shimo bring equipment, set up as much as I could, and even helped with the video while he got audience shots.

    After each event, and taking down everything, he'd be very tired. At the end of the day, he would make sure the batteries were charging, tapes marked, new tapes ready and he then would put a towel over his eyes and would instantly fall asleep, snoring, usually within 30 seconds. (I timed it one day). Then, after we got back to New York, he'd spent days editing the entire event into a documentary to be shown to True Parents and for use at other events.

    Throughout my forty-one years in the church, thirty-three years at New Future Photo, I worked with Shimo the longest and the closest of any member I knew. He became my brother I never had.

    I knew that True Parents loved him very much. I hope the brothers and sisters from the last forty years can understand how valuable he was. And, I hope the Second Generation can someday understand the man who filmed our True Parents for over thirty-four years, and know him as well.

    Thank you, Shimo!!!

    I will miss him dearly.

Chapter 38

Last Times I Saw True Father
Las Vegas

In 2009, the first Original Divine Principle Workshop (or "Education Session Proclaiming the Completion of the Liberated Realm of the Portion of Responsibility in God's Providential History") took place in Las Vegas. Several hundred members participated in the event. We knew that True Parents were in Las Vegas, but were not sure if they would visit the workshop.

On the last morning, we were all surprised to learn that True Parents were indeed coming. When they entered the ballroom, they were met with a thunderous applause. First, True Father spoke a little bit, then, both True Father and True Mother stood up and sang very happy songs.

Figure 154 True Father singing a happy song

After they sang, True Father wanted a group photo taken. So, they walked into the crowd and as several hundred joyous members crowded around them, I took photos, screaming my usual 'Smile, Please" in several languages, as loud as I could, all the while True Parents and the members smiling more and more. After the photos were taken, we thought True Parents would say goodbye and leave. But, they surprised us again. This time they sat on the edge of the stage and True Father announced: "You can take all the pictures you want!" For almost thirty years, this was the first time I ever heard True Father say: "Take all the photos you want!" So, several hundred cameras and cell phones reached toward True Parents, who were smiling and waving, and hundreds of flashes started firing over and over again for at least several minutes. I was in front of them for the first few minutes, taking my share of photos, and then I went behind them on the stage to photograph all the members, still taking photos.

When True Parents started to rise, I motioned to all the members to open up the middle, so True Parents can go through the parting of the audience, just like Moses.

With the echoes of three manseis, True Parents departed and everyone was so happy because they saw True Parents were happy.

Figure 155 True Father said "Take all the photos you want!"

90th Birthday

At the closing of True Father's ninetieth birthday, True Parents were on the stage singing and dancing. The entire audience of members were clapping and singing, as well. Then, True Father went over to the birthday cake and instead of cutting it, he took a couple of handfuls and threw them out the surprised members. I was directly in front of him, as usual, and when he started to take the pieces of cake, I knew what he was going to do. As he was in the midst of throwing the cake, I took a photo and quickly ducked down so the cake wouldn't hit the lens. Then, I straightened up and aimed again, taking another photo and ducking again. I got the shot, and kept my camera clean.

Chapter 39

True Father's Seung Hwa

In 2012, I was asked by Headquarters to photograph True Father's Seung Hwa in Korea. When I arrived at Cheong Pyeong, I met with Graeme Carmichael who was also sent to help do photography.

The day after we arrived, we were given the blessing to go up to the Cheon Jeong Palace with other American leaders to give our final respects to True Father personally as he lied-in-state on the third floor. We all went to the second floor where we took off our shoes and in groups of about fifteen to twenty people; we eventually entered the room where True Father was lying. We were all very quiet, tearful and repentful as we faced True Father for the last time. Peter Kim gave us brief words, and then we bowed all together. The Korean film crew and

Mr. Kim the photographer documented our visit. Hyung Jin Nim and Yun Ah Nim were there to thank us, most especially the East Garden staff with big hugs. As we left the room, we took one last look at True Father.

The next day, I went to the arena where the main ceremony was to be held. A large portrait of True Father, posing at his desk with the Divine Principle, was on the stage. In front was a long table in which hundreds of members and VIPs from all around the world bowed and offered a flower to True Father. Then, each would turn and offer bow to the True Children who represented True Mother.

The day of the Seung Hwa ceremony, Graeme and I arrived early. We decided that he would remain inside and wait for the casket to arrive, while I went to the street in front of the arena and photograph the procession as it passed in front.

Figure 156 True Father's hearse arriving

After I took photos of True Father's car, I ran as fast as I could to try to get inside. But, luckily, I was able to get to True Father's car just as it arrived. I was able to photograph the pallbearers bringing the big, red casket out of the car and prepare to bring it in. Kwon Jin Nim held up True Father's portrait, with True Mother, her daughters, and WonJu McDevitt just behind them.

Figure 157 True Father's red casket

For the next hour and a half, I was totally focused on photographing the event from every angle I could. It was a very emotional experience, but difficult to photograph, especially at True Mother on the stage and the True Children who sat in the front row.

Even though everyone knew that someday True Father would ascend to the spirit world, it was still a deep, emotional, and even shock that it happened.

As the event was concluding, I was told that all the American documentary team, video and photographers, would not be allowed to the Palace for the final ceremony. So, being from a military background, I unhappily obeyed. I followed True Father's casket back to the hearse and then I ran as fast as I could back out to the other side of the street, and waited for True Father's car to pass by one last time. As the car passed, with True Father's huge portrait on top, and many members waving and bowing, I took many photographs as I prayed my goodbye to True Father. Then, I saw True Mother's car and bowed to her. After True Mother passed by, the bus carrying the True Family passed me. I stood there, watching, as the motorcade started the long climb up the hill to True Father's final resting place.

Figure 158 True Father's final farewell

It was a very emotional and tiring day. As I walked up the hill to the seminary dorm, I would remember True Father's smile, love and his earnest desire to bring victory for God. As I walked, I kept looking up to the Palace hoping I could see True Father one last time.

Chapter 40

Final Thoughts and Prayers

Through the years, I came to realize that True Father was more than a leader, or even the Messiah. I came to feel him to be my real father, my real parent.

I had a revelation from God in 1976 about how He has felt for the last 6,000 years and how His heart feels towards True Father:

My prayer:

What is wrong? Why can't I feel God's heart, True Parents' heart, and the heart of an innocent child?

God's prayer:

"Why can't you realize how hurt I've been, seeing you suffer, hearing your screams, feeling your deep wounds? Why can't you realize that there is a barrier between us, a barrier of death, a spiritual death? I can't stand the smell of it, I never have and I never will. It's been with me ever since you left me, and you never realized how much it was really hurting. I love you so much. And, I cry from the deepest depths of my heart to you. But, it's so hard to let you know that I'm crying, that I'm shedding tears of sorrow, tears of misery. I can't cry out like you can. I can't let loose the flood of all my tears of love out of my heart, to pour over each one of you. I feel so alone, so helpless. I want to cry out to you, scream to you, but all I can do is cry in my heart the tears of a lonely, rejected, broken father for his long, lost children. But, it's so difficult for you to understand, for you to be where I am, to feel the weight of my tear-filled heart that carries the over-burdened responsibility of my children's lives, to know that my precious ones, whom I brought into the world, have been and are suffering under the terrible pain of a dust-filled death. You would cry so much from just one tear of my sorrow. I feel your tear stained hearts, but you can't feel my universal,

suffering heart, which is so sensitive to even the slightest pain, the slightest bit of sadness.

Now, my son is with you. Only he can show you how my heart really feels. He knows me so well, because he knows how I feel, and how all of you feel. Oh, how I want to make you happy, but I can't with this heavy, miserable heart that I now have. Please look to him, please listen to him, please feel him. You see him, you see me. You hear him, you hear me. You feel him, you feel me. You cry with him, you cry with me. He is your father. You are his children. But, I am his father, so all of you are my children. I don't want to see my family suffer. I don't like seeing my children cry. I cry when you cry, but even more so, because I made you, you came from me. I want to love you with all my heart. I want you to be my children, again. I want you to feel joy. I want to love you and I want you to love me. I want to become one with all of you, to embrace you, and cry tears of love together, as father and children, as one family. That is all you've ever wanted. That is all I ever wanted. I am praying for you."

Remember I mentioned there is no future in history? Please believe that there is a future in history, because True Parents are connecting the past and present and creating a new future. Each moment we attend them is precious. Please do your best to attend and love them while you are still able to.

To the First Generation: the Completed Testament Age Book of Acts is still being written. You have sacrificed and accomplished so much in the past, but there is no such thing as retirement, so continue to do your best, because you still have so much to offer.

To the Second and Third Generations: Your parents sacrificed their youth attending True Parents. They went through many difficulties and did great things to build the Heavenly Kingdom. Please learn from them. They have tremendous hope for you. Please cherish this time with True Parents; please pray to understand their hearts and their desire for you. Please see and hear them as much as you can. Love and attend the True Family who is attending True Parents, for they are finishing what True Parents have started. No matter where your talents take you, please be blessed and create beautiful blessed families of your own and continue building God's Kingdom.

For new members and guests: those of us who followed True Parents for thirty, forty, even fifty years, we understand what you are going through. Search for God in your hearts.

I have photographed True Parents for thirty-three years, seeing them with their family, with members, teaching Heads-of-State, leaders of the world religions, scholars, scientists and citizens from countries on every continent about God's heart and how to build the Kingdom of Heaven. I've witnessed God's revelation to be true. I assure you, you are on the right path.

Photographing our True Parents was a great honor, privilege and blessing. I wish I had done a lot more to make them happy. My heart has deepened tremendously through witnessing their love for God, for each other, for their children and for all of us. They have put all their hopes, desires and dreams upon us. Let's make them happy! My greatest joy is that I was able to make our True Parents happy, especially when I said "Smile Please" in my funny Korean.

Brothers and sisters, let's continue loving and attending our True Parents, and we will complete building God's Kingdom.

Figure 159 True Father's thumbs up

Addendum

Madison Square Garden 1974

I wrote this testimony of the Madison Square Garden event in 1974. Since it is very long, I have included here as an addendum.

It all started way back when, on the 2nd of September 1974, Carmela Acohido and I, on leave from my ship in Pearl Harbor, flew to Los Angeles, landing at about 7 pm. The moon was just rising with the color of brilliant orange. Actually, it's very beautiful in a sense. But, there's just one thing wrong. Normally, the moon would seem white because of the rays of the sun bouncing off of it. But, when you have miles upon miles, and tons upon tons of smog in the way, the Moon will be of an orange color, and you're not breathing fresh air any more. You're inhaling all of these polluted elements, which should not be there in the first place. So, you cough a lot. Also, all this polluted junk invades the eyes, and you are constantly having your eyes bathed in tears. It's not a good place to be if you want to live longer than the age of two. But, there have been some specimens that somehow have a longer life span than the normal inhabitants.

The church center where we stayed at, and where Keith Chow and Debbie Nanod from Hawaii were, used to be a motel lot with six cabins and a six-car garage. Now, it's just a cozy church center with 15 people, with Phillip Schanker leading and singing us all the way, and using it as a base of operations to conquer Los Angeles in a heavenly way. Keith and Debbie were in great spirits and happy we arrived. Keith, in fact, met us at the airport.

For the next three days, the three of us sold candy to raise enough money for future expenses. Keith had to stay behind since he was still getting over pneumonia. He painted one of the offices while we were gone. We usually went to shopping centers and chased after people most of the day.

The strangest and most disturbing incident I had was the first night of selling. At about 7:15pm, I walked up to this lady in her car, from behind like a crazy fool and I got an instant reaction from her. She turned toward the store, screamed her head off, not literally, started the engine and was revving it up something fierce. So, I calmly and innocently walked away from the car, letting her know that I didn't want to harm her and that I too was scared to death. I walked to a gas station and waited over an hour for the police to come. But, they never did. I wonder why she didn't blow her horn like other normal people do? Strange!

The next day, two of us stayed in the parking lot all day. Now, this wasn't bad except that we were in San Fernando Valley, smog everywhere, the sun beating down on us, bringing the temperature up to 102 degrees (just a smidge hot) and I didn't have a hat. Believe me, I was mighty glad when night came. So, as you can see, it wasn't all peaches and sauerkraut being in Los Angeles.

On Friday, the 6th, we got two Dodge vans together, and 16 of us started our journey to another smoggy city on the other side of the country. At 12 o'clock Noon, we headed toward the desert area west of the city.

Rolling through the hot, sandy hills and plains of Death Valley, we come to beautiful, downtown Needles, California. This majestic and tranquil little desert community has, more often than not, set the daily temperatures as the highest in all the land. I lived in the desert for two years, but it gets pretty cotton-picking hot here.

As we leave this majestic place in this land-locked beach, we bid farewell to this sauna-bath of Southern California.

As the miles roll by: we sing, eat, drive, study and sleep.

Ah, it's night, and we arrive into exciting Flagstaff, Arizona. A family member from Phoenix is here, and we bring her along on our journey.

During the night, we cross into New Mexico, and at 9am, arrive in Albuquerque to freshen up and prepare our breakfast.

We're off by 10pm, eating a hearty meal of granola and 2-day old hard-boiled eggs, which fall apart when we peal them. The tall, rolling hills begin to stretch out to form mesas with a reddish tint to liven up the beauty of the desert land. You cannot imagine the beauty, the color, the loneliness, and yet, you almost feel at home here. A desert can be exhilarating and utterly mysterious. It's just fantastic.

Moving on, the mesas get fewer and fewer and soon we're driving across the rolling plains of the Texas Panhandle and come to a city called Amarillo. The people here are just about the sweetest, hot-diggity-dangedest bunch of people in the whole wide cotton-pickin' world. One gas attendant chased us all over town to return our gas cap that we forgot. We sold most of our stock of candy here. The people are friendly, courteous, and we really wanted to stay so we could be with them longer. The people of Amarillo will forever be in our hearts. They're just something else.

Leaving Amarillo about nine at night, we continue our trek through the unseen plains of the panhandle of Texas and into Oklahoma, reaching Oklahoma City about 4am. An hour later we stop to have a short Sunday Service.

We lined up in two sections, five rows of three's. We bowed three times, said the Children's Pledge, prayed in unison, and Diana Swank (future Mrs. Ken Weber) closed with a prayer. Then, we sang "Shining Fatherland" while looking east. It was extremely moving. From where I was standing, far left of the second row, the dark blue sky filled with stars, and small trees rising above the scattered mist along the horizon, with our leader in the foreground, in front of the group, all of us looking, feeling, experiencing, and loving Heavenly Father externally, within ourselves and with each other.

Now on the Will Rogers Turnpike, the plains turn into green hills and trees, scattered farms with barns built in the 19th Century still in use, swiftly go by our sightseeing eyes. The air is clean; the sky is clear and everything in green, green, green.

As we see the last few feet of the turnpike, we enter the hills of Missouri. At about 3pm, we arrive in St. Louis. And again, smog enters our journey. Here, we sell some candy in a suburb called Webster Groves. The first house I go to had a heavy feeling to it. It was a church of Mysticism. As I left, some words were painted on the side of the house that read, "Witches live here." For the rest of the time there, the atmosphere was really heavy and a bad feeling all around. Hardly anyone smiled, not even the children.

A few hours later, we cross the Mississippi River into Illinois.

As the day rambles on, the two vans pass mile after mile of rolling farmland. As we breathe the fresh air, cattle graze lazily near the roadside caring only how good the grass is.

We come to Springfield, Lincoln's final resting place. But, we move on, rushing to get to our destination.

It's 11:30pm, half an hour before midnight. Most of us in the second van are asleep, when suddenly our left rear tire blows. We slowly reach the side of the road as the first van moves steadily onwards, unaware of our plight. A big, flatbed truck stops in front of our van, and gives us his help in replacing the blown tire. We give him our thanks as he speeds on his own journey.

Now, we wait till Midnight, hoping the first van had noticed that we weren't with them. But, they do not come.

By putting into action a pre-arranged plan in case of an emergency such as this, we eventually unite with number one van in Indianapolis, 45 miles away. After refueling and exchange greetings, we continue our trek into the blackness of an Indiana night.

It's now 6:30am, Monday morning, as we enter the town of New Philadelphia, Ohio. There, we freshen up at the home of one of the team member's relatives. Also, we sell the rest of the candies that we brought, repair the blown tire and make more food that will last us until New York.

We're off again by 3am, heading for Dubois, Pennsylvania where we will meet with five other vans from California and Utah.

Five hours later, we arrive in this small Pennsylvania town and we meet two vans from California. We all eat dinner at good old American MacDonald's!

At 11:30 in the evening, we are able to enter a YMCA and have some recreation before we start our work in the Big City: pool, ping-pong and basketball. I, myself, participated in the basketball game. Since, we didn't have tennis shoes, we played without any shoes or socks.

Before I had to leave the game, my feet not only developed many fine blisters, but when I made my only basket of the night, I rammed my big right toe into a stage near the basket. I sprained it pretty good. At about 1:30am, we all went back to the vans to get some much needed sleep.

I was the first one up at 7am. It was a sight to see. Three new vans were parked near us. It was densely foggy, and it was COLD. I woke practically everyone up and guess where we ate breakfast? That's a right, good old MacDonald's.

At 10:30am, the caravan of seven vehicles started out into the fog, trying to keep in touch and not losing each other.

At about 2:30pm, we ate lunch at a rest stop. We sang, prayed and ate together. The police came by and told us not to make too much noise. And we didn't, until we left saying three cheers quietly scrambled for the vans. We drove for the next five hours through the endless sea of green hills of Pennsylvania and New Jersey.

At Eight O'clock, on the night of September 10th, we crossed the George Washington Bridge and entered Manhattan Island. And guess who drove us in, Keith himself. After driving in the wide-open spaces of Hawaii, he's the one to first experience the quagmire, the tension, the stupidity and the craziness of New York and its drivers. And to top it off, he became an official driver to one of the vans and rove around New York for the week we were there.

As soon as we got onto the island, we already were in a traffic jam. We were just dumb-founded at everything: the old buildings, planted trees, the atmosphere and the people.

But, what really amazed us was that we found our posters for the event on a street corner billboard. It was three rows high and about twenty across, so about sixty of our posters that read, "Sept. 18th Could be your Re-birthday" were on one street corner.

As we continued on, we saw dozens, hundreds, literally thousands of three feet high posters, row upon rows, strewn all over the city. Wherever there was a billboard or a construction site, there our posters were, staring at all the people going by.

Our two vans stopped in front of the Taft Hotel on 51st and 7th Avenue. Within four minutes, not only were 17 people out of the vans, but also our entire luggage, both inside and on top of the vans, was on the sidewalk, ready to venture forth into the hotel.

By ten O'clock, we were all snug in our rooms, a little hungry perhaps, but ready to sleep without anything moving underneath us. And did we sleep in the big, comfortable beds that went with the rooms? Utter nonsense? Really! Why sleep in a soft bed when we got our trusty-dusty sleeping bags and a floor to get our sleep?

Rrinnggg, "What time is it?" Eee-gads, its 4:30am! We all got dressed in fifteen minutes to get ready to go to St. Michael's Church on 34th Street to hear Father speak.

Dozens of vans pull up to the church, and hundreds of family members assemble inside. There is loud, beautiful singing. Then, Father talks to us, giving us inspiration and some of the reason why Madison Square Garden is so important to Heavenly Father, True Parents and the world. If we fill the Madison Square Garden, it would be one of the most victorious events in world history. We begin to feel honored to participate in this great event. Sixty to seventy people are then chosen to go straight to Philadelphia to start on the "Day of Hope" event there. Traudl Stempfl is one of those chosen.

After Father spoke, we piled into our vans and headed for our assigned areas. Our group of eleven landed on Lexington Avenue, between 58th and 71st Streets. The Upper East Side of Manhattan is a very wealthy neighborhood: a lot of businesses and a Catholic school were between 65th and 66th Streets.

I stayed at the corner of the church, 65th and Lexington, most of the day. It was utterly amazing. I would say that about 99 per cent of the people we met knew about Rev. Moon and September 18th, from little old ladies to school kids, businessmen, housewives, secretaries, street cleaners, vendors, delivery boys, policemen, women traffic cops, shoppers, hair stylists, girls in very high elevator shoes, priests, nuns, visitors to the city, and, of course, us. This would be our territory for 8 days. Out there by 7am in the morning, we would first go to the front of a library, with a revolving circular disk standing on its side in front. We would sing some songs, pray for success, and charge bravely forward into the streets, passing out flyers and tickets as we go.

Most of the people wouldn't take the flyers because they would be sick of seeing us at every corner. They would always see these well-dressed, smiling young people at a corner, and they'd probably say to themselves: "Oh no, here we go again!" Some of them would walk by smiling; some wouldn't give any kind of expression at all; others would look away, mostly at the sky, as they walked by; some would give us dirty looks; some say impolite words (even by some old ladies); threaten us; tell us to go back home and live normal lives like they do' tell us that we are being misguided' and many times, people would walk in the middle of the street, risking their lives with speeding taxis, and go to the other side just so we wouldn't bother them for the hundred-upteenth time. And several people would just go flakey. After being stopped so many times, they would start giving strange looks on their faces, as if they had never seen us before. Then, they would go off screaming "Rev. Moon, Rev. Moon!" to other people, as if questioning them who Rev. Moon is.

Then, there would always be those who would say that they were going to the event, and would always smile whenever approached. Some, after being approached so many times, would stop and ask questions.

You really find a lot about people this way. But, they were more than just people to us. We really felt love for them, because we were actually helping every one of them, even though they didn't know it, no matter who they were. Those who smiled, threatened, ignored and hated us, we loved them. It may sound crazy to love total strangers, be we did just that, because we knew how they are living, what was effecting their lives, and that they will soon feel exactly as we do. That, they too, will soon feel Heavenly Father coming into their hearts and they would start to feel for other people as we do. They would soon see that we really are brothers and sisters, and God is our Father. And that, indeed: war, hatred, jealousy, greed, selfishness, bigotry and everything that is against God's Will, will soon be vanished. They soon will discover that the ideal world will become a reality in their own lifetimes. It is within their grasp, and they don't even know it. But, they will. They will soon feel, for the first time in their hearts, true love for God, True Parents, the world, their nation, their society, their family and lastly, their original selves. This is why we stayed on the streets for the fifteen hours a day, because we're feeling God's heart and we wanted to show this to the people of New York. What I'm trying to say is that Heavenly Father, True Parents, Unification Church, Divine Principle; everything is true, all true.

All day long, I stopped in front of people, with a big smile and very humbly asking them if they were going to Madison Square Garden. I had a lot of rejections, some took the flyers I had, and very few people would stop and talk. This went on pretty much all day and into the night. Then, at about 8:30pm, the best experience of the day occurred, outside of seeing Rev. Moon, of course.

I stopped a group of people, a man and two women, in front of a drug store at 65th and Lexington. The man was really curious about what we were doing. There was a good reason why he was. He was a journalist for CBS's 60 Minutes named Mike Wallace. I knew who he was, but I didn't let him know that I knew. I told them that we were a Christian group who had the belief that the ideal world can be realized very soon with the Lord of the Second Advent, and that Madison Square Garden was an important step in the realization of his Second Coming. I also told him that members from over forty countries, a total of about 4,000, were in New York just for the event, and that all the other family members around the world were working for, raising money for and praying for the success of Madison Square Garden.

Not only that, but I told him that I was on leave from the Navy, coming to New York from Hawaii just for this event. He seemed more curious now, since he was a former World War Two submariner himself, and I gave him my address in town, and also my ship's address. Before, he didn't intend to go or have anything to say about us. But, whatever I said to him or the way I acted or both, he decided to go to Madison Square Garden.

I knew he was an important contact, so I contacted our Public Relations people the next morning. A few days later, I was told that he not only was going to go, but also planned to film it and do an interview with Father. So, I feel I have contributed much to the entire Eight-1City Tour because of this one person. I am very happy that I was able to not only meet Mike Wallace, but also persuade him to go and become really interested in the movement.

Ta-daa, It's 5:30am! Everybody up! Scramble, scramble, bump-grind! Where's the toothpaste? I don't know, look in the TV set! Bump, zonk, 6:30, downstairs! Scramble, scramble to the elevators! The doors open, yeeah! Charge for the rotating doors. Swing, swish, and bammm; it's COLD. Scramble, scramble back inside.

Each morning, we would line up in front of the hotel, in different teams of 12 people per team. We'd get the flyers, our lunches and walk over fifteen blocks to a corner where we would spend the rest of the day. At about 1:30-2:00pm, we'd eat our lunch, talk about the morning's experiences and wonder what was going to happen the rest of the day.

At 8:30 at night, we all join up and eat at a MacDonald's, Burger King, or a small hot sandwich snack-bar called Charlie's Corner. By Ten O'clock, we'd be back at the hotel, where all the teams would gather for a meeting to find out what happened during the day. We'd sing, learn of each other's experiences and what ever news overall about the upcoming event. Then, we would all sing one last song, pray and say good night.

Now there's one thing about New York City you have to be aware of: whatever you do, never, ever ride in a taxi in New York. They are professional, skilled, fearless maniacs who do not have any set speed limit. There could be cars, trucks, people, buildings, trees, cows, bicycles, horse-carriages and motorized street cleaners all over the place, and the cab drivers would find some way to get through or around, over or under them. I even saw one cab drive the entire length of sidewalk on the west side of 45th Street. They may have scars of past battles, but they still venture forth with undaunted and unwavering courage to overcome its foe. In other words, whenever you see a cab, anywhere, stay out of its way. Taxis fear nothing, not even the foot and a half deep potholes that numerously mark every few feet of road space. I would ride in one only on the condition that it was a life and death situation, and that I would be able to survive the trip. Other than that, I see nothing wrong with them.

Early Sunday morning, with darkness still covering the city, we all line up in front of the hotel, ready to pile into the vans that will take us to Saint Michael's Church.

After entering the vehicles and are on our way, each group of people conducts a short service to Heavenly Father for everything that he has given us, and rededicating ourselves to Him, True Parents and the world to bring about God's goal of the Kingdom of Heaven.

At 5:15am, as the blackness of the night starts to break up into a dark blue, we arrive at the church and race to get inside. As everyone enters, the sisters go to the left and the brothers to the right. All Blessed Couples present sit in the front of the stage.

With True Parents arriving in about 30 minutes, we all start singing to bring up a spiritually happy atmosphere.

As we sing, I begin to sense a feeling that I've never felt before. I feel love and brotherhood towards all of these people who came from all parts of the world. I never met most of them, but I do know them. We are all alike, with one purpose, desire, will and ambition. And, that is to accomplish God's plan, to make Heavenly Father and his children happy. I begin to feel for all of those people who don't know what is going to happen because of our efforts. I begin to feel a love for our True Parents that I've never experienced before. I feel that they are really happy and anxious for the success of Madison Square Garden.

As we continue to sing, the spiritual atmosphere rises, the voices become harmonious. The songs are beautiful, serious and meaningful. And, I begin to choke and I can't continue on singing. I take several deep breaths, look at all those around me and those on the stage, and I try to sing again, but choking soon afterward. My eyes begin to water. For the first time in ten years, I'm on the verge of tears. But, I hold them back smiling, and I begin to feel God's heart as I begin to sing again. I am happy being here, because I am one of Father's followers who is in this city to help change history. This is the happiest and the most serious moment for our True Parents. I am deeply honored, just as everyone else here. It is 5:50 in the morning.

They're here! Father and Mother have arrived, and the atmosphere zooms to a higher level. They walk down the aisle and onto the stage. Mother is beginning to show that she is bearing a child. A hush of wind is heard throughout the church. Father and Colonel Bo Hi Pak begin speaking.

For two and a half hours, Father talks to us, inspires us, make us laugh, tells us the importance of Madison Square Garden and how we should act as God's children. We are relaxed, yet our eyes and ears are glued to the two men on the stage. It is kind of hard to imagine that one of those two men is the long awaited Messiah. A few minutes after eight o'clock, the pastor of St. Michael's walks to the front, onto the stage and talks to Father, who is in the middle of speaking. Then, the pastor walks off the stage and out of sight. We are in awe and smile because the man doesn't know to whom he was really talking to. So, Father starts speaking again, but a few minutes later, an organ starts playing, and the pastor tells us that we overstayed our time by forty-five minutes and that we must keep our end of the agreement by leaving, now! Mr. Kim, the president of the international movement of the church, tries to get one more minute to introduce some leaders of the Korean and Japanese churches, but the pastor is insistent. So, President Kim says alright, asks all of us to rise and say three manseis, and we immediately part, clapping happily.

As everyone gathers outside, our team forms across the street and we go to the subway to head back to Lexington Avenue.

Being Sunday, it is not very busy and many stores are closed. But, some are open, and people slowly emerge later in the day. My partner, David Lowe, and I start at 66th Street and Lexington and we just ask the people if they have any questions about Rev. Moon. Some people do and some don't.

As the day crawls on, David and I begin to have a happy time asking people and our spirits are high. During this day, I talk to more people than I have in the past four days. All in all, it is a good day. Monday certainly will be much busier.

By 7:30 the next morning, we are all about in the streets again, passing out literature and still asking people if they have any questions.

By Eleven O'clock, we boarded our van and went to Wall Street where members of the church were having a rally. Hundreds of our people were on the steps of the Federal Hall Memorial Building, singing and waving signs. In front of the George Washington Statue, in the middle of the steps, was the platform where our speakers talked to the crowd. Then, most of the teams, including mine, mingled among the spectators, trying to make the rally as lively as possible. We blocked Wall Street for several hours. Traffic was at a standstill. It was a complete success. Among the speakers were: two Catholic ministers, one from Southeast Asia and the other from Ireland; Rev. Paul Werner, who is in charge of our region of California and Hawaii; a German sister, Ann Marie Manke, who was raised in Canada and was in Honolulu for the Day of Hope in April and whose bright red sunburn was healed by now; and the regional director of New York area, who spoke about his experience before coming into the family. It was good publicity for Madison Square Garden. After the rally, we all went back to hit the streets for six more hours.

The next day, we pounded the streets hard because it was the last full day for passing out leaflets, for tomorrow is September 18th. It could be one of the greatest days in history, or one of the worst. It's just a matter of hours away.

Some of the team members stayed on Lexington Avenue, while the rest of us went to Plaza Square near Central park. This is one of the landmarks of New York City and also where the horse carriages are if you wish to ride around the park for ten dollars (remember, this is 1974).

For most of the day, my partner, Bill Mitchell, and I stayed and talked to people. Some wouldn't want to talk with us, but those who did were good people and we were able to persuade a few to go to the event the next night. I talked to one couple that really cared about young people and tried to convince me that I should work for a particular cause, like in a hospital or something, and to beware of people like Rev. Moon. I told them that we were helping the needy causes, but in a more important way that affected all causes, all people and all nations. It was hard to convince them of this, but they are a really fine couple. They will soon find out.

I talked to a hippie in a way that seemed I was kind of on his level of thinking. After all, I did live on the same street as the singing group "Jefferson Airplane." We got really together on many things and we learned many things. But, basically we agreed that God is all around us and in us, and that there will be no need of churches and religions because we would be in God and God in us. We would feel him, be able to talk to him like I would talk to you. It was a good talk and I felt really high afterwards.

Then, I met this girl, a teacher, who just came back from Hawaii. She was really curious about Rev. Moon and the movement and was going to go and hear him speak. Then, an old man walked up to us to listen, and began to tell her that she shouldn't listen to me. He said that I was following a quack, a fraud that only wanted people's money. He based his information on government reports because he said he was a "G" man, and he knew the real truth and was trying to protect her. After he left, we both smiled and I said that I wasn't going to say anything since he wasn't there to defend himself, just to go to the rally and judge for herself. She said that she was going to go anyway and that the old man didn't change her mind at all. I later learned that the FBI had done an investigation on Rev. Moon and found that he was clean in all respects. So, I feel the old man had just read an article in the New York Times and was passing himself off as a "G" man. All in all, it was a good day, and we all turned in after our nightly meeting.

It's September 18th, possibly the greatest day in modern history. All the teams line up by 6am. We get new flyers that say: "Today is September 18th, Will you be there?" And we are at our posts within the hour.

Some people pass out the new flyers at subway exit and others stand a block apart, on the corners. My partner, Mathew Morrison, and I walked on one side of the street for about six blocks. We just walk back and forth passing out flyers. All morning we did this, and thousands of flyers are handed out. At about One O'clock, we gather and catch the subway for Madison Square Garden.

Now, for those who have never ridden one of these beauties of transportation, I shall etch a picture of one such vehicle into your memory bank for future reference. As you go down some stairs, you come to this booth. There, you pay for a token that permits you access to an area of platforms where you can board these city trains. It is relatively quiet and big with dark gaping holes to the sides. Then, hark, a noise! It must be, it's got to be, yes! Then you cover your ears, and if the situation warrants, your dress too, and you wait for it to stop. A long silver beauty, which is covered with various, unrecognizable graffiti, sits a few seconds before opening its sliding doors, dumping people out and letting people in. Then, its doors close as quickly as they opened, and slowly speeds off for the next stop. Gaining speed, the wind gets-a-breezing and you wish you could cover your ears hard enough. The car is moving in every direction, you pray you don't get sick until you can reach the proper facilities for such happenings. As you occupy one car, you lazily glance to the car ahead of you and discover, with much fear of heat failure, that it is jumping all over the track and the people don't seem to mind. You could get sick just watching it bounce in every direction. Then, the train begins to slow down, and you walk to the doors, much happier at the thought that you will be on dry, steady cement in a minute or two. And then, the big cavern lights up your destination. The train stops, the doors open and you hurry out before you get stuck inside, since the doors are timed and all. With the journey finished, you suddenly discover you still have to get to the street. But, that's easy, since all you have to do is follow the crowd. The scene reminds you of a movie you once saw about cattle being herded somewhere to be disinfected or something. And, that's what if feels like to travel on a railroad under New York City.

We arrived at Madison Square Garden at about 1:35pm. We had about an hour to wait, so we went to, well you know, for lunch. After we ate, we crossed the street and went to the front of the humongous arena. There were already hundreds of family members waiting in lines before entering.

Beneath the Garden is the entrance to Pennsylvania Station. Most of the teams were lined up in the area adjacent to the entrance. We stood outside for about two and a half hours, so that the other members could get to the Garden, and for final preparations inside. During this time, most of the members were looking for old friends and finding some. There were people from all fifty states and from many countries: Japan, Korea, Germany, France, Holland, Italy, England, Canada and more!

I saw several members from Mr. Sudo's team. They are the ones who helped prepare for the "Day of Hope' Banquet in Honolulu last April. I saw Traudl Stempl, the German sister who stayed with us for a month. And, I saw Bill Miho, whom we gave to Rev. Sudo's team as a gift, and he eventually found Keith. So, they talked for a long time.

There were also two naval officers that weren't from the US Navy. In fact, it turned out that they are part of Father' navy. He has a forty-eight foot boat in which he takes VIP's out to go fishing. One of the officers had been a fisherman up in Alaska, but he was never in the regular navy.

Then, the "opposition" started to arrive. First, came the guy who had poster-boards all over him saying "Husband power" and "Wives must OBEY husbands." There were also street preachers who were trying to keep people from going in. But, they didn't know that they were preaching to family members. And, some were passing out literature to "Read your Bible and forget Rev Moon." Then, the family members began to sing in order to drown out the street preachers. It was a peaceful battle with singing covering the speeches.

A little after Five O'clock, those who were security guards began to file into the building. And guess who two of the security guards were? Yep, one Keith Chow and one Ken Owens.

Before we entered, we saw Bruce Brown in one of the lines. It was good to seem him again. He looked thinner than before he left Hawaii. It was strange, but during the trip, it was the sisters who gained weight and the brothers who lost it. Can't figure that one out.

After the security guards filed in, we had a short meeting on what to look for. We were chosen into two man teams and placed in different areas of the building. We were told that we had to look out for people who came for the sole purpose of killing Father. If we spotted such a person, we were to notify the official security guard at once. But, we had to remember that that security guard wasn't about to sacrifice his life for someone he didn't know. So, in a since, we were the first line of defense, and if it came down to where we had to sacrifice our lives, we would to it. Our main job was to do just that and not even listen to what is happening on stage. We would always find that out later. And, being a military man, I took those directions literally.

My partner, Mathew Morrison, and I were at section 23, behind the stage. We had a signal, that in case of danger, we could inform another team, and we were all set to give our lives for Father. I had actually convinced myself that I was expendable, and that I would do all I could to stop a potential assassination.

At 6pm, the people began running into the Garden, trying to get the best seats possible. The security guards were looking for possible suspects, mainly, if a person seems too nervous and trying to hide something. The usherettes, who were family members, tried to sit these people as best they could. At about twenty minutes to seven, one of these girls told me about a girl sitting near the gate. The person was completely out of her mind and there was no way of knowing what she might do. We didn't think she would be dangerous, but she could be a distraction. We tried our best to persuade her to leave. But, decided in the end that a brother in the family would sit next to her and keep an eye on her throughout the night. It turned out that she was really quiet and did a lot of clapping.

As it approached Seven O'clock, we could see that every seat in the house was going to be filled, and our worries about success were over. But, the job of protecting True Parents had just begun, and it was going to be a very long and interesting night.

A marching band came out onto the stage and they played to live-in up the atmosphere and make it a happy one.

At 7pm, the lights went out, the searchlight lit up the side podium. A lady announcer came onstage and welcomed everyone, and hoped that everyone would have a happy experience.

Figure 160 True Father speaking at Madison Square Garden. I was standing at the upper left doing security.

First, the entertainment would begin. A combo group, consisting of five or six instrumentalists and a girl singer did several songs. They were quite good and the audience clapped loudly.

Then, the Korean Folk Ballet came on. These were just girls, ranging from fourteen to seventeen, and most of them had never danced before joining the ballet. They were a smash hit. The audience loved them.

During this whole time, and until the talk had concluded, I steadfastly watched the audience for potential troublemakers. Being in the Navy taught me many things. One was that if I was told to do something, I followed it to the letter. I glued myself to that audience, and scarcely at the stage.

The New Hope Singers next appeared onstage. They sang some hymns and family songs. They were great and got a loud reception from the people.

Then, the moment came when Rev. Moon and Colonel Pak arrived on stage to begin the two and a half hour talk. This is when all the security guards really began to work, because anything might happen.

Father began by welcoming everyone and hoped that they would learn to begin to work for God's Kingdom of Heaven on Earth.

The next thing he said surprised everyone, even family members. He said; "Anyone who opposes me, please stand up!" There was silence. No one stood up.

But, after he began to speak again, a heckler rose up in the center of the ground level seats and was forcibly removed from the premises.

This made the atmosphere very low and people began to get very nervous. So, Father requested to the audience that he sing a song. He sang a Korean lullaby. The audience was very moved by his singing and the atmosphere rose up again.

Then, he began speaking once more, with Col. Pak interpreting.

Father said that he had received a message from God in 1970 to come to America and help save this beautiful land. That he was going to reveal part of that message tonight.

He talked about how God's heart was broken because of the Fall. God has been grieving for man all these years and how God has been trying to bring his children back to Him.

He said that the Bible is a codebook, full of symbolism that should not be taken completely literally. That we must interpret the Bible the way the writers wanted it to be interpreted.

He discussed the failure of Adam and Eve and how it was Lucifer who seduced Eve by fornication. That it was Lucifer's idea for the Fall, not God's.

He spoke of how God had prepared the Jews for four thousand years to receive and accept the Messiah. And, how the Jews failed miserable by rejecting Jesus and killing him.

Father talked of what Jesus' mission was. He was to eventually take a bride and start a family, and then a world full of perfected individuals. Jesus was to live and obtain the Kingdom of Heaven and not be crucified as many wrongly believe.

He argued that John the Baptist had the greatest mission of all the previous prophets because he was the living witness to Jesus and to tell the people that Jesus was the Messiah and to unite around him. Instead, John failed in his mission by not following Jesus and that was the main cause of why the Jews rejected Jesus.

He revealed that the Christians must not blindly follow the Bible literally, but to interpret it correctly and be prepared for the Second Messiah.

The role of the Christians today is not to make the same mistake that the Jews made, but to unite around the Second Messiah when he does come, not reject him. We must prevent another crucifixion from occurring and delaying for another two thousand years the Kingdom of Heaven.

Father spoke for two and a half hours, from 7:30 till about 10pm.

Twice during the speech, hecklers had their say and both were in my general area behind the stage. The first heckler was about 40 yards away from me, and some commotion developed, but it was quelled very quickly.

The second heckler happened to be in my section and I quickly ran up the steps to where she was heckling herself. I moved towards her to within about ten feet and I put my finger to my lips and happily went "shhh!" It took ten seconds and an official security guard to get her quiet.

She erupted again minutes later, but was told by the security guard to either keep quiet or leave. She remained quiet after that. What was strange about her, though, was that she was wearing dark sunglasses inside. Strange!

By the time Father finished, he was given a standing ovation as he left the stage. He had come to deliver a message from God to the people of New York, and he had done just that.

My job was finished because he had left and there was no need to look at the people anymore. Everything had gone according to plan. So, I enjoyed the rest of the show in which the New Hope Singers and the Korean Folk Ballet performed again.

All the family members were happy, because they had worked so hard. The rally was a success.

On the Sunday before, Father said that he not only wanted Madison Square Garden filled, but he also wanted thousands of people outside to have a riot, to break glass and everything, trying to get in, and he would pay for all the damage. Believe it or not, while he was speaking at the rally, there were indeed thousands outside rioting, trying to get in. The glass doors to Penn Station were cracked, all of them.

After the rally, our team gathered under the flagpoles on 7th Avenue. The street preachers were still working, even at 11:00 at night. Family members began to sing again, loudly to drown out the speakers, who had bullhorns to magnify their words. We couldn't hear them because of the singing.

Hundreds of people were still in front of the huge arena. Lights from the street lamps and buildings lighting up much of the area. Sidewalks littered with handbills. Street preachers still preaching, people from the hotels across the way watching everything far below, cars rolling by and passengers in the buses trying to figure out what was happening, and hundreds of well-dressed young people singing harmoniously into the night. What a way to end a very successful evening.

But, that was not the end.

Our team and another, one in which Debbie Nanod was in, took the subway back to the hotel. Once there, we put on some old clothes and gathered for a meeting of all the teams.

Once we were assembled, we were told how True Parents were overjoyed at the success of Madison Square Garden and that we must now fulfill one of Father's promises to the city of New York.

In order for New York to know about Rev. Moon and Madison Square Garden, we put up over three hundred thousand posters all over Manhattan. There were many gripes from the citizens and legal action was being taken to stop it. So, Rev. Moon promised the people of New York that as soon as the rally at Madison Square Garden was over, every family member would go throughout the city, at night, while everyone was sleeping, and take down every poster that exists. This is why we were in our old clothes, because we were going to do just that.

All through the night, thousands of members stormed through New York, taking every one of these posters down. The police saw us doing this and were utterly shocked. Passersby walked on in disbelief. A television news team came and photographed us as we worked, peeling the posters down with scrapers, water and fingernails, and using the vans and ourselves as ladders. We were doing this for the people of New York. They'll be in shock once they notice there aren't any posters staring at them in the morning. It took us all night till seven in the morning, to complete the job. It had been a long and glorious night.

But, now, we must leave. Our work is done. We have been successful and have won a great battle.

We all packed and got ready to leave for Belvedere to hear True Father and onward to our home states to resume work.

But, I must say farewell to all my new friends and companions, for I must return early, not being able to make the journey with them, for my ship in Pearl Harbor awaits me.

Everyone bids goodbye to old and newfound friends alike. Tears are shed, laughter is heard and love is felt. But, no matter where you are from, where you are going, whatever your mission, difficult or not, it is plain to see that we will always be a unified family, always together in love centered on Heavenly Father and True Parents.

Well, this is what I witnessed, the event leading up to and including Madison Square Garden. I learned many things in these eighteen days.

I began to feel more for people and how urgent it is to bring them into the family. The more you work within the family, the closer you come to God. You become more aware of God, the world, the nation, the society, your family and yourself. And you begin to see your Original Self coming out and have a desire to attain fully your True Self. Then, this desire spreads to where you want to help others to attain their true selves and by helping others, you'll be able to grow, too. Through this, you discover that it's all to help Heavenly Father bring his children back. That is the main reason why we do this, because He is our Father. He is our primary concern, above everything else, nothing else matters. His happiness is our first goal. And we are achieving that goal by serving his son. So, please try to study the Divine Principle, pray and work hard. By doing these three things and helping other people, you will become a true child of God.

Made in the USA
San Bernardino, CA
07 May 2017

Copyright @The Professional Speakers Academy 2025 Breakfree forever Publishing

ALL RIGHTS RESERVED: No part of this book may be reproduced or transmitted in any form whatsoever, electronic or mechanical, including photocopying, recording, or by any informational storage or retrieval system without the express written, dated, and signed permission from the author.

Title: The Changemakers: Entrepreneurs With a Mission, Voices With a Message

ISBN: 978-1-917815-09-3

Category: Speaking / Business / Motivational

LIMITS OF LIABILITY/DISCLAIMER OF WARRANTY: This anthology is a collection of personal stories written by individual contributors. The views and opinions expressed are those of the respective authors and do not necessarily reflect those of the editor or publisher. The content is intended for inspirational and informational purposes only and does not constitute professional, medical, legal, or financial advice. Readers are encouraged to seek appropriate professional guidance for their personal circumstances. Some chapters contain references to trauma, abuse, and violence which may be distressing. Reader discretion is advised. While every effort has been made to ensure accuracy, the authors and publisher accept no responsibility for any errors, omissions, or consequences arising from the use of this book. All rights reserved. No part of this publication may be reproduced, stored, or transmitted in any form without prior written permission from the publisher, except as permitted under fair use.

DEDICATION

To all the change makers in the world, the ones who refuse to settle for 'how it's always been,' who stand tall when it would be easier to shrink, who speak truth when silence would be safer, and who dare to believe that their voice, their work, and courage can spark transformation.

This book is for you.

May your light never dim, and may your ripple become a wave.

> "Every message shared in courage becomes a ripple that touches shores far beyond what the messenger can see."
>
> — From The Changemakers

CONTENTS

INTRODUCTION — 6

CHAPTER 1: From Pain To Purpose — 8

CHAPTER 2: It's Never Too Late To Be Great — 19

CHAPTER 3: Cracked But Not Broken — 37

CHAPTER 4: Breaking Beyond Your Barriers — 51

CHAPTER 5: The Future Of Leadership — 63

CHAPTER 6: Grip To Growth — 79

CHAPTER 7: From Invisible To Irresistible — 93

CHAPTER 8: Freedom Forged In Fire — 115

CHAPTER 9: Life Lessons From The Big C — 129

CHAPTER 10: Moves Of The Infinite Player In This Game Called Life — 149

CHAPTER 11: Unlocking The Magic Of Irish Traditional Music — 159

CHAPTER 12: A Journey To Freedom — 173

CHAPTER 13: Built To Run Without You — 189

CHAPTER 14: The Cost Of Someone Else's Dream — 199

CHAPTER 15: A Journey Into Wholeness — 215

CHAPTER 16: The Art Of Simplified Scaling — 229

CHAPTER 17: The Whole Self Advantage For Neurobrilliant Success — 243

CONCLUSION — 263

INTRODUCTION

The Changemakers:
Entrepreneurs With a Mission, Voices With a Message.

In every generation, there rises a collective of bold souls who refuse to blend in - visionaries who challenge the status quo, break ceilings, and turn their personal trials into platforms of transformation.
The Changemakers is a testament to that spirit. It's not just a book; it's a movement - a gathering of 17 powerful voices from **The Professional Speakers Academy,** each one forged in the fire of experience and refined through the pursuit of purpose.

These are not ordinary entrepreneurs. They are builders of legacies, creators of movements, and carriers of messages that matter.
Each has faced their own crucible - moments that tested their resilience, questioned their identity, and demanded their growth. Yet, through those moments, they discovered a truth that unites them all: business is not just about profit; it's about purpose.

Within these pages, you'll walk alongside founders, mentors, speakers, and thought leaders who turned pain into platforms, and setbacks into setups for something far greater. You'll encounter stories that will stir your courage, strategies that will stretch your thinking, and insights that will remind you that transformation isn't reserved for the elite - it's the birthright of anyone willing to rise.

Each author in this collection has not only built a business but also embraced a mission - to influence, to inspire, and to ignite change in others. Their words are raw, real, and refreshingly authentic. They'll take you behind the glossy highlight reels and into the gritty reality of entrepreneurship - the long nights, the self-doubt, the divine nudges, and the relentless pursuit of impact. But this isn't merely a compilation of success stories. **It's a ripple effect in print.** Every chapter is a spark - an invitation for you to reflect, realign, and reignite your own mission.

Whether you're a seasoned entrepreneur, a leader in transition, or someone standing on the edge of a new beginning, this book is your call to action: to step into your voice, own your message, and make your mark.

The world doesn't change just through titles or talks, it changes through action. And in Changemakers, you'll find 17 action takers who are not only talking the talk but walking the walk - of what happens when courage meets calling.

So, take a deep breath, turn the page, and prepare to be moved. Because once you hear these voices, you won't see business - or yourself - the same way again.

This is the Changemakers.
17 Voices. 17 Journeys. One ripple effect that can transform your life and business.

CHAPTER 1
FROM PAIN TO PURPOSE

> "To be successful you MUST give up the need for approval from others, and trust yourself.
>
> - Andy Harrington"

Changemakers

It's November 2012, and I'm standing at the back of the ballroom in London's Grosvenor House Hotel. Crystal chandeliers shimmer above a crowd of the wealthy and well-connected, but my focus is elsewhere.

From my vantage point, I can see him - larger than life even while seated. Ten years I've waited for this moment. Dreamed of it. Doubted it. Fought for it. And now, here I am.

On stage, comedian Ruby Wax is warming up the audience, her trademark wit cutting through the air. To her left and right stand four members of the U.S. Secret Service, their dark suits and earpieces making the scene look like a movie set.

"Ladies and gentlemen," Ruby announces in that unmistakable voice, "please welcome to the stage, former President of the United States of America, Bill Clinton."

Three hundred people rise to their feet in thunderous applause. But I stay seated. My mind isn't on Clinton. It's on the man sitting at the top table - six foot seven, broad-shouldered, unmistakable. Tony Robbins. This is it. The moment to end a cycle that began more than a decade ago.

As Clinton speaks, my mind drifts back to where it all started - the Old Bailey, London, November 2001.

The Beginning of Change

I'm sitting in the gallery of Court No. 4, looking down on the dark oak panels, the barristers in wigs, and formality of the space. The air is thick with tension.

In the dock sits a young woman I'm close to - early twenties, small, fragile-looking, but brave beyond belief. She's giving evidence against the man who violated her trust and shattered her sense of safety.

As she finishes, her counsel asks quietly, "Is there anything you'd like to add?"

She grips the rail, trembling but determined. "Yes," she says. "I'm going to say something I didn't have the courage to say before."

The courtroom stills.

"No longer am I going to believe it was my fault. No longer am I going to keep your secret. It's over. The truth is out."

The words echo around the chamber, and in that instant, I realise courage isn't the absence of fear - it's action in spite of it.

The verdict comes later: guilty. Relief floods through us both, but what follows isn't peace. It's silence - the kind that fills a house when someone you love has shut down completely.

Despite running a £21 million recruitment company at the time, I felt utterly powerless. All the money in the world meant nothing when I couldn't help the person I loved to find herself again.

When I checked her into the Priory Clinic, the consultant said she was clinically depressed and prescribed medication. But deep down, I knew pills weren't the answer.

A Late-Night Spark

One night, exhausted and desperate, I flicked on the TV. A late-night infomercial caught my attention - an American giant named Anthony Robbins was talking about mastering your emotions, transforming your life, and reclaiming your power.

Something about his conviction pierced the fog. I picked up the phone and called the number on the screen.

Changemakers

"Thank you for calling the Anthony Robbins Companies," said a cheerful voice. "This is Marshonda - how may I help you?"

Forty minutes later, I'd enrolled in Tony's Mastery University. I didn't know exactly what I was buying - only that I was buying hope.

Against all advice, I checked her out of hospital, and we flew to Florida for *Unleash the Power Within*.

Thousands of people filled the arena. Tony stormed the stage, booming: *"You already have the power to change!"*

That night, my partner was one of those chosen for a live intervention in front of 5,000 people. I held my breath as Tony worked with her, guiding her from pain to laughter, from despair to joy - right there on stage.

In that single session, everything changed. She realised she could choose meaning over memory, focus over fear. And I realised something too: I was meant to help others find that same power.

A thought whispered inside me: "Maybe that's why you're here, Andy. Maybe it's meant to be you on that stage too."

But almost as soon as I heard it, I dismissed it. "Don't be ridiculous. Who's going to listen to you?"

A Date with Destiny

Months later, we attended Tony's Date with Destiny event in South Carolina. On the final day, participants were asked to pair up and hold eye contact - to truly see one another.

I hesitated. Everyone quickly found a partner - except me.
And one other person.

Tony Robbins.

When our eyes met, I gestured awkwardly, asking if he'd partner with me. To my shock, he nodded.

We sat opposite each other for what felt like forever - five minutes of silence that said everything.

Tears welled up. I thought of what his work had done for us, and how, through him, we'd found hope again. To my surprise, I saw tears in his eyes too.

In that moment, I made a decision that changed my life.

Even though I wasn't yet a speaker, author, or coach, I vowed to learn, grow, and one day inspire others the way he had inspired me. And perhaps - just perhaps - share a stage with him.

Ten Years Later

July 2011. Backstage at London's Excel Centre.

Nine thousand people fill the arena. I can hear the low hum of excitement beyond the curtain.

Beside me stands Beckie - the woman who would soon become my wife - whispering, "This is your moment. You've got this."

I step onto the stage to a roar of applause. I'm about to speak alongside Tony Robbins.

It's hard to describe what that moment felt like - the full circle of a decade's journey. The failures, the rebuilding, the doubts, the grit. All of it leading here.

Since then, I've shared stages with world leaders, entrepreneurs, and

Changemakers

icons – from Sir Richard Branson to Robert Kiyosaki, from Steve Wozniak to Bill Clinton.

And that brings me back to this ballroom in 2012.

Clinton finishes his speech. The audience rises again. My heart races. I stride toward Tony, tap him on the shoulder, and as he turns to face me, I find myself once again looking into those same eyes that once changed everything.

"Hi Tony," I say. "I'm Andy Harrington. We've shared the stage a few times, but I wanted to thank you – because ten years ago, you inspired me to change my life."

We shake hands. And in that instant, I realise: the cycle is complete. I am no longer the student seeking change – I am the changemaker.

Why You Should Read This Book

Every great transformation begins with a decision – a line in the sand where you say, enough is enough.

For me, that decision began in a courtroom and ended on a stage. For you, it might begin on this page.

This book, Changemakers, is written for those who know they're meant for more. People who have overcome challenges, gained wisdom, and now feel a calling to use their story – not as a wound, but as a weapon for good.

Because the truth is:

Right now, there are people in the world who want to know what you already know – and they're waiting for you to show up.

Every one of the changemakers you'll meet in these pages has walked through their own fire. They didn't just learn something - they lived it. They found meaning in their struggle, turned it into a method, and now use it to transform lives.

In these chapters, you'll learn how they did it - their step-by-step frameworks, mindsets, and models that help people change faster, go further, and live fuller.

You'll discover how to:

Turn your life lessons into lasting impact.

Transform your expertise into a real business that serves others.

Build influence, income, and inner fulfilment - all at once.

And as you do, you'll see that **you too are a changemaker in waiting.** You don't need letters after your name. You don't need to be "qualified" by anyone but life itself. Your qualification is your experience, your empathy, and your energy to serve.

We live in an era where your message can reach millions from your phone, your stage, or your story. The question is: will you use what happened to you to make something happen through you?
Because this isn't just a book - it's an invitation.

An invitation to rise. To lead. To use your life to light the way for others. If you're ready to make a difference - in your business, your relationships, your community, or even your own sense of purpose -
then turn the page.

Changemakers

Your story is waiting to be written. And who knows? One day, perhaps someone will read your chapter... and find in it the spark that changes everything.

ANDY HARRINGTON

CHAPTER 2
IT'S NEVER TOO LATE
TO BE GREAT

REDISCOVERING IDENTITY, PURPOSE AND JOY

> "It's only too late if you've taken your last breath!"
>
> – Ali Gordon

Have you ever felt your identity, purpose, or joy quietly slip away as you pass through life?

Have you ever wondered if maybe your chance to start over has also passed you by?

If so, then this chapter is for you!

I want to start by reminding you - you are not too old, and it is not too late.

God sees you. He knows your story, and He can breathe new life into your dreams. Even now, there's a path ahead filled with meaning, hope, and joy, just waiting for you to take the first step; even if you cannot see it or feel it right now.

For me, my journey began the moment I realised my lowest point wasn't the end, it was the place God chose to start something new.

From aloha to ashes

I feel it in my bones; life is about to change forever.

Eighteen months of training in Hawaii, Plumeria on the breeze, waves on the shore… then six months in Papua New Guinea as a Medical Missionary. My dream is finally real, I can taste the salty air, feel the promise ahead.

Then, in a heartbeat, it shatters. After just six weeks, I'm asked to leave.

The colour drains from my world. Confidence, hope, belief in the future, all vanish, leaving me in the shadow of the life I thought was mine.

Changemakers

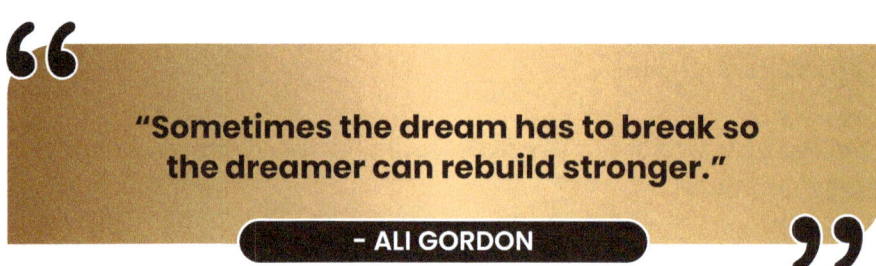

"Sometimes the dream has to break so the dreamer can rebuild stronger."

– ALI GORDON

When the wheel isn't mine!

Back in Madrid, I'm fighting to hold myself together, desperate for help. I know I need professional support, but doors slam shut. Calls go unanswered. Referrals drag on for months. My life is crumbling while the system shrugs.

I tell myself to be patient. It takes time, they say. But my patience is gone. My mind spirals, each day another brick in the wall trapping me inside my own head.

When I finally enter The Priory in London, I think, "At last, I'm in charge of my healing!".

But I'm not!

The steering wheel of my life has been taken, and not by choice.

Control is comforting – but freedom comes when you learn to trust the hands holding you.

– ALI GORDON

Home Front Heartaches

If you've ever been in crisis, you'll know, family can be both your greatest comfort and your greatest challenge.

Mine is in open conflict. Arguments over who is "right," who "understands" me best, me or them; whose opinion "matters."

Instead of focusing on healing, I'm fielding emotional grenades from the people I love. It's exhausting to be in the middle of a war I never asked for.

Is love for me?

In my darkest moments, I wonder if God has abandoned me.

If He truly loves me, why am I still in pain? Why has He allowed my dreams to shatter? Maybe I'm not worth rescuing.
Maybe I'm too broken.

If you've ever felt unseen, unheard, or forgotten by people or God, you'll understand the weight of these questions.

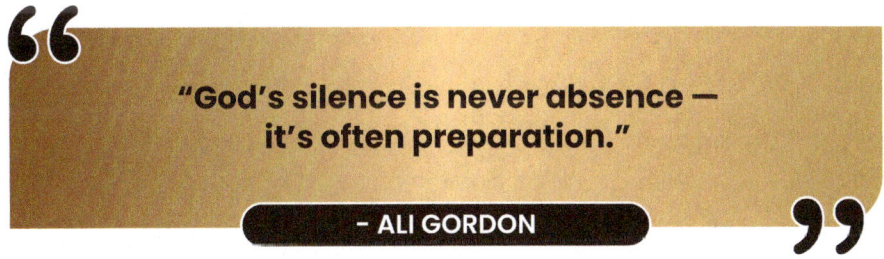

> "God's silence is never absence — it's often preparation."
>
> — ALI GORDON

A messenger in disguise the day choice disappeared

Then comes the gut punch!

My voluntary status at The Priory is removed. Simply because I am a little too keen to leave the hospital to be able to make my own rules again! I am officially "sectioned" under the Mental Health Act (1983).

In plain English? I cannot leave, even if I want to.

I am now terrified! Totally, physically, spiritually terrified. This is my worst-case scenario. All I wanted to do was go home, but instead I feel trapped with even less control than before!

And then... he appears, "the man with the kind eyes".
He doesn't lecture or judge. He just sits with me in a disused corridor and truly sees me. His calm presence steadies me.

Later, staff insist no one was there with me on the security camera footage, but I know he was real. An angel. A whisper from God, "You are not abandoned. I am here."

God Has a Plan

Meeting "the man with the kind eyes" changes me. I see that no matter how lost I feel, a turning point is always possible.

God isn't punishing me, He's redirecting me. He doesn't "fix" me instantly; He walks beside me as I rebuild, step by step.

I choose to trust Him again, to treat hospital staff with kindness, and to return to Madrid, not to resume life, but to start anew.

Leaving The Priory, sunlight warms my face. No fireworks, just a quiet certainty, life isn't over. Madrid awaits, and so is the woman I'm becoming.

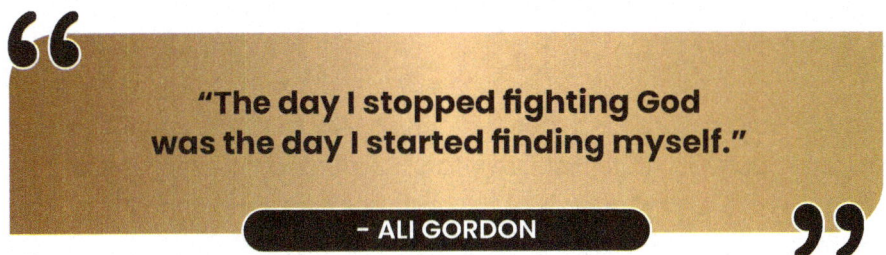

"The day I stopped fighting God was the day I started finding myself."

- ALI GORDON

Success in Disguise

I'd love to tell you that from this day forward, everything goes smoothly, but it doesn't.

I make poor relationship choices again, as if to prove I can still "control" my own life. I resist letting God have total control. Inevitably, I end up back in hospital in Madrid for yet more "psych Obs" (psychiatric observations)!

But along the way, there are significant wins, milestones on my journey to becoming whole again.

Slowly, things begin to shift. I train as a Transformation Coach and a Fire walk Instructor, because I want to pay forward the breakthroughs I've had.

I launch LUXINOR Coaching and Training, and later, LUXINOR Publishing. They become my way of helping others step out of their comfort zones, just as I have.

Finally, I start to dream again! A published author; TV appearances; speaking at international conferences; and my proudest creation, **"The F.L.A.M.E.S. Rediscovery Roadmap."** ™

The Critics Arrive

Isn't it interesting that when you start something great, the critics come out?

My father calls my training trips "ridiculous." My brother reminds me that most start-ups fail in the first five years. Some people even whisper they don't believe I've ever been ill at all, and that it was all orchestrated to gain attention.

Also, as well as other people having their say, I start to notice that my own inner critic voice starts chipping in too! "Who are you to be doing this?" "They are right, listen to them!" "Just get a proper job with a regular salary!" As if I don't have enough to deal with!

It all stings, but it gives me great chances to learn and change! For example, I learned that criticism from others often says more about the critic than the one being criticised! I also learn that I can work with my inner critic to create a new conversation about who I truly am!

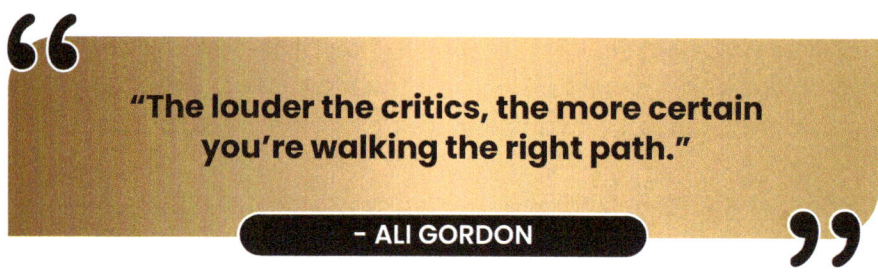

> "The louder the critics, the more certain you're walking the right path."
>
> — ALI GORDON

Here's the Truth

Can you relate to any of the following?...

Maybe you wake up one morning, look in the mirror, and barely recognise the person looking back.

The titles and roles that once defined you: parent, partner, professional, have faded or shifted. Without them, it's easy to feel invisible. When you stop recognising you, it chips away at your confidence and makes you question whether you still matter.

Or perhaps you've lost that sense of why. The goals that once got you out of bed don't fit anymore, and the old routines feel like wearing someone else's shoes, uncomfortable and awkward. Without purpose, the days can start to blend into one another, leaving you feeling restless and uncertain.

Or possibly even the things that should bring joy start to feel muted. You smile politely at good news, but inside it doesn't quite land. Life starts to feel more like surviving than truly living. So, wouldn't you rather be experiencing any, or even better, all, of the following instead?

Imagine waking up and feeling an unshakable sense of "This is who I am!" You see yourself with fresh eyes – strong, valuable, and deeply worthy, and you carry yourself with a quiet pride that others can't help but notice. Every choice you make comes from a place of self-respect, and it feels good… really good… to finally stand in your own truth again.

Now picture opening your eyes each morning with a burst of excitement in your chest, knowing exactly what you're moving towards. You have a reason to leap out of bed, something that lights you up from the inside out. Every day feels like a step towards a vision that matters to you, and you go to bed each night with a smile, knowing you've lived on purpose.

Finally, envision feeling that fizz of happiness in your chest again, like bubbles rising in a glass. You wake up curious about what the day will bring, and you find yourself laughing more, noticing beauty in small things, and embracing opportunities without hesitation. Life feels rich, colourful, and deliciously worth living, and the best part is, you know the joy is here to stay.

Changemakers

"OK, but how do I move from the pain to the joy of life?" I hear you asking!

Well, I believe you can achieve this by reclaiming your identity, rediscovering your purpose, and reigniting your joy.

So, what do I mean by this?

Reclaim Your Identity: Let go of old labels and roles. Remember who you are at your core and stand tall in it.

Rediscover Your Purpose: Find what matters to you now. Create fresh goals that light you up.

Reignite Your Joy: Bring back your spark. Notice the little things, say yes to new experiences, and let happiness flow again.

"The F.L.A.M.E.S. Rediscovery Roadmap."™

With your permission, I would love to share a little on how **"The F.L.A.M.E.S. Rediscovery Roadmap."™** can help you achieve reclaimed identity, rediscovered purpose, and reignited joy!

"The F.L.A.M.E.S. Rediscovery Roadmap."™ is a 6-month online group coaching program specifically designed for people aged 55 to 75 who are ready to rise again after "later-life" challenges.

It's your chance to reconnect with your true self, rebuild confidence, and find fresh purpose. A space to dust yourself off, stand tall, and set out on life's next chapter, no matter your age, no matter where you're starting from.

Each module focuses on a different area of knowledge, skills, and actions to take.

These are shown below!

FOUNDATIONS:

We start gently, no rush, no pressure. This is your space, a place where you can breathe, exhale, and reconnect with you. Not the roles you've had to play, not the titles you've carried, not the expectations that have been placed on your shoulders, but the real you.

We'll look at your skills, your strengths, and the parts of yourself that may have been tucked away under years of labels, responsibilities, and "shoulds." It's like opening a forgotten drawer and finding treasures you didn't realise you still owned, abilities you'd written off, talents you didn't know you still had, sparks of curiosity and creativity that are ready to be brought back to life. Together, we'll gently peel those layers back, letting you stand in your own name again, confident, grounded, and clear about who you are and what you bring to the table. This is where the groundwork is laid, the solid foundation that will support everything that comes next on your journey.

LIBERTY:

Once you've got your footing, it's time to loosen the grip of those invisible chains, the limitations that have been holding you back for far too long. In the **LIBERTY** module, we gently but deliberately start dismantling the old stories you've been told (and maybe even told yourself) about what you can and cannot do.

You'll begin to recognise the fears that have been quietly steering your choices, the ones that whisper, "you're too old," "you're not ready," or "it's too risky." Instead of letting those voices control the narrative, you'll learn how to face them, challenge them, and release them. This isn't about pretending those fears never existed, it's about taking away their power. It's about giving yourself permission to dream without boundaries, to imagine a life that feels lighter, freer, and more you than it has in years.

ADVENTURE:

This is the stage where we throw open the doors to possibility and let fresh air flood in. This is where you step beyond the familiar and give yourself permission to explore, to play, and to say "yes" to things that stir your curiosity. Maybe it's trying a creative pursuit you've always admired from a distance, learning a skill that feels delightfully outside your comfort zone, travelling somewhere new, or even pursuing a passion you'd quietly buried under years of "maybe someday."

It's not about reckless leaps, it's about thoughtful, courageous steps that awaken parts of you that have been sleeping. In this module, you start to rediscover that spark inside, the one that still craves excitement, growth, and joy, and you learn how to nurture it, so it becomes part of your everyday life.

MASTERY:

The **MASTERY** module is where confidence really starts to grow. You'll be learning and developing new skills, not just because it's good for you, but because it makes life richer, more independent, and a lot more fun.

You'll take on challenges that once felt intimidating and turn them into small, satisfying wins. Whether it's conquering a bit of tech, picking up a creative talent, or deepening your knowledge in something you love, this module proves to you that you're still growing, still capable, and still able to surprise yourself, and that's a great feeling.

ENGAGEMENT:

The **ENGAGEMENT** module is where you start weaving this new energy, freedom, and curiosity into everyday life. You begin showing up for the things, and the people, that matter to you.

It could mean joining a local group, volunteering for a cause close to your heart, or simply connecting more deeply with the friends and family you already have. **ENGAGEMENT** says, "I'm here, I'm involved, and I'm part of something bigger than me." It's about building a life that feels connected, purposeful, and satisfying, on your own terms.

SUPPORT:

This is where you establish your safety net, and your Elite F1 Pit Crew rolled into one. This is where you connect with people who understand you, who believe in you, and are there to remind you why you started, even on the tough days. It's about having a circle that celebrates your wins, lifts you when you stumble, and walks beside you every step of the way. **SUPPORT** turns this from a lonely climb into a shared adventure. Let's face it, life is just better when you've got the right people in your corner!

Each Module also has its own Programme Title, see below!

Changemakers

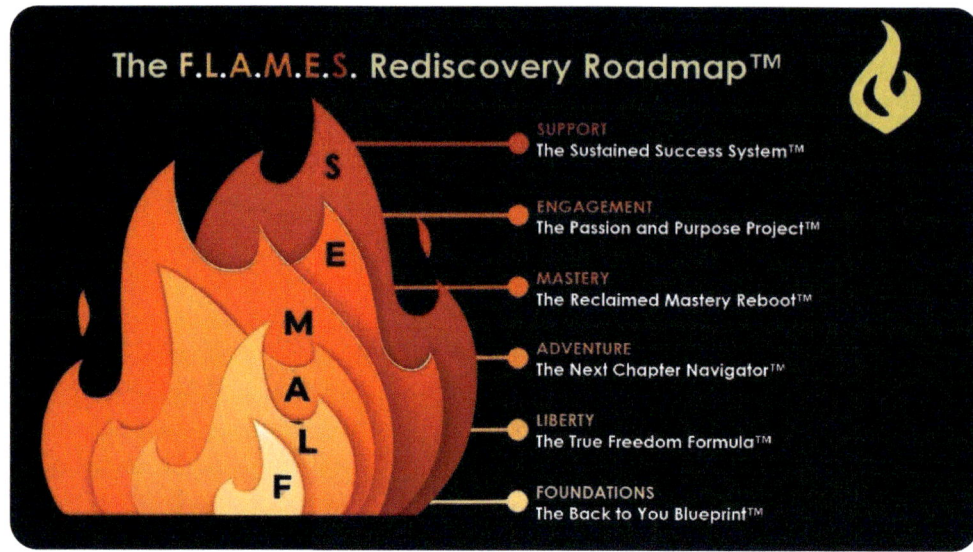

For example, **FOUNDATIONS** is **"The Back to You Blueprint"**™

I would love to introduce this programme in a little more depth. Here we cover FOUR themes:

FOCUS – *Make space for you.* Shift your attention inward. Put life on mute, silence the to-do lists, roles and expectations, so you can tune into yourself. Using techniques such as Introductions to: "Ideal Average Day" visualisation, mindfulness exercises, and breathing exercises.

Pause. Breathe. Begin again.

FIND – *Rediscover hidden treasures.* Dig beneath the layers to uncover forgotten strengths, talents and sparks of curiosity waiting to come alive again. Using techniques such as Introductions to: childhood strengths and talents exercise, and comparison with today's identified strengths and talents.

Uncover the gold within.

FREE – *Release what isn't really you.* Let go of the "shoulds" and old expectations that weigh you down, creating space for authenticity. Using techniques such as Introductions to: inner voices, identification, reframing from "should" to "get to".

Let go! Feel lighter!

FIRM – *Stand strong in your own name.* Root yourself in clarity and confidence. Stand tall, grounded in who you are and what you bring. Using techniques such as Introductions to: the concept of our true core self, the "Who am I?" exercise.

Rooted. Ready. Rocking it!

Each of the other Programmes follow a similar structure, with its own relevant sub steps to follow.

Here's why this course is unique!

What makes **The F.L.A.M.E.S. Rediscovery Roadmap™** stand out is that we don't just throw piles of information at you. Most people finish a course with a notebook full of half-scribbled ideas that get tucked away and forgotten.

Sound familiar? I've done it too!

With LUXINOR Coaching and Training, change happens differently. You're given time to absorb what you learn, reflect on how it fits your life, and most importantly, put it into action.

Throughout **"The F.L.A.M.E.S. Rediscovery Roadmap"** ™, information, reflection, and application are woven together, so transformation isn't just a hope at the end, it's happening every step of the way.

Changemakers

> "Reclaiming your life isn't about going back - it's about moving forward with purpose.
>
> — ALI GORDON

So, to Wrap Up...

If having read this chapter you resonate with anything I have said, you can see how this programme might help you move from the pains you are experiencing to your dream life, or you can hear the words on these pages calling to you, then I encourage you to get in touch to have an **"Ignite The Fire"** chat with me in person. Here we can get to know each other better. You can also find out more about what's needed to change your life from hurting to healing and how **"The F.L.A.M.E.S. Rediscovery Roadmap."**™ can help you with this.

I hit 60 this year. I've been "sectioned", broken, misunderstood, and written off because of my age and emotion regulation issues more times than I care to mention...

...but I am here - and so are you!

Remember: it's never too late for being great! If I can rise from my lowest point in a locked ward to creating a life filled with purpose, joy, and impact... then you can too!

All it takes is that first, trembling step; and I'll walk it with you!

Ali Gordon is a Transformation Coach and Fire walk Instructor who empowers people aged 55 –75 to rediscover their identity, purpose, and joy no matter what life throws their way.

Her book, **"Hope in the Darkness: One Heart's Journey to Becoming Whole"**, charts the messy, miraculous path from breakdown to breakthrough, with a few divine nudges and guinea pig cuddle breaks along the way.

Based in Madrid with her four furry flatmates and an overly generous fridge, she now passionately shares her life journey to inspire others that they too can create fulfilling, exciting, and joy-filled lives.

Discover more at: **www.luxinorcoachingandtraining.com.**

Take that first step now!

Scan the QR code to sign up for an "Ignite the Fire" chat so you can start writing the next chapter of your life with energy, purpose, and joy!

"Your next chapter starts right here!"

- ALI GORDON

CHAPTER 3
CRACKED BUT NOT BROKEN

AN ORTHOPAEDIC SURGEON'S JOURNEY FROM INJURY TO INSIGHT

> "Pain was my teacher, silence my challenge, and advocacy my mission – together they became the fire that shaped my voice."
>
> – George Zarifopoulos

Changemakers

We all carry cracks.

Some are in the bones we've pushed too far. Others are in the trust we've given to systems that promised to protect us. Most are invisible, hairline fractures in the spirit, hidden behind professional smiles and steady hands.

This is my journey, from the surgeon's table to the patient's bed, from physical collapse to professional redemption. Along the way, I meet the forgotten workers whose stories are rarely told, and the rare managers who dare to listen. This work is for them. For us. For everyone caught between the grind of duty and the weight of pain. Back pain doesn't clock out when your shift ends. It follows you like a shadow, creeping into your most intimate spaces. It interrupts your sleep, dulls your concentration, dampens your joy. It chips away at the foundation of your identity.

It doesn't matter whether you're lifting, driving, sitting, or standing for hours, the toll isn't just physical. It grinds down the spirit. Before the injury, my life was a rhythm of theatre lights, scalpel handles, and the quiet hum of suction machines. The smell of antiseptic was as familiar as my morning coffee, and the weight of surgical gloves felt like a second skin. Most people imagine surgery as constant adrenaline, but in truth, it's equal parts focus and patience. There are stretches where you're as still as a statue, your back inclined at an awkward angle, your neck bent just so, while you work through layers of muscle and bone. The operating table becomes your universe, everything beyond its sterile perimeter fades into irrelevance. I thrived in it. The quiet concentration broken only by the steady beep of monitors. The unspoken choreography between scrub nurse and surgeon, where a raised eyebrow meant "suture" and a slight nod indicated "retractor." There was a pride in knowing that for those hours, someone's life was literally in my hands, and that I could change their tomorrow with precision and care. In those days, I was invincible. Or so I believed.

Changemakers

My typical day began at 7:30 AM with rounds, checking on post-operative patients before the hospital stirred to full life. By 9.00 AM, I was scrubbing in for the first case. The ritual was like meditation as arms are raised, water cascading from elbows, the methodical cleansing that separated the ordinary world from the sacred space of surgery.

Between cases, I'd grab coffee from the machine that perpetually needed repair, its motor grinding like an old man's joints.
The orthopaedic department was a tight community, we shared gallows humour about difficult cases, celebrated successful outcomes with quiet satisfaction, and carried each other through the inevitable losses that came with our profession. There's a saying in surgery: "Your body will remember before your mind does." The hours of standing, twisting, and lifting leave their mark like sediment in a riverbed. We all joked about our sore backs after a twelve-hour shift, comparing ourselves to the rugby players we'd patched up, warriors bearing honourable scars. But deep down, we thought we were indestructible.

After all, we were the ones who fixed broken bones, not the ones who broke them.

But there is this paradox; we treat people who are in pain with more pain.

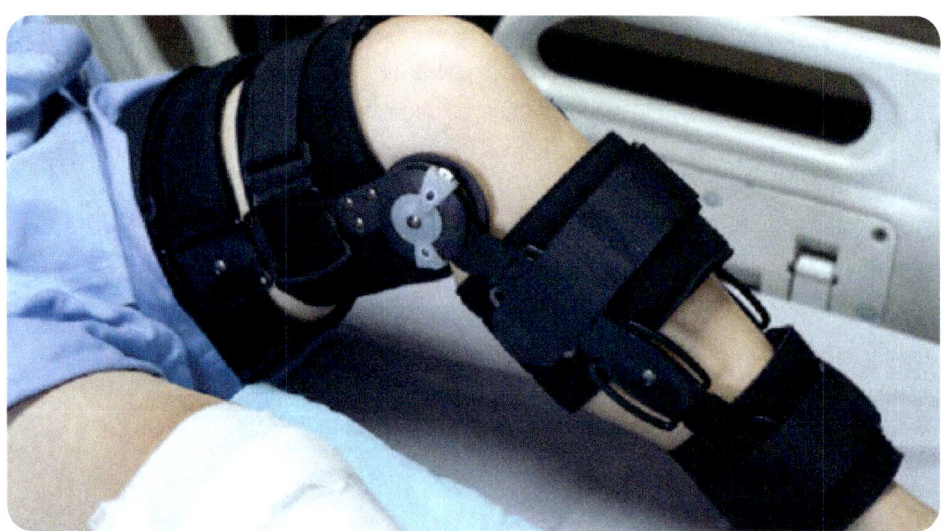

But here's the truth most don't hear, back pain is not always a life sentence. It's a signal. A challenge. And with the right knowledge, small daily adjustments, and a commitment to change, it can be managed, softened, and often reversed.

What follows is more than a memoir. It's part personal account, part practical manual, and part cultural critique. It's about the science of back pain, yes, but it's also about the human cost of neglect, when people are left to fight their battles alone.

It begins just after Christmas, twenty-five winters ago. The air is sharp enough to sting the lungs; daylight fades by mid-afternoon. I'm in the hospital's administrative wing. The waiting room is stark, metal filing cabinets, dull faux-leather chairs, faded posters promising better health systems. The air smells faintly of ink and bureaucracy.

The receptionist looks up. "You can sit, Mr. Zee."

I shake my head. "Standing hurts less."

The intercom crackles: "Send George in."

The hospital manager sits behind a desk large enough to stage an operation. Shoulders like a retired rugby player, face grey, eyes like granite, mouth rarely bent into a smile.

Without looking up: "Well, George, what's the matter?"

I steady myself, my spine protesting every breath. "Six months ago, in theatre, we were repositioning a massive patient. The timing failed. The others dropped away. I took the full weight. Something cracked. I finished the surgery, but I left the theatre in pain, and it's never stopped. I've only been given painkillers. If I go on sick leave the Department will suffer, and you know it. I need physiotherapy.
Please send me to Occupational health."

Changemakers

He raises a hand. "First, don't blackmail me by saying the Department won't function without you. Second, your doctor says it's muscular. Refer yourself to physio."

"I can't. Regulations won't allow it."

He picks up his pen. He is not even looking at me. "You can go now. I'm busy."

Dismissed.

I walk out hollow; my plea dissolved into the walls. Something in my spine had cracked that day in theatre, but it's my faith in the system that feels broken. Six months pass. The pain becomes constant, less a sharp cry, more a dull companion. My body curves into new shapes. My stride shortens. My moods changed. At the dinner table I am absent. In bed I growl like a wounded animal. Nobody wants to be around me. My family feels the shift, my children tread lightly, my wife grows quiet, even the dog greets me with a cautious wag.

I stop looking in mirrors. I stop asking for help. Like a fractured bone left unattended, I begin to set wrong.

Until one August afternoon, walking toward the canteen, drawn by the smell of roast beef, I hear behind me: "George?"

Turn like a log. The spine is not following what the brain is telling it to do. It's Mike, an old friend, now a metabolic physician.
"You've vanished," he says.

I shrug. "Back pain. No one's helping. I'm surviving."

He studies me for a moment. "Come to my clinic. Now. Before lunch."

Two days later: "Borderline diabetic. Hypertension's starting. You need a total change, or medication for life."

Something in me snaps again, but this time it's not defeat, it's defiance. "Me? Pills for life? I'm a doctor. I prescribe them, I don't take them."
That was my line in the sand.

The next six months are my proving ground.
Recovery isn't cinematic. It's not a quick montage. It's awkward, slow, and often lonely. I walk, first to the end of the street, then around the block, then miles. I read everything: pain science, posture mechanics, metabolic health. I rebuild not just my body, but my understanding.

Slowly, stiffness loosens. My blood pressure settles. My energy returns. My family smiles more. At work, I lose the nickname "Papa Smurf" for my hunched, blue-scrubbed frame.

The crack in my body is healing. The crack in my confidence begins to knit too.
Then a nurse comes into my clinic. She lifts patients daily, smiles through every shift—but pops painkillers in the break room. Nobody asks. Nobody notices. Until she ends up in surgery herself.

Her story mirrors mine. And I realise, there are thousands like us. Drivers. Nurses. Warehouse staff. All enduring quietly. All underserved.

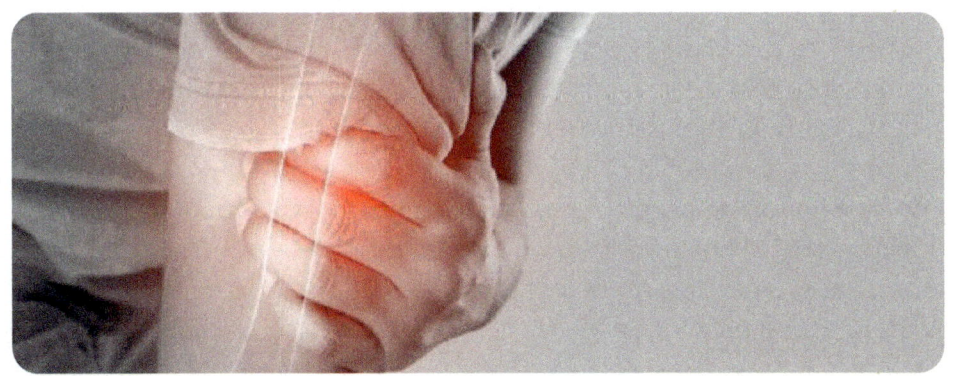

Changemakers

So, I built something: The **E.R.A.S.E.** Low Back Pain Formula.

It's not theory - it's lived. Tested. Proven.

Mike and Sara, owners of a 25-driver transport company, were losing nearly £200,000 a year in costs related to back pain. They applied the E.R.A.S.E. Formula, those losses almost disappeared.

Donna, who ran an administrative services company, was haemorrhaging half a million annually from sick leave and staff turnover due to musculoskeletal issues. Within a year of applying the formula, her costs dropped dramatically.

These aren't abstract successes; they are proof that cracks can be repaired when the right care and attention are applied.

My spine cracked. But I was not broken. Pain became my teacher. Silence became my challenge. Advocacy became my mission.

If you're a leader, this work will give you tools to protect your people, and your bottom line. If you're a worker, it will give you strategies to reclaim your body and your life. Recovery isn't about "getting back to where you were." It's about moving forward with wisdom you didn't have before.

Because sometimes, a crack doesn't mean collapse.
Sometimes, it's where the light gets in.

Even in pain, there is strength.
Even in silence, there is a voice.
Even in the hardest moments, there is hope.

We all carry cracks. But cracked is not broken.

And the very place where you think you've fractured, might be the place you begin again.

Let's begin. Let's walk this road together.

But let's approach one of the subjects and answer the question, **Why Movement Matters?**

Let's begin with it.

Do people move when they are in pain? The answer is, NO. Because when pain arrives, the first instinct is stillness. Even the breath is stopped. We freeze. We guard. We avoid. We stay in bed, skip the gym, decline invitations, stop walking the dog. It's natural. Pain sends a primal warning: *stay still or you'll make it worse.*

Changemakers

But for back pain, especially mechanical back pain – this message is misleading. Prolonged immobility doesn't heal. It hurts.

The spine, like all joints, is designed to move. Motion nourishes the discs, lubricates the joints, strengthens the supporting muscles, and signals to the brain that the body is safe. When we don't move, we stiffen. We weaken. We become more sensitive to pain, not less.

The phrase "motion is lotion" isn't just a cliché, it's neurobiology. Regular, varied movement reduces the threat signals the brain interprets as pain. Movement improves circulation, encourages lymphatic drainage, and provides your intervertebral discs with the fluid exchange they require to remain healthy. Without movement, those sponge-like discs become brittle. The muscles that support your spine begin to atrophy. The fascia stiffens.

And it's not only the musculoskeletal system that benefits, but movement also directly influences the body's hormonal system. Every step, every stretch, every rotation sets off a cascade of biochemical signals. Exercise increases the production of endorphins, natural painkillers that elevate mood and dull discomfort. It reduces cortisol, the stress hormone that, when elevated chronically, contributes to inflammation and sensitises the nervous system to pain. Gentle movement increases levels of dopamine and serotonin, two neurotransmitters associated with motivation, focus, and emotional regulation.

Perhaps most striking is the effect on insulin sensitivity. Physical activity enhances the muscles' ability to uptake glucose without insulin, thereby reducing blood sugar levels and improving metabolic flexibility. For individuals who like I was, are teetering on the edge of type 2 diabetes, this is more than a bonus. It's a lifeline.

When you move, you're not just stretching a joint. You're activating an entire endocrine orchestra: lowering blood pressure, balancing hormones, and promoting an internal chemistry that supports healing.

I saw this in myself. I see it in my patients. And the research agrees. Clinical guidelines from the National Institute for Health and Care Excellence (NICE) recommend staying active as one of the most effective treatments for non-specific low back pain. A landmark study published in The Lancet reinforced the evidence that bed rest delays recovery, while movement accelerates it.

Yet, culturally, we resist this truth. Patients are often told by well-meaning friends or even outdated practitioners to rest. To lie flat. To "take it easy." But for how long? And at what cost?

This doesn't mean reckless movement. It doesn't mean ignoring pain or pushing through red flags. It means the kind of intentional, progressive movement that meets your body where it is and nudges it, gently, forward. During my own recovery, I started with ten steps. That's all I could manage. But those ten became twenty. Twenty became a stroll. A stroll became a brisk walk. Each day, I wrote it down. I tracked not just distance, but how I felt. Was my posture better? Was my breathing deeper? Did I feel more human?

Because pain does something strange to time. It shrinks your world. You measure life by minutes, until the next dose of painkillers, until the next spasm. Movement, done wisely, starts to widen that world again. I learned to carry resistance bands in my coat pocket. I stretched against lampposts. I practiced hip rolls at traffic lights. Movement wasn't a gym appointment. It was survival.

I shared this with my patients. I told them how the shock absorbers of their body are faulty and how to activate the additional ones. Drivers were delighted with the explanation as this was so easy for them to understand. They were laughing, asking me what brand of shock absorbers they need to buy from the store. One elderly man, a retired lorry driver, began setting an alarm to stand every hour. He'd walk around the garden, regardless of weather. After six weeks, his back pain eased. His blood pressure dropped. His smile returned.

Changemakers

Another patient, a midwife, started incorporating micro-breaks between appointments. Ten squats. A shoulder roll. Deep diaphragmatic breathing. Her headaches diminished. Her back spasms stopped.

Mike and Sara's drivers added a 3-minute movement sequence at every delivery stop: spinal rotations, leg swings, shoulder shrugs. At first, they laughed. It felt silly. They were teasing each other for the peculiar movements they were doing. They felt that they were part of a choreography. They thought that they were in Broadway. But the attitude changed. Within weeks, the laughter was joined by relief. They were competing. They were comparing their "positions" and their techniques. Younger drivers were instructing some older and the camaraderie and networking grew stronger. By month three, their health records had changed.

Movement reclaims what pain tries to steal. Motion is fun.

It gives you agency. It gives you rhythm. It gives you choice. But perhaps most powerfully, it restores trust.

Because chronic pain erodes trust in the body. You feel betrayed by the very frame you live in. Movement, approached with kindness and consistency, helps repair that relationship. It says: "I can move, and nothing terrible happens." It rebuilds the broken contract between body and brain.

So, here's what I offer, not as a prescription, but as a promise:

Move every hour, even if just to change position.

Walk outside daily, no matter how short the distance.

Reintroduce safe spinal motion, side bends, rotations, pelvic tilts.

Changemakers

Use breath to support movement: inhale to lengthen, exhale to release.

Track your wins. Even tiny ones.

This is not about reclaiming youth or chasing athleticism. No one is asking you to become a marathon runner or a vault jumper. It's about regaining belonging in your body. It's about walking back into your life, step by step.

Because recovery doesn't always roar. Sometimes, it whispers, "Move." And when you listen - your body remembers.

Let's keep going.

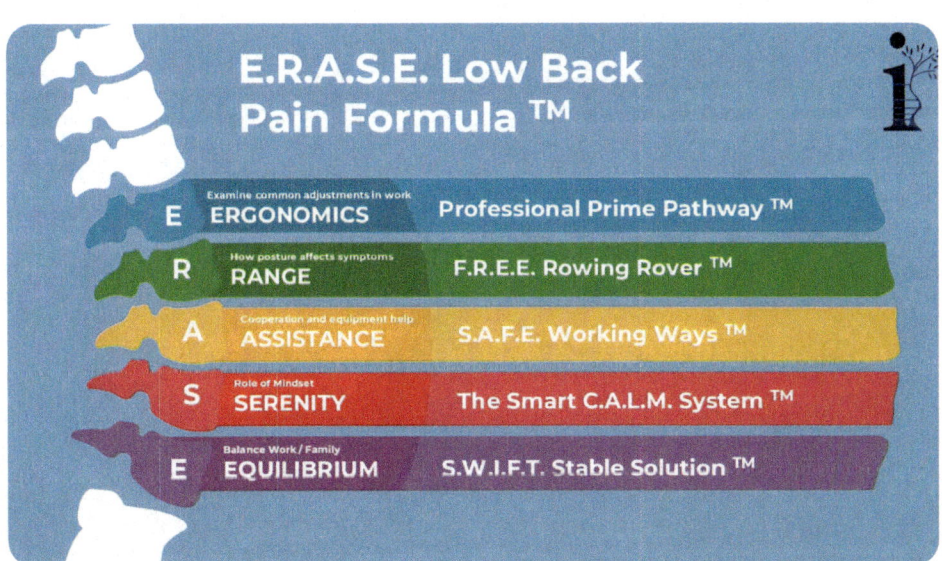

49

George Zafiropolous is a Senior Consultant Orthopaedic Surgeon, Researcher, Author and Educator. Trained in the EU, UK, and USA. Awarded a scholarship by the British Orthopaedic Association. Conducted research on the biomechanics of the musculoskeletal system, leading to further training at the Hospital for Special Surgery, New York and Mayo Clinic, Rochester, USA. Visiting Lecturer (University in Greece), where he established a course on the Biomechanics of the Musculoskeletal System. University Lecturer and Visiting Professor in United Kingdom. Led Orthopaedic Department with strong skills in management, organisation, and communication, committed to achieving goals. Member of several national and international Scientific Societies and Speaker at numerous scientific conferences. Author of scientific books, including Healthcare Heroes: A Comprehensive Guide for Future Health Professionals and Functional Anatomy and Basic Biomechanics for the Musculoskeletal System, and multiple peer-reviewed articles published in scientific journals. In recent years, following personal experience, committed to in-depth research on chronic low back pain management and the holistic impact of symptoms on individuals and their environment—particularly in corporations. Member of Professional Speakers Academy. Author of series of books on low back pain management, including Pain Management for Chronic Back Pain Sufferers, From Back Pain to Productivity, Back Pain Management Guide for Professional Drivers, Questions and Answers for Back Pain Sufferers, Kamasutra for Back Pain Sufferers, and Menopause and Back Pain – A Woman's Guide to Managing the Transition. Awarded the **Best Author Award** in 2024. Continues to serve communities and has developed materials to help companies minimise the costs associated with back pain, improving organisational efficiency.

Scan the QR code for More!

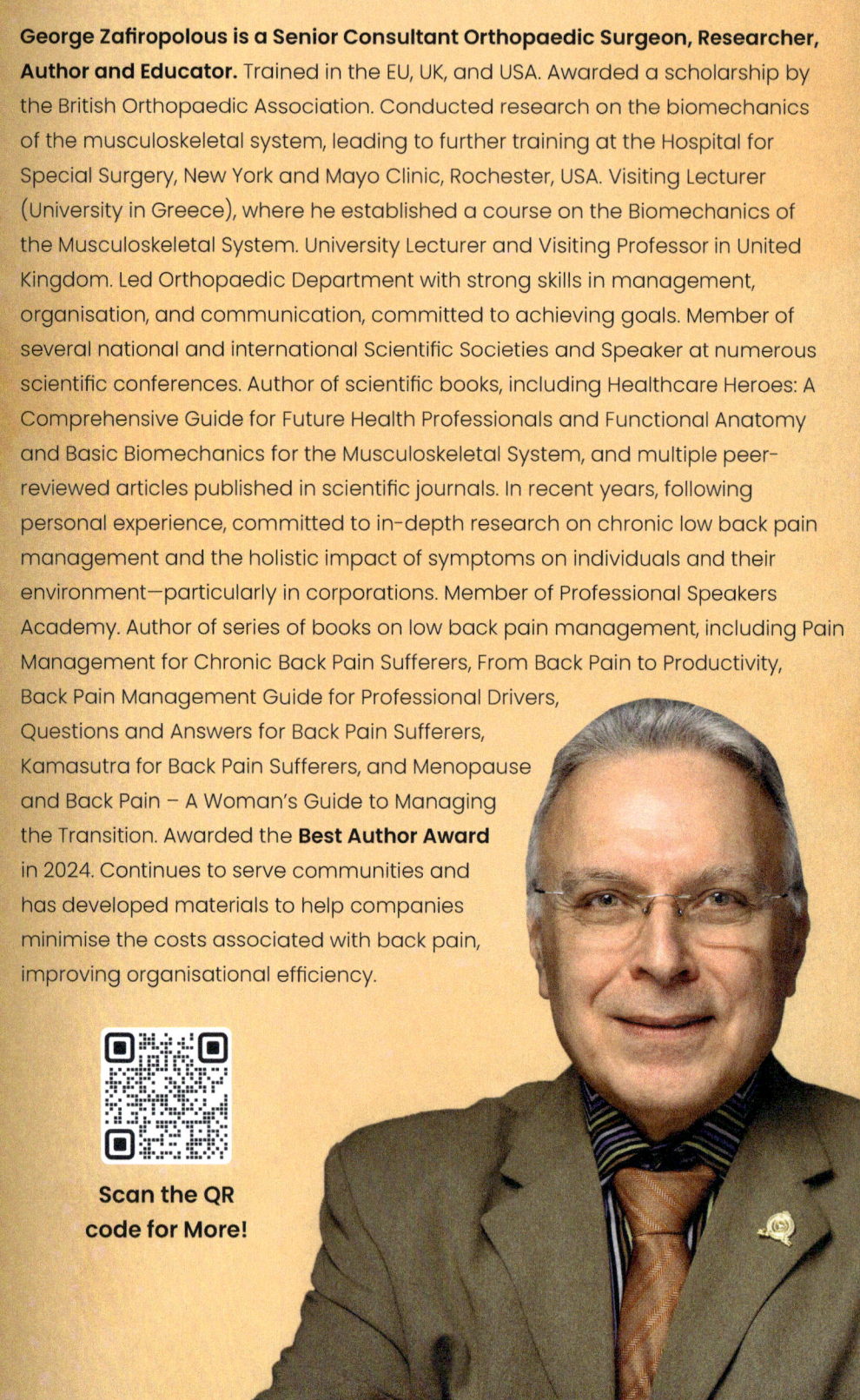

CHAPTER 4
BREAKING BEYOND YOUR BARRIERS

> "Living life to your full potential means living life on YOUR terms."
>
> - Colleen Stevenson

Have you ever carried a secret so deep it feels sewn into your skin? Not just hidden in your mind but woven through your bones. You've built a life around keeping it contained with years of silence, shame, and survival. On the outside, you look fine. You smile in photos. You laugh at the right times. You keep going. Maybe people even envy you, thinking you've "got it together."

But inside, it's like you're moving through water, everything heavy, muffled, slow.

The truth is, it's not always the event itself that hurts the most. It's the weight of keeping it locked away, unspoken and unresolved. The longer you carry it, the heavier it gets, until your body feels like it's holding its breath all the time.

You find ways to cope, wine that warms you just enough to dull the edges, food that comforts for a moment, endless scrolling, shopping, keeping yourself so busy you don't have to feel a thing. You tell yourself "This is just life."

But deep down, you know it's not. You can feel it in the knot in your stomach, the tightness in your chest, the way your shoulders never quite relax.

Pain that sits in the body too long doesn't just stay pain – it becomes tension, exhaustion. And if left there, it can turn into something far more dangerous. Dis-ease becomes disease.

I'm not here to "fix" you. I'm here to tell you your story matters. Your secret deserves to be heard. And healing is possible.

I know – because I've lived it.

It's September 1993. I'm eleven-years-old, standing barefoot at the top of a staircase. The house is quiet, but it's the wrong kind of quiet – the kind that makes you strain to hear what's coming.

Changemakers

Behind me, my bedroom door is closed, though I know a flimsy door isn't much of a barrier. To my left, a small window looks out onto a street washed in sunlight, but in here the air feels stale.

The carpet beneath my toes is stained, crawling with fleas. The walls are patched with damp. My stomach is twisting, because downstairs, I hear it - the sound of a key turning in the lock.

The smell comes first, before he even steps inside: that sharp, sickly-sweet Joop aftershave. It hits me like a warning.

Then I see him - greasy brown hair hanging over his forehead, gap between his teeth, ears that stick out like they're tuned to my fear. He doesn't have to say a word. My pulse is already hammering. My hands tremble so hard I clasp them together just to hide it.

I feel the weight of everything that's already happened pressing down on my chest. And then, something inside me snaps.

"DON'T YOU EVER TOUCH ME AGAIN!" The words tear out of my throat before I can second-guess them. "IF YOU DO, I'LL CALL THE POLICE!"

The silence after is louder than the shout. His face hardens, but he doesn't move. My heart feels like it's going to burst. Part of me wants to run past him and out the door, but my feet are frozen.

In my head, the thoughts come fast: What if he comes upstairs? What if he hurts me again? But then another voice cuts through: Not this time. Not now.

I think about telling my mum, but I picture her - slumped in her chair, drink in hand, eyes glazed. She wouldn't hear me. And even if she did, she'd twist it into something that fits her version of reality. I think about a teacher. Maybe they'd listen. But what if they told the police? What if they took me away from everything I know - even the bad parts?

Changemakers

The fear of losing my fragile stability outweighs the fear of staying silent.

So, I make the choice: I tell no one. Not Mum. Not Dad. Not a friend. I wrap my shame around me like a blanket and bury the truth deep inside, where I think no one will find it.

But burying a secret doesn't kill it. It just grows roots.

My older brother didn't just take my innocence – he locked away the girl I was meant to be. I was like a bird with wings made for the sky, trapped behind bars. I didn't just hide the memories. I hid me.

As the years passed, I tried so many things to break free….therapists, counsellors, and yes there was an element of this that served me – So much so that I became a mum to two beautiful girls and for a moment, I hoped their love will heal me… But motherhood doesn't erase pain…

Nothing seemed to help me move forward. In those years I had one loyal companion, my dear friend Oyster Bay, New Zealand's finest white wine, and then one day, life throws me something I didn't see coming.

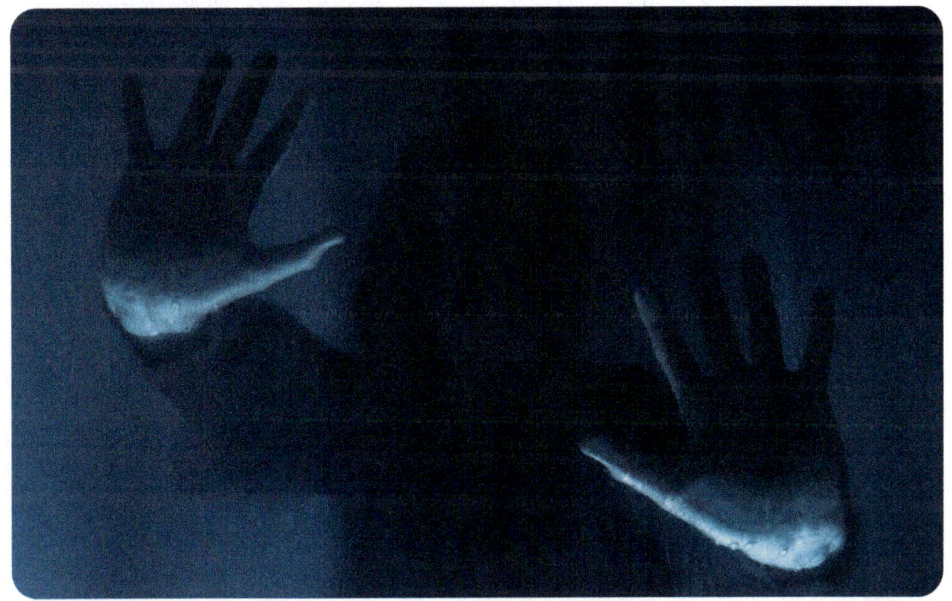

Changemakers

It's November 18th, 2014. The hospital waiting room is full of glowing, pregnant women. I feel out of place among their laughter and round bellies. The smell of disinfectant is sharp in my nose and the phone at the front desk rings endlessly.

Dr. Andrew Prentice steps out – a short man, greying hair, warm smile behind thick glasses. "Hi, Colleen. Take a seat. I wasn't expecting to see you today."

"Oh? I thought we had a follow-up. You removed the polyps from my womb, remember?"

"Yes, I remember… but your notes are with the oncology team. You have been informed of that?"

"The oncology team? No… what's that?"

He pauses, and my stomach drops before he even speaks. "Colleen… the results show you have cancer of the womb."

The words float in the air, and I wait for them to land, to make sense.

They don't. "You must have made a mistake. I'm thirty-three. I'm here for a check-up. Cancer? No. Not me."

But the look in his eyes tells me there's no mistake.

For two weeks, I don't leave my bed. I cry. I rage. I ask the universe, "Why me? Haven't I been through enough?" I replay my life like a film I wish I could rewrite.

Then, one morning, my eight-year-old daughter Jaz stands in the doorway, ready for school. Her dad waits outside. She looks at me, her small face serious, and asks, "Mummy… are you going to die?"

Changemakers

Something in me shifts. "No, darling," I say, pulling her into my arms. "I'm not going anywhere."

After she leaves, I face the bathroom mirror. My reflection is pale and tired, yet beneath the weariness, a faint flicker still remains.

You've survived worse, I tell myself. If you can live through the pain of your past, you can live through this. Those girls need you.

No one will open this cage for you, Colleen—you have to unlock it yourself.

The road back isn't easy. People I thought would support me vanish. Some mock me "You're boring now, why aren't you drinking?" Others make jokes "Are you a rabbit? All you eat is greens!" Their words sting, but they don't break me.

I keep going. I read every self-development book I can get my hands on: The Secret, The Monk Who Sold His Ferrari, Feel the Fear and Do It

Anyway. But reading isn't enough. I find a coach who teaches me how to go deeper – to face the parts of me I've avoided my whole life.

I meet my inner child. I listen to her. I tell her she matters. Slowly, the bars around my cage begin to bend. I forgive my brother – not because what he did was okay, but because I refuse to carry the poison any longer. Forgiveness becomes freedom.

That freedom lights a fire in me. I train as a coach. I start helping women unlock their own cages. And now ten years cancer-free, I love nothing more than knowing that I've guided hundreds of women into living life to the fullest.

That's why I created my **Break Beyond Your Barriers Blueprint**™ – to help women reconnect with who they truly are, so they can stop surviving and start living.

One of them is Emily. When she came to me, she was convinced she wasn't "good enough" for a promotion she wanted. We traced that belief back to a single comment from a teacher when she was eleven. We reframed the story, gave her the tools to rewrite it. She applied for the job – and got it. Now she leads a team of ten.

How did she do it? By shifting her mindset. Your mindset is the lens through which you see and experience the world. It influences your thoughts, emotions, actions and ultimately shapes your reality. But the first step to shifting your mindset is AWARENESS!

The aim of AWARENESS is to gain clarity on our reactive behaviours and patterns which are rooted in the beliefs we hold. Our beliefs come from our past conditioning and life experiences…and what if there are conscious patterns or behaviours that feel normal to us but at the same time (without realising) limit us?

NOW WHY IS THAT IMPORTANT TO UNDERSTAND?

Well, without the awareness of your reactive behaviours and patterns, you will be limited from the life that you deserve. You limit yourself from your potential successes and stop yourself from pursuing your goals.

For instance, a long time ago, I believed that money was the root of all evil (which wasn't my own belief in the first place, but I'll explain that in a moment) but because that belief was so deeply rooted, the moment I received money was the moment I'd let go of it. I'd either spend it recklessly , gift it away etc, and I had no savings because a part of me truly believed that if I have money then people would see me as selfish or greedy, particularly my Dad, because he was the one that used to say it aloud when I was a little girl. It was never my belief to have and hold onto...and you know what maybe it wasn't my dad's either, maybe it was just a family loyalty passed down in ancestry.

And I wonder how many others are out there with the same unconscious belief, spending money recklessly on unnecessary things rather than investing it into what really matters and using it to help them achieve their goals.

And once I realised I had no AWARENESS of what I was doing (unconsciously), I soon changed the narrative.

"Until you make the unconscious conscious it will rule your life, and you will continue to call it fate" - Carl Jung

A common mistake I see is people confuse awareness with action, because whilst awareness is essential, it's only the first step, and some people think that once they have the understanding about themselves, things will automatically change for them.

Changemakers

But here's the thing, without looking inward, without taking an honest look at ourselves, without looking under the carpet at what dust, junk and shit is hiding there, it's only going to get worse, because you may potentially trip over it causing more damage, or it might be harder for you to clean up in the long run.

How do I know this? Because it happened to me. I refused to look under that carpet. Why didn't I? Because it felt scary at the time, I didn't want to think about re-living the sexual abuse I'd endured in childhood, it was the unknown, but guess what? My lack of self-awareness was holding me back from a whole load of unknown opportunities. Unknown opportunities that have created a better life for me!

So, I knew that when Emily came to me after her free clarity call, I had to share the 3 C's of self-awareness with her.

CLARIFY

Emily clarified every self-limiting belief she had about herself (i.e. I'm not good enough).

CONSIDER

Emily considered where the self-limiting beliefs came from, (i.e. Past Experience or Past Conditioning).

CONSEQUENCE

Emily looked at what had been the consequences of having this limiting belief.

Once Emily had found the awareness, she was ready to take the next step (BIG ACTION). So, with her permission I took her through a 1:1 deep hypnotherapy session called The Time Lens Method™. The awareness became clearer, and she could gain a deeper understanding of how and why this limiting belief was holding her back. This also helped her reframe her thought process and create an empowering belief, rather than a limiting one.

So, when it comes to awareness think of it this way....

Imagine you're driving on a foggy road. At first everything is hazy, and you can barely see what's ahead, making it hard to navigate. But slowly the fog begins to lift. As it clears, the road becomes more visible and you can see the turns and obstacles ahead, making your destination much clearer.

Awareness is like a fog lifting. The clearer your awareness the easier it is to move forward with purpose, avoiding roadblocks and making confident decisions.

Living life to the fullest is a choice. I chose it. Emily chose it. And you can choose it too.

Healing isn't just about surviving the worst days; it's about creating the best ones. Every scar you carry can be the foundation for something beautiful.

Your fullest life is waiting, but it won't come knocking, you have to open the door.

So, if my story has stirred something in you, don't ignore it. That's your inner child, calling you home.

The question is - will you answer to her?

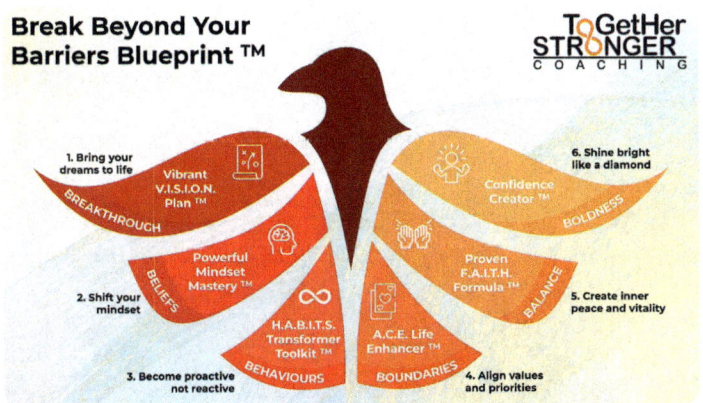

Colleen Stevenson is a Level 7 Holistic Mindset Coach, NLP Practitioner, and author who knows first-hand the power of turning pain into purpose. After surviving childhood trauma and a life-threatening cancer diagnosis, Colleen rebuilt her life from the inside out - and now helps women worldwide do the same. Through her award-winning *Break Beyond Your Barriers Blueprint*™, she empowers clients to heal, reclaim their confidence, and create a life they truly love. Colleen's mission is to show women that no matter their past, they can rise, thrive, and live life to the fullest - unapologetically and on their own terms.

Scan the QR code for More!

CHAPTER 5
THE FUTURE OF LEADERSHIP

"The future of leadership will not be measured by titles or control, but by the power to inspire, the purpose to serve, and the prosperity we create together."

- Simone Heinzelmann

When we drive a car, we're required to pass both theory and practice. Why? Because without it, accidents happen. But how much more complex is a human being? And how many accidents do we create every day? Emotional crashes, mental meltdowns, broken trust, lost clients…

My vision is that one day, the High IMPACT Leadership License will be a standard for everyone in a leading position. Until then, let me share a few short stories with you. Maybe you'll recognise yourself in one of them and become part of the movement.

There's the **snooze-button morning:** the alarm rings, but you hit snooze again. Last night was restless, and today you're dragging yourself into the office, hoping not to make that one wrong move that could cost you everything you've worked for, your position, your career, even your business.

Or the **rat-race glacier:** every step you take, the ice cracks and another crevasse open. Your to-do list multiplies like hidden crevasses under fresh snow. You help everyone else cross, but wonder, "Who's checking the rope for me?" And sometimes you catch yourself whispering, "Is this really all there is? What about my potential?"

Then there's **the promotion illusion:** you thought the summit would bring relief. Instead, the air is thinner. Yes, the title is higher, the salary larger, but so are the bills, the expectations, the lifestyle.

And finally, the **time trap,** your child asks for just one hour on a hot summer day to enjoy some ice cream together. Your partner longs to go to a weekend dance festival, which was once your shared passion. And your answer stays the same "Sorry, I don't have time." Each "no" feels like a rope you cut, and once cut, it's hard to tie back in.

If one of these stories' stings, you're not alone. **77% of senior executives report symptoms of burnout (KPMG).** The World Health Organisation even calls it a workplace syndrome. These are not weaknesses; they're

Changemakers

signals that to climb today's peaks; your current equipment needs an upgrade.

But here's the good news, every expedition has a basecamp. A place where you can regroup, pick better gear, and choose a smarter route. That's what the **High IMPACT Leadership License** is: a rope system, a high-tech GPS, a set of human technologies that allow you to climb higher, without burning out.

And maybe you're wondering, "why should I trust you to lead me on this expedition?" Fair enough. Come along and see for yourself. Let me begin with a few questions.

Which mountain are you actually climbing?
What would tell you it's the right one?
And if you discover it's the wrong one - what would you do?

It is May 2001.
I can see sunlight shining through the window, white flowers on the sill leaning toward it, and images of 8,000 meter peaks smiling back at me from the walls.
I can smell hot coffee steaming beside me.
I can hear the easy morning, a laugh in the corridor, then quick, purposeful footsteps pounding toward my door.
I feel cold sweat on my skin as if the world is steady but something inside me is already cracking, like a glacier shifting before it breaks.
I am in my thirties, with a well-curved body in a bright summer dress, but no one who knew me ever mistook me for fragile. I am a **chamois** through and through, an elegant mountain antelope, nimble on ridges, stubborn in storms, happiest where the air thins. A woman of contrasts, laughter and lipstick one day, ropes and crampons the next. A woman in Munich wearing high heels on a mountain bike.

Then Bogdan bursts into my office like someone crashing into basecamp at dawn, 1.90 meters tall, in his fifties, brown curls slightly unruly, a three-day stubble on a face carved by wind. His grey shirt clings from travel, his trekking trousers already dusted with the road. He radiates the kinetic energy of a man who's always halfway up a mountain, even when he's indoors.

If you need a movie reference think Liam Neeson in Taken, but with crampons and an ice axe. Charisma and danger in one.

Bogdan: "I got the permit for the First ascent for our 7000m peak in India. I want you to be part of my expedition. You could be the first woman on the summit. Believe me, this will be your legacy. You'll be remembered worldwide. You'd make history."

Simone: (Taking a deep breath) "I know. I know I could make it. But is this really my path? Is this what I should do with my life? The mountains already gave me everything - taught me about fear, about leadership, about bringing people home.

Changemakers

It breaks me to walk away. But it would cost me more to climb. My path ends here, and I have to let it go." (I tell him with my eyes filled with tears).

"Have you ever been on the road to success, with everything lined up, the famous summit almost in reach, when suddenly you felt "this is not my mountain? This path is over!"

What do you do? Push on, hoping it would feel right at the top? Or step back, even if it meant leaving part of yourself behind.

I kept managing our extreme treks and expeditions in the company I´m working for, pretending nothing had changed. Everyone knew my career was over, everyone except me. Then I ended my 10 year-relationship with Michael, a German mountain guide. It felt like an avalanche. I quit high-altitude expeditions, hiding instead in seaside cliffs, pretending chalk and sea breeze could cover the void. My life was falling apart, and the tsunami was still to come.

It is a Monday morning in September 2001.

I step into the office of the CEO and Shareholder of the Market leader for trekking and expeditions in the German-speaking region.

I can see stacks of papers, a framed photo with Sir Edmund Hillary, and the empty chair I'm walking toward.

I can smell lemon cleaner, and that metallic hint that means a storm is coming, only this one isn't on any weather chart.

He is already waiting for me, Andreas is in his mid forties, his legs crossed, one foot bouncing nervously, I can hear his fingers tapping on the wooden table like a metronome.

Andreas: "You went too far with the training of our Guides last weekend. Fear, identity, boundaries, that's therapy. Not our job."

Simone: "Above 4,000 meters, pretending there's a line between personal and professional makes Guides fail. I'm not doing therapy, I'm teaching leadership under pressure. The same tools that bring a rope team back alive, naming the storm, probing crevasses, setting a turn-back time, are what our guides need."

Andreas: "Nice metaphor. But not our business. We sell trips, logistics, safety. Drop this idea." – (Silence)

Simone: "But… ahm…(my voice is thin and trembling) then I need to cut the rope. I quit, Andreas. I'll take this work on my own now, my expedition, my summit, no matter the risk."

The tsunami hit me, sudden, unstoppable. "Oh my Gosh, what did I just do?" But I had no choice, I had to quit my job.

This was my first expedition without a rope team, just me. Six months of self-leadership, day by day. I saw that every human already carries four tools to reach any summit: **Words, Thoughts, Emotions, Actions.** That was the birth of Human Technology.

Later came another truth, three levels of consciousness, and the superconscious awakens the genius in us all. I had touched it in the mountains, but only now did I recognise it.

From there came the **High IMPACT Leadership License.** Too many leaders ignore their own human technology, sacrificing health, neglecting wealth, trapped in layers of limitation.

That's the moment you stand alone on the glacier. No rope team. No fixed lines. Just you and your tools.

And maybe you've been there too, when no one else can carry you across. *"Which tools do you trust when the ground cracks under your feet?"*

Extracting the strategies I once used unconsciously was one climb. Building a business from nothing, that was steeper.

And the chorus came quickly,

Michael my ex-partner in life and in the mountains: "Your salary was among the highest. You coached guides, even families who lost loved ones. Not a single lawsuit. You throw it all away!

Anita a friend of mine told me: "You had the dream job – first ascents, treks, global partners. What could be better?"

My mother, close to tears, said: "I told everyone you will become the female Reinhold Messner, a famous star, and now, you are a nobody!"

Step by step I built a new basecamp, a small practice translating high-altitude disciplines into everyday leadership. At first individuals and couples, real lives at real edges. Then parents. Soon, managers, living at an altitude without leaving their desks.

The first success stories were written. The inefficient meetings of John F. became ascents with defined routes, not blind slogs. His work became a rope people could trust.

I watched how Peter D's depression lifts, momentum returned, and his KPIs not just met but surpassed. I still remember the first quantum leap, Christian A. made millions, yes, but more than that, he rerouted his whole life. Foot pain gone. Six nightly wake-ups turned into sleeping like a child.

I wasn't treating symptoms. We rebuilt his self-leadership, habits, decisions and stress. His body followed.

I didn't become the first woman on that Indian peak. Instead, I became the guide who helps others reach theirs, and return safely to what matters most. Do I regret saying no? I don't. Sometimes the bravest ascent is a well-chosen descent. The mountain I didn't climb gave me a clearer view, success isn't standing alone on a ridge; it's standing with a rope team that make high impact decisions because they learned to lead themselves first.

Today, all of this is distilled into the **High IMPACT Leadership License,** a path to empower yourself and your teams. Made for leaders, game changers, and future builders who want altitude without the oxygen mask, leading expeditions and climbing peaks called teams, targets, board rooms and tough conversations. This is where the journey becomes practical. Let me take you step by step into the **High IMPACT Leadership License.**

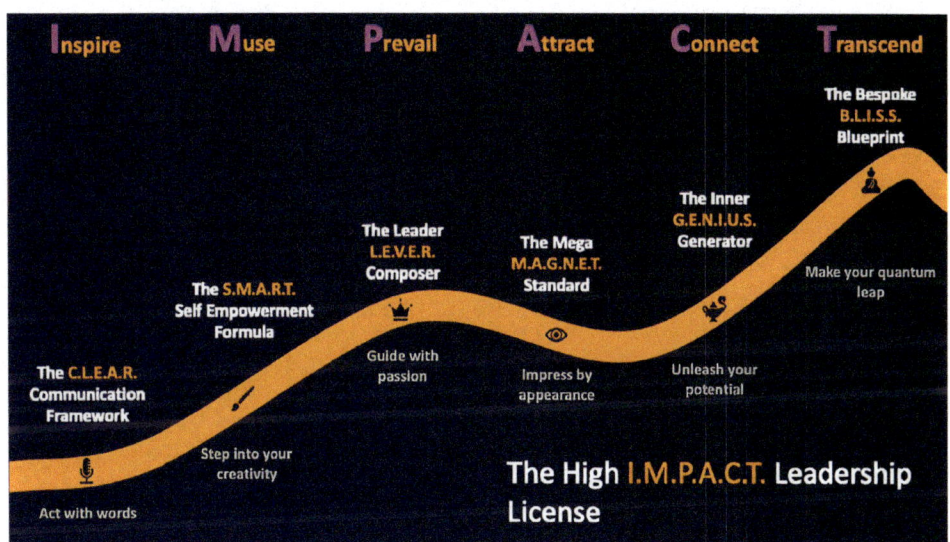

The High Impact Leadership License

Stage 1: Act with Words – Inspire

Every expedition begins with words: the calls across a ridge, the map briefing before the climb, the quiet reassurance on the rope.

Yet most managers overwhelm their teams with noise. The average person speaks about seven thousand words a day. The average manager? Between thirty and fifty thousand. That's six hours of monologue. Too many words, too little clarity. The result? Confusion, low quality, lost clients.

I once coached a director who proudly told me he "kept everyone informed" by sending daily emails. His team confessed they stopped reading them. He thought he was leading; in reality, he was burying his people in an avalanche of words.

Here's the truth: your words are your rope. They can secure trust – or they can tangle the entire team.

That's why the leaders I work with apply the C.L.E.A.R Communication Framework. They grow their people with words that empower and inspire, transform negativity into possibility, and run meetings that feel like summits reached together—not avalanches of slides. Productivity rises. Leaders gain not just digital followers on LinkedIn, but real-life loyalty. Sales increase naturally, because clarity always converts.

💡 *Reflection for you:* Before speaking, run it through three filters: Is it true? Can I say it positively? Is it necessary for the job?

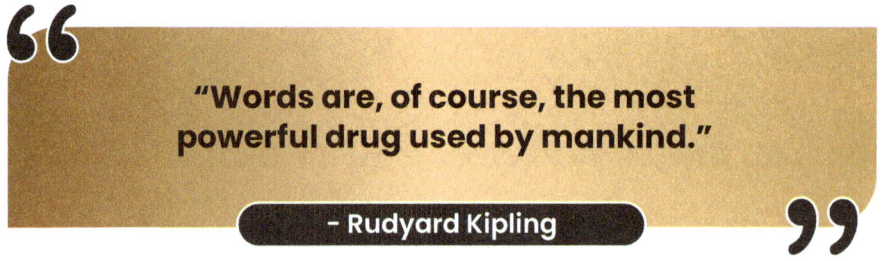

"Words are, of course, the most powerful drug used by mankind."

— Rudyard Kipling

When you master words, you become more than a manager. You become an inspirer – a climber others trust to tie in with.

Stage 2: Step into Creativity - Muse

Sooner or later, the trail steepens. Logic alone won't get you across a crevasse. You need creativity - the ability to see a route where others see only a dead end.

But many leaders tell me:

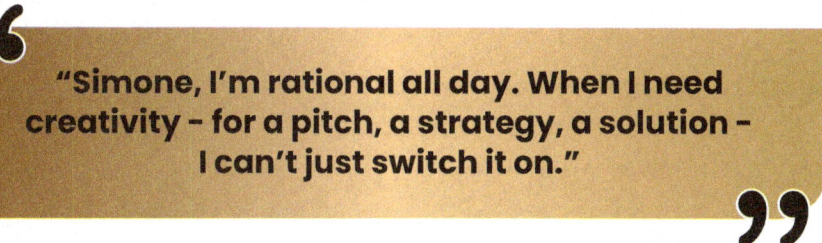

> "Simone, I'm rational all day. When I need creativity - for a pitch, a strategy, a solution - I can't just switch it on."

So, they delay. Deadlines slip. Presentations bore. Stress builds. Creativity isn't a luxury - it's the oxygen of innovation.
And it can be trained.

My clients practice The S.M.A.R.T. Self-Empowerment Formula mental procedures that unlock creativity in seconds.

Einstein himself relied on "thought experiments." The theory of relativity was born not in a lab, but in his imagination. Leaders can do the same.

One CEO dreaded presenting to investors. He claimed he "wasn't creative." We tried a simple exercise: Imagine it's one year later, and your investors are celebrating you. What exactly are they applauding? In minutes, his tone shifted from dry to inspired, When he finally stood in front of his investors, they felt that inspiration too."

💡 *Reflection for you:* Before your next strategy session, close your eyes. Imagine the project is already a wild success. Ask: What did we do differently to make it work?

Changemakers

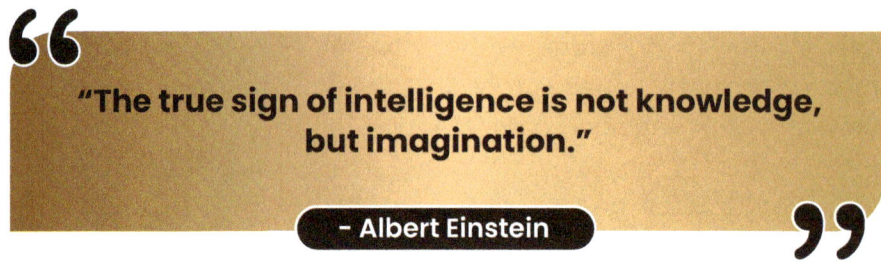

> "The true sign of intelligence is not knowledge, but imagination."
>
> – Albert Einstein

Stage 3: Guide with Passion – Prevail

Every climber faces storms. The question is not if emotions hit, but how you prevail when they do.

Far too many leaders still believe emotions have no place in business. So, they take one of two dangerous paths: the poker face, suppressing emotions until they collapse inside; or the floodgate, expressing everything and exhausting everyone. Both lead to what doctors' call "Manager's Disease": a list of symptoms like stress, high blood pressure, depression, burnout—even heart disease or stroke.
Science is clear: negative emotions release stress hormones that make us sick if unprocessed. Positive emotions, on the other hand, boost resilience and extend life expectancy.

One senior partner admitted his silence made people feel invisible. Another confessed his team feared his outbursts. Both were burning out. With The Leader L.E.V.E.R. Composer, they learned to let go of harmful emotions and generate positive ones — sometimes in the middle of a meeting. The change was visible: calmer breathing, clearer eyes, a room that felt safe again.

💡 *Reflection for you:* Next time stress hits, pause for thirty seconds. Ask yourself: What emotion would serve me better right now? Calm? Curiosity? Courage?

Decisions made in good mood are more successful, science has proven it. And a culture of smiles reduces sick leave, lowers turnover, and turns teams into rope parties that actually enjoy the climb.

When you prevail in this way, storms don't destroy your expedition — they test and strengthen it. Your rope team follows you with trust, knowing that even in chaos, you keep the line steady.

Stage 4: Impress by Appearance — Attract

Research by Albert Mehrabian showed that words account for only seven percent of impact. The rest is tone, body language, and presence. Yet many managers think appearance is only about a suit or a haircut. They forget that presence is also how you walk through the office, how you breathe when you enter, how you look at your people. Too often, leaders carry an invisible shield on their backs that says: 'Do Not Disturb.' The result? People stop approaching. Conversations shrink into rumours. Trust erodes. Careers derail.

But when leaders apply The Mega M.A.G.N.E.T. Standard, something shifts. They radiate confidence without arrogance. They attract top talent not through charisma alone, but through integrity — because they do what they say. They walk like climbers who know their rope is solid, and everyone senses it.

💡 *Reflection for you:* Before your next meeting, stop at the door. Plant your feet. Take a deep breath. Lift your chest. Step in as if you're tying the rope for the whole team.

On the rope, presence is the difference between panic and calm. In business, it's what turns a manager into a magnet.

Stage 5: Unleash Potential — Connect

The higher you climb, the more awareness and consciousness matter. Most managers operate on autopilot—guided by the subconscious, replaying fears and past experiences in reaction mode. This creates over-control, micromanagement, and stagnation. Teams suffocate. Relationships fracture.

Changemakers

Leaders who connect with their super-consciousness access something extraordinary: their inner genius. I call this The Inner G.E.N.I.U.S. Generator. And yes, there's a simple, step-by-step way to do it. We go into this in more detail at the High IMPACT Leadership Academy. Most managers lead as if they were navigating a glacier blindfolded. But when you connect with super-consciousness, it's like pulling off the blindfold and finally seeing the markers to cross safely.

A division head was notorious for micromanaging. Almost every decision had to go through him, and the business stalled. Through consciousness connection training, he shifted into leading from vision instead of fear. Within six months, not only did his business line grow, but his marriage—on the brink of collapse—began to heal.

💡 *Reflection for you:* Before deciding on something critical, ask:
Am I choosing from limitation, or from vision?

On a glacier, this is the moment you trust the ground under your feet—and yourself—to find a safe crossing where no map exists. In leadership, it's the moment where potential turns into power.

Stage 6: Transcend Limits — Make Your Quantum Leap

Every expedition reaches a point where old gear won't cut it. Certifications, titles, even decades of experience—they're useful, but they don't carry you higher anymore.

Too many leaders remain stuck—new jobs, same problems, new partners, old conflicts. Different summit, same storm.

The way forward is leadership transformation. The Business Owners and Top Managers I work with use The B.L.I.S.S. Blueprint—a series of processes that rewire limitations into strengths, upgrade beliefs about energy and money, build a millionaire's mindset, and reframe relationships with statistics and probabilities so numbers no longer hold them back.

Changemakers

One entrepreneur had all the external signs of success: revenue in the millions, a corner office, recognition in the industry. Yet he confessed he felt trapped in a cage of golden bars. Through the B.L.I.S.S. Blueprint, he let go of old scripts around money and failure.

The result? Not just groundbreaking new visions, but genuine freedom—a deep sense of independence. He began investing in social projects, dancing again with his wife, even taking his son on expeditions. That was his quantum leap.

💡 *Reflection for you:* Write down the summit you're chasing. Then ask yourself: What limiting belief do I need to let go to get there?
The moment when the fixed ropes end, and you must climb on your own, skill and courage is where your leadership stops being only about you. It's when your limits dissolve and your journey becomes legacy.

If there is only one thing you carry with you from this climb, let it be this: Laughter is the best medicine.

Keep your rope team smiling, and you'll be a Game Changer—bringing Health, Wealth, and Happiness not only to yourself, but to everyone tied to your rope.

Simone Heinzelmann didn't start out brave. As a child, she hid under tables, too shy to even speak to neighbours. Years later, she would be clinging to icy ridges and gasping for air above 6,000 meters, on mountains that became mirrors of her inner fears. Living and traveling through Nepal, Bangkok, Singapore, Malaysia, and Japan transformed those outward expeditions into a journey of inner discovery.

Out of those lessons, Simone created the Human Technology Platform, her professional basecamp. Anchored by a degree in Business Administration, she launched her first brand, The High IMPACT Leadership License - a powerful fusion of business logic, extreme adventure, and Eastern wisdom.

Today, as an award-winning keynote speaker, executive coach, and founder, Simone guides leaders to transform fear into strength and pressure into clarity. Her mission is simple but profound: to help people climb their own summits through **People Powered Performance -** because even superheroes need a team.

Your Basecamp Awaits
Scan the code to join my 90-minute live session. Upgrade your human technology, choose your route, and climb without burning out. High Impact Leadership starts here.

Scan the QR code for More!

CHAPTER 6
GRIP TO GROWTH
THE UNSPOKEN PATH TO HEALING

> "When we grip the roots of our pain with courage, we discover the hidden wisdom to grow beyond it – healing is not loud, it is the quiet power of presence."
>
> - Rick Charlton

Changemakers

Have you ever wondered how to help when someone tells you "I'm fine" and you know it really means "I'm broken"?

Let me take you back to December 2009, a road traffic collision in the north of England. I can smell the blood first. That unforgettable scent of blood in traumatic vehicle accidents is sharp, metallic, and suffused with an eerie stillness. It's not just the iron-rich scent of haemoglobin that hits you; it's the way it blends with burnt rubber, leaked fuel, and the acrid tang of fractured plastic and metal. That coppery odour becomes thick and humid when mixed with adrenaline, shock, and heat. There's also a psychological layering to it. In the immediacy of trauma, the scent carries weight, registering not just in the nose but somewhere deeper, evoking primal alertness or grief. It's not unlike a forge, metallic, heated, and hanging in the air like something working but broken at the same time.

I can see twisted metal and shattered glass glinting under flashing beacons that cut through the haze, blue, strobing against the pale faces and wreckage, and the stark brightness of the portable scene lights. The airbags are deflated, smeared red and white, crumpled like used tissues. Debris is scattered like fragments of a story violently torn apart, wheel trims, personal items, ripped upholstery. I see people moving erratically, some helping, some stunned, others just frozen. Steam rises from engines, mingling with cold December drizzling rain.

I can hear sirens swelling and fading, an auditory lighthouse drawing responders in. Panic-sharp cries and strained voices form a human soundscape of urgency and confusion. The shouts of responders use clipped, command tones: *"Clear the area!"* *"Can you hear me?"* The crackle of radios relay instructions in clipped bursts. Groans from twisted metal, cooling and shifting after the force of impact. Footsteps crunching over broken glass and gravel, each one deliberate, invasive. It's a soundscape not unlike war or collapse, every noise a punctuation mark in a narrative of sudden trauma.

Changemakers

I arrived and stepped into the scene as the fire service commander with a mix of instinct, training, and a burdensome clarity. Two fire crews are already here and have started work supervised by the crew commanders, waiting for me to take overall incident command.

I feel hyper-focused urgency; my senses narrow not to shut out chaos, but to interpret it fast. I'm absorbing the layout, risks, positions of casualties, vehicle types, and spill patterns. The weight of responsibility bears down. Every decision could mean life or death. I feel the invisible pull of command, the need to protect, to lead, to act. I also feel the tug of empathic tension deep in my stomach. There's the horror of this scene, yes, for me this is normal, this is my work! But I also feel the need to shield my crews emotionally while keeping them effective. I'm subconsciously registering the human moral cost, then boxing it away for later.

Almost like magic, I'm overcome with a familiar calculated calm …. practiced, almost ritualistic. Calm is currency in chaos. I speak clearly, not loudly, with eye contact, giving quick assessments, triaging with voice and gestures.

Then the moral gravity hits. Not just the five people trapped in the taxi, but *I realise that I know the taxi driver;* his son plays rugby with my own boy. He doesn't recognise me in my fire kit and helmet; he's in a bad way. Then there's the young lad trapped in the other crumpled car, disfigured by the impact, wheezing to take a breath… there's a visceral ache that lodges deep and quiet. I know this job's different to all the others, the effects of this one won't surface until later when the job is done.

My crew's safety is paramount. I feel every risk as a possible misstep with real consequences. My internal monologue is echoing "Absorb. Decide. Move. Debrief later.", layered beneath is my personal mantra: "do what you can, with what you have got, to help as many as you can". This isn't just command; it's communion with chaos.

Changemakers

A crew manager I know approaches. "Rick... the lad in the second car... he's John's nephew". "What?" My eyes flick briefly toward the wreckage. Recognition flickers, then solidifies. "John was meant to be on tonight. Christmas party. Switched shifts last-minute". "Shit... I trained John from scratch. Watched him find his feet in this job. God". My voice trails off, the professional shell cracking under a personal quake. There's a moment of silence, just the distant thrum of a siren and the snap of a cutting tool. "He'll carry that. For years". "We all will".

I now experience a collision between duty and relationship. Reality distorts when faces in the wreckage relate to people from memory. I feel a deep moral ache. The "what if" drills into my mind, had the party not happened, had the shift not changed. I'm overcome with protective sorrow, wanting to shield John from the knowledge, yet knowing it'll find him soon enough. Amidst it all, I need to stay focused, to lead with clarity while carrying personal grief silently.

This moment marks a fracture line between command and humanity. That moment... sharp, aching, defiant, is the kind of truth that doesn't fit neatly into any protocol. A rupture in the rhythm of command, and I've stepped into it not just as a leader, but as a human tethered to duty and heart.

The metal groans as the cutters finish their work, peeling the roof away like the lid of a beans tin. Steam rises from fractured radiator. The boy's body lies crumpled inside, lifeless yet not gone, the air around him thick with the scent of fuel and coolant. I climb in, boots slipping on the wet, grinding glass and grit, settling gently onto the dashboard. It's a break from command protocol, but no voice objects. They see it in my face. This isn't interference. This is presence. "Stay with us, lad. You're not alone. You're safe now". My hands hold his head, opening his airway, every rasp from his lungs a thunderclap inside my own chest. Unconscious, yet still fighting. I speak quietly, not to wake him, to anchor him. Thoughts of my own children at home tucked up safe in bed are quickly subdued and suppressed. *"You're doing fine. We're right here. Your uncle trained with me... he's family. Just stay a little longer".*

Changemakers

The paramedics slide the board in. I shift carefully, lifting with them, making space only when the last strap clicks. I hold his hand. "Squeeze, lad. Show me you're still in this". His fingers curl faintly around mine, tremoring, not with strength, but with will. "That's it. Hold on. Grip hard. We're nearly there". I'm walking now, fast, toward the ambulance. The scene around me blurs. Lights strobe on my visor, but my eyes never leave his face. As I step up into the back, his hand tightens one last time. "We've got you. We've got you". And then, the grip fades. A silence worse than sirens. He dies holding my hand. And I don't let go.

In certain Indigenous traditions, holding someone physically during transition is sacred. It's believed the last breath travels not just through the mouth, but through the skin. That breath doesn't vanish; it transfers. My hand became more than a conduit; it became the bridge between presence and passing. In that instant, I wasn't just a firefighter or commander; I was the grip bearer, who steadies the soul at the edge. Little did I know, this was to become a metaphor for my life's work and purpose:

"The role of a leader isn't only to command during crisis, but to offer the last grip in moments of passage, whether from trauma to recovery, chaos to clarity, or pain to peace".

Just as traditional healers might sit beside those crossing thresholds, I was within the breach, holding what protocol usually avoids, the raw truth of closeness. I didn't instruct from a distance; I entered the moment, became its witness and its weight-bearer.

The Fracture Begins: After the Incident

In the aftermath of that Christmas night, something cracked, not loudly, but relentlessly. Each emergency call became a summon to relive that boy's final breath. My body suited up, my voice commanded, my boots still walked into chaos, but inside, a quiet dread nested. PTSD crept in slowly, wearing the face of insomnia, hypervigilance, and emotional numbness. I found myself replaying scenes not just in memory, but in muscle, clenched fists, shallow breathing, a thudding heart for no reason but ghosts. Frustration was high: "I've been a soldier, I've been to war! This shouldn't be bothering me so much!".

I began to dread the very thing I'd once been forged for, the sound of the pager, the smell of smoke, the weight of leadership. Protocol was no longer a shield, but a trapdoor. I was performing the motions, but my soul was elsewhere, dragged back into that crushed vehicle every time I saw a young person driving or heard the stuttered rasp of strained breath.

Eventually, the uniform came off. Not as triumph, but as quiet surrender.

The Illusion of Escape: Ten Years of Masked Success

I moved into a different industry, hoping that distance would bring healing. The salary grew, the title gleamed, and from the outside, I looked like a man who'd mastered transition. But internally, the mask tightened. Corporate success offered no balm for soul-wounds. My marriage ended, communication frayed, intimacy hollowed out. I was present but partitioned. I was even homeless for a while, and nobody knew; the mask was on tight. Friends praised my resilience, but they never met the sleepless version of me or the one who flinched at loud noises and silent thoughts. Despair became quiet companionship. I didn't speak to it, but I carried it. Hidden behind PowerPoints and leadership meetings was a man who'd once held a dying boy's hand and never let go of that final grip.

Changemakers

The Turning Point: Meeting Andy
Then came Andy, also a former firefighter. A Trauma Incident Reduction (TIR) facilitator. His journey was similar and relatable, his own path decided in the aftermath of 9/11 where he was recovering the deceased from the rubble of the World Trade Centre in New York. He didn't just talk about trauma; he invited me to trace it, sit with it, dialogue with it. Something opened, not immediately, but with enough space for curiosity. I qualified as a coach, studied trauma, mental health, and the scaffolding of recovery.

Coaching became more than a profession; it became a language to reclaim the unspeakable. I found that my pain had grammar, my memories had rhythm, and my experiences had tools embedded in them. I wasn't broken. I was coded for growth, but my system hadn't been shown how.

The Kalahari Reckoning: Journey into the wilderness
I grew up in Botswana, Southern Africa, and I decided I needed to return home to find myself. I stepped into Botswana's central Kalahari Desert, alone, unconnected by technology, with no duty, just silence and presence. Alone with the bush, the animals, the wind, and the stars, gazing into my campfire, I unlearned the noise of 'leadership-as-performance'. I remembered myself not as a victim of trauma, but as a witness to sacred passage. The desert didn't offer escape; it offered 'mirror and medicine'. Each footprint became a metaphor. Each dawn a reminder. There, stripped of performance and rank, the clarity emerged, "post-traumatic stress is a wound. Post-traumatic growth is a vow". I saw myself not just as a survivor, but as a 'torchbearer,' ... forged in war and in fire, whose path now led not into danger but into healing others.

The Meeting with the San Bushman Elder
Around a low fire that crackled like time itself, I spoke with an elderly San bushman guide, his eyes as weathered and watchful as the desert stones. He shared ancient wisdom that trauma leaves spiritual echoes, not just psychological scars. That healing is not

achieved by erasing pain, but by witnessing it communally, rhythmically, with breath and ritual. That even sorrow must dance, through stories, songs, and silence. "In our way," he said, "the soul staggers until it finds its tribe. Then it begins to walk again".

This conversation didn't just resonate, it reframed everything. I saw the Western model of trauma as linear, but the Indigenous way was cyclical, ritualised, and relational.

Reclaimed Purpose: Turning Pain into a Compass

My professional journey from soldier to firefighter to coach taught me to stand in transitions, hold the "grip others can't". I create frameworks of resilience, inspired by my revelation. In the Kalahari's deep hush, where silence speaks in ancient rhythms, I found not just solitude, but revelation. Beneath the Baobabs and beneath my own skin, I learned that trauma isn't a rupture to fix, it's a passage to honour.

The Shift to Coaching and Facilitation

Returning from Botswana, I decided to transform my trauma instead of escaping it. I trained as a Trauma-Informed Mindset Coach and TIR Facilitator. I studied Shinrin Yoku (Forest Bathing) enabling well-being through nature. I approached coaching with the resilience of a warrior, the wisdom of an elder, the structure of a clinician. Integrating Indigenous wisdom, modern coaching psychology, and Applied Metapsychology to create a holistic healing framework.

Here's what I learned, a beautiful irony.

This isn't therapy, it's structured, person-led resolution. No digging. No diagnosis. Just a safe way to revisit trauma until the emotional charge dissolves. Whilst backed by modern neuroscience and operational rigour, its philosophy is ancient.

Changemakers

In African cultures, they say, "Ubuntu." I am because we are. Healing is communal. In the Zulu tradition, after a traumatic event, the village gathers. There is ritual, rhythm, and release through movement, music, and storytelling. The community don't analyse the pain; they witness it. The Dagara people of Burkina Faso perform grief rituals to release unspoken sorrow. The burden is shared, not buried.

In Native American cultures, ceremonies like the "wiping of tears" provide sacred structure for mourning and moving forward. In talking circles, people speak without interruption, because being heard is the first step to being healed. What these traditions knew, and what my approach affirms, is this, healing doesn't happen through labels. Healing happens through process, presence, and permission.

Then, in the universe's mystical way, a LinkedIn message from a Kenyan practitioner, Munene, led me to observe anti-poaching rangers in Kenya. I saw their trauma, flashbacks, hyper-vigilance, and grief from armed confrontations and moral injury which mirrored my own experiences. By sharing models from my private practice, I provided visible relief to the rangers. This inspired us to co-found Strong Ranger Resilience (SRR) CIC, a non-profit dedicated to supporting rangers with trauma recovery.

After returning to the UK, my experiences in Kenya and my personal journey became the catalyst for my private practice. I recognised that trauma is everywhere, affecting people from all walks of life, including high-profile professionals like celebrities, sportspeople, and ordinary individuals. However, when people attempt to discuss trauma, they are often met with resistance and phrases like, "we're fine," or "move on". Often, facilitation is dismissed as "therapy talk" that's unnecessary for those who are considered "tough". My experience is that this scepticism ignores the unspoken burdens and quiet devastation that trauma inflicts, fracturing lives beneath a polished exterior.

My journey, from holding a dying boy's hand at a car crash to guiding rangers in Africa, taught me how trauma hides behind brave faces.

Changemakers

This journey inspired the creation of my system, a unique branded solution for healing that helps people move from survival to growth.

My mission is to help people heal from trauma using the 'Rising P.H.O.E.N.I.X. Framework,' a seven-stage model for personal and communal growth. Combining Indigenous wisdom, mindset coaching, and Applied Metapsychology, it's designed for anyone whose courage is unspoken, pain unseen. My vow is to create a "sacred space" for people to be held, heard, and healed, guiding them from post-traumatic stress to post-traumatic growth.

Before I take you through my system, lets address the question I asked at the start, how do you help someone who says, "I'm fine," but is "broken"? Well, 'I'm fine' is a survival skill, not a status report. Helping someone in this state is like tracking a shadow animal, you must walk alongside it rather than chase it. The deepest form of help is to reconnect them to their "sacred breath" and honour their pain as part of their soul, rather than trying to fix them.

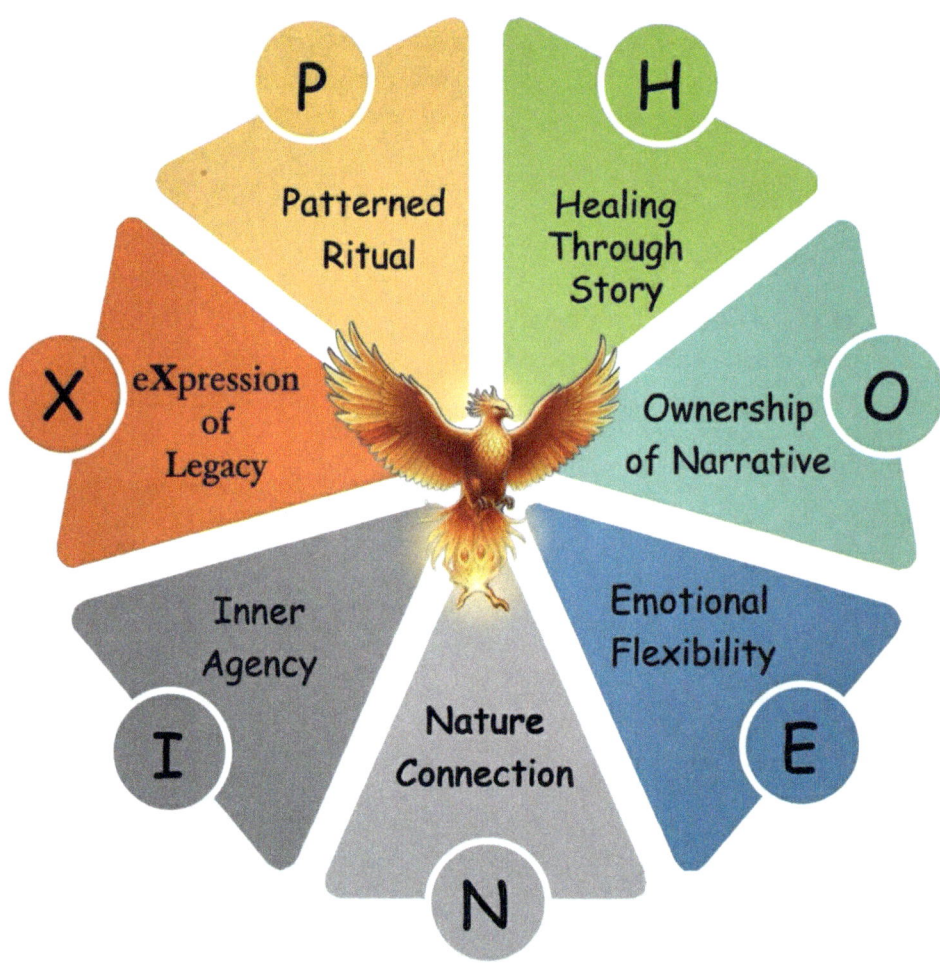

The 'Rising P.H.O.E.N.I.X. Framework'

Patterned Ritual & Presence: Addresses how traditional talking therapy often fails because trauma is a non-verbal, bodily experience. The framework uses patterned practices to help clients regain control and regulate emotions.

Healing Through Story & Symbol: Recognises that trauma shatters a person's life story. Clients use the **'3 Mountains Story Model'** to create a new, organised narrative and use symbols to process feelings.

Ownership of Narrative: Focuses on helping clients move beyond being defined by a "trauma story" by using the **'Ownership Activator'** to integrate past events into a new narrative of resilience and meaning.

Emotional Flexibility & Expression: Uses the **'Mind Gym'** to help clients overcome emotional constriction and a cycle of fear or numbness.

Nature Connection & Non-Linear Wisdom: Counters the rigid thinking associated with trauma by using the **'Wilderness shift system'** to help clients connect with nature's non-linear wisdom and process emotions without words.

Inner Agency & Integration: Addresses the loss of control and fractured self that trauma causes. The **'Agency Integrator System'** helps clients develop a sense of inner agency and accept different parts of themselves.

eXpression of Legacy & Communal Witnessing: Counters the isolation of privatised trauma. Clients learn that communal healing and creating a legacy are essential for transforming pain into something that benefits others, allowing them to move from surviving to thriving.

Rick has over 30 years of experience in leadership, operations, and coaching within diverse and challenging environments. His career spans roles in the British Army, the Fire and Rescue Service, HM Government, Corporate leadership, and supporting Anti-Poaching Operations in Africa. After years of silently struggling with PTSD, Rick's journey led him back to his childhood home in Botswana, where he fused his personal experiences with Indigenous wisdom, modern psychology, and Applied Metapsychology. Today, he helps people across all walks of life move from post-traumatic stress to post-traumatic growth, creating a "sacred space" for them to be held, heard, and healed.

Scan the QR code for More!

CHAPTER 7
FROM INVISIBLE TO IRRESISTIBLE

THE GEMS WITHIN EVERY WOMAN

BUILDING AN AUTHENTIC PERSONAL BRAND THAT SHINES AND ATTRACTS FROM THE INSIDE OUT

> "In a marketplace full of manufactured personas that profit from our insecurity, authenticity has become the rarest and most valuable currency"
>
> – Marianna Penna

Changemakers

"I am exhausted!

I've worked hard for years, built a career, raised a family, created a home. I've achieved what I've always dreamed of, yet I still feel incomplete. In midlife, demands pile up and expectations grow heavier. On the other side, energy, joy, spontaneity, everything seems to vanish. Bit by bit, I feel I have lost myself.

I've been looking toward a brighter future, hoping for comfort, while losing sight of the present, the very moment where my true self resides. In chasing success and validation outside myself, I've overlooked the most important part: my own soul. I poured energy into every role, every demand, yet left myself thirsty. And if I cannot truly see and honour the gems within me, how can I expect the world to see them?

And my business? I feel like I'm losing my mind. I am a leader, running my own company. People rely on me. I feel lonely and overwhelmed on this journey. I should have all the answers. I work hard, long hours; I read business books, follow trends, push myself to be resilient, capable, invincible. On top of that, I'm told I must look polished, fit, glamorous, and socially active. That's supposedly what it takes to be seen as an expert, a woman of influence.

Since Covid the market feels unpredictable, almost hostile. Social media demands endless performance: content, podcasts, books, events. Push, push, push. Run, run, run. Fast, fast, fast! How long can I keep going like this before I break?

AI is everywhere, and I know it's an opportunity. Yet I feel unsure how to use it while remaining authentic. I want to come across as genuine, but I don't know how. And honestly, I feel too old for social media. I dislike how I look; I'm uncomfortable on camera. I check every detail before posting, but even then, I wonder, "how can I attract new clients if I don't look great, if my script isn't perfect, and if, even when I put myself out there, I still don't feel seen?"

Changemakers

I search for work-life balance. Health gurus preach balance. Nutritionists promise quick fixes. Coaches demand discipline. Marketing experts shout consistency. I feel pulled in every direction, tumbling inside a washing machine. While I spin, my message blurs, my presence weakens, my brand loses coherence.

My mentor tells me, 'Focus. Not every door needs to be opened.' Yet I chase every opportunity, thinking one might finally lead to success. In that chase I create only stress and distraction.

STOP. I've had enough! Sometimes I think I should quit. Why stretch myself thin, trying to be everything to everyone, when the reward is stress, sleepless nights, and a business that feels like a burden and doesn't make the money I wish for?

So, I stand here asking: "Who am I? What do I want? What do I need?"

How often do women talk to themselves this way?
I know exactly how it sounds; I've lived it myself.

The Weight of Being Too Human

Naples, September 1989.
The September sun streams through the tall windows of our chemistry classroom, casting golden rectangles across worn wooden desks. I'm fifteen, chatting with a classmate about our holidays, when suddenly, "PENNA!"

Professoressa "Freeda," our chemistry teacher, moves through the room like a predator. Short, angular, short steel-grey hair pulled back, highlighting her sharp cheekbones and prominent, aquiline nose. Her black-rimmed glasses magnify eyes that never seem to blink. She wears the same dark wool suit every day, smelling faintly of stale coffee and antiseptic.

Every movement is deliberate, slow, terrifyingly controlled. Her voice cuts through conversation like a blade. Every head turns. The hum of students fades into silence.

She has asked a question about chemical bonds to Miss "Rainbow", a classmate of mine repeating the year. Frozen beside me, Miss "Rainbow" stares at her textbook. Professoressa "Freeda's" gaze sweeps the room, sharp and calculating.

"Penna, as you are human, because you are just human," she continues, approaching my desk, "help Miss "Rainbow"!"

The message is unmistakable: Miss "Rainbow" is hopeless. Me? Merely human, mediocre - just enough to highlight her failure.

Time stops. Twenty-five pairs of eyes fix on me. Blood rushes to my cheeks. Her lips curl in a faint, cold smile. She has made her point: "You are ordinary. Nothing special. Just human. Nothing more."

But what if those moments when we're told we're "human" "too emotional," or "too much", are actually revealing the precious materials from which our authentic brands will be built?

The Clash with Convention

London, February 2020.
A West London studio buzzes with nervous energy. I adjust my blazer, feeling a flutter of creative excitement. As the newly appointed female Managing Partner of a tax law firm, I hold what some might call an "unusual" vision, professionals can have personality; and expertise doesn't require emotional sterility. Today's team photoshoot is not about headshots, it's about showing that humanity and authority can coexist.
He doesn't just walk in, he arrives. His shoes click against the studio floor like a gavel declaring judgment before anyone else can speak. His navy suit is cut so sharply it could cross-examine you; his tie is knotted with surgical precision, his confident, daring smile reveals teeth of dazzling

Changemakers

white that amplify his proud gaze — as though even gravity wouldn't dare argue with him. Determination radiates from him, but not the quiet, steady kind, it's the I've-already-won-before-you-open-your-mouth kind. His chin tilts a fraction too high, the universal sign for "I don't take advice, I give it." Mr."I Know Best," the Senior Partner, steps into the spotlight first.

The photographer asks: "What's your guilty pleasure? What makes you human outside legal credentials?"

Mr. "I Know Best," smirks, leaning into the lens with the confidence of a man who thinks the world is his jury: "I like sex and alcohol!"

The words drop like an unredacted footnote in a Supreme Court ruling. The room bursts out laughing, not because it's funny, but because he expects it to be. He revels in the reaction, eyes twinkling with the self-assuredness of someone convinced their wit is as bulletproof as their litigation skills.

But I don't laugh. Weeks of creative thought dissolve into a cheap punchline.
The sting is familiar — my work, my worth, reduced once again.

"Stop!" I say, steady. Inside, I'm screaming. "This is about showing who we are professionally, can't you see that?"

He waves me off casually, like a judge striking irrelevant evidence from the record: "Oh, come on. You're too serious. This is boring, and the campaign is a waste of time. You and your crazy ideas, this is going nowhere."

There it is. "Crazy ideas!" The same dismissal I've heard 30 years ago. What if the very qualities the world discourages you from expressing sensitivity, empathy, 'crazy' creativity, are actually raw gems waiting to become your greatest professional assets?

When Pressure Creates Brilliance

In that studio, watching my vision crumble, I had what I call my "Diamond Moment", a flash of clarity: *"I refuse to be squeezed into something that does not belong to me. I want to express my worth, be truly seen, appreciated, and build a business grounded in my own unique assets. I will uncover my strengths, reveal my gems, and build upon them!"*

That moment changed everything. I realised that the **qualities the world often tells us to hide, empathy, creativity, humanity, are actually the raw gems of our personal brand.** Gems that, when uncovered and polished, become the foundation for a business that is not just visible, but magnetic and successful.

Women today are building businesses faster than ever, yet many crumble inside. For decades, society has told them that, "empathy is weakness, creativity is impractical, and humanity does not belong in the business world." Now, paradoxically, authenticity is demanded, yet the very traits that make women extraordinary are often hidden, suppressed, or dismissed.

Hiding behind an image is exhausting and damaging. When you lose yourself, your personal brand, a reflection of who you truly are, becomes hollow. Masks crack, revealing doubt, exhaustion, and disillusionment. Without an authentic brand, business falters. Clients don't just buy services, they buy you. So, when "you" is hidden, opportunities slip by, and influence remains limited. Personal and professional are inseparable; your brand is not an accessory, it is the engine of **visibility, authority, and growth.**

This is where **brand clarity** becomes critical. Your brand is not just what you do, it is **who you are.** When your unique qualities are uncovered, refined, and expressed, you stop chasing opportunities and begin attracting them. A polished, authentic brand shines like a beacon, drawing the right clients, collaborators, and growth toward you. **Pressure doesn't destroy, it reveals.**

Changemakers

Every role, responsibility, doubt, and triumph applies pressure. Like ordinary stones transformed into diamonds, rubies, and emeralds, these pressures shape your hidden gems. Your personal brand journey mirrors this process: discover, align, and polish who you already are. The challenges you've faced, the doubts you've endured, and the "crazy" ideas you've been told to abandon are the very materials that will make your brand unique, powerful, and irresistible.

This is where authenticity becomes your compass. It is not a strategy, it is your essence revealed. When embraced fully, authenticity transforms these raw materials into a personal brand that doesn't just reflect who you are, it propels your business forward. Your story, values, and strengths become a magnet, naturally attracting opportunities, recognition, and influence.

And to guide this transformation, I built **The Brand YOU GemsCraft Journey ™** a step-by-step journey that helps women uncover, align, and polish their unique gems so their authentic brand can shine brilliantly in the marketplace.

So, the question is no longer, *"Should I quit?"*

The real question is, "Am I ready to uncover my gems and let them shine?"

Your journey to build a personal brand with authenticity begins here. Below is an overview of the precious recious journey, highlighting the common challenges women face in building their personal brand, how our solutions address them, and the benefits they deliver.

Shine from the inside out. The Brand YOU GemsCraft Journey ™.
Every woman carries her own gems, unique and precious. This is where my **Brand YOU GemsCraft Journey ™** begins, seven gems, seven steps to help women create a personal brand from Essence to Brilliance. Each gem represents a part of you, that pressure, and life, that needs to be crafted.

Each one is waiting to be discovered, crafted, and polished until your authentic brand shines.

Balance is essential in the professional life of women. It addresses the female struggle working from the outside-in. That is why I've integrated **the chakra system principles** into the **Brand YOU GemsCraft Journey™** because building a business isn't just strategy, it's energy alignment. When your root (security) is unstable, you hustle from fear. When your heart (connection) is blocked, your message falls flat. When your crown (vision) is ignored, your brand feels soulless. True personal branding isn't about adding layers, it's about removing them until your energy, values, and vision align. Work-life balance isn't a luxury; in today's fast-paced, demanding work world, it's the foundation of sustainable growth.
The journey covers the seven-energy centres that when aligned, create harmony and flow. But I've translated these esoteric concepts into practical personal branding terms that resonate with accomplished women who don't have time for just abstract theory.

The Brand YOU GemsCraft Journey ™ has a diamond shape, with the seven gems placed along its structure representing your journey from Essence, where you boldly embrace who you truly are, to Brilliance, where your authentic self shines fully. At the base, you have three gems representing your inner foundation. At the peak, three gems representing your outer expression. And running horizontally through the centre, the crucial fourth gem that bonds inner and outer into authentic alignment.

Changemakers

Ruby (Root Chakra) – **Boldness: The Discovery Truth Ruby™**
Problem: Many women start their journey feeling disconnected from who they truly are. They mimic others' success, follow trends, or present a curated version of themselves that doesn't reflect their authentic essence. Too often, their personal brand and external style - from brand visuals to personal style - are misaligned, making their communication inconsistent and less trustworthy. This lack of coherence weakens their presence and confuses their audience about who they truly are.

Challenges: Confusion about core values, lack of clarity in identity, and difficulty distinguishing themselves from peers. Pressure to "fit in" overrides their intuition and voice, leading to inconsistency between who they are and how they present themselves to the world.

Consequences: Without a solid, grounded foundation, personal branding feels hollow. Women often experience imposter syndrome, inconsistency in messaging, and low visibility because their brand is not anchored in authenticity or expressed with stylistic coherence.

Solution: **The Discovery Truth Ruby™** methodology focuses on **Knowing Your Essence.** By exploring life experiences, values, and unique strengths, women uncover what makes them genuinely different - not superficially unique. This is about **embodying authenticity** in every aspect of communication, from tone of voice to visual and personal style, ensuring every expression reflects their true self.

Advantage: A strong Ruby foundation ensures that all branding and style decisions - from messaging and design to dress and presentation - are **authentically aligned.** This deep coherence between inner essence and outer expression builds **trust, magnetism, and unmistakable presence,** allowing women to communicate with precision and confidence while radiating a consistent, authentic style that sets them apart.

Carnelian (Sacral Chakra) – Bloom: The Creative Flow Carnelian™

Problem: Women often suppress their creativity or dismiss their innovative ideas as "too risky," "impractical," or "crazy." They feel pressure to conform to conventional expectations.

Challenges: Fear of judgment, self-censorship, lack of confidence in creative ideas, and difficulty expressing individuality in a crowded marketplace.

Consequences: Suppressed creativity leads to brand stagnation, loss of differentiation, and missed opportunities to stand out. Unique approaches remain hidden, leaving women invisible among competitors.

Solution: Carnelian helps **Ignite Your Creativity.** The methodology transforms ideas into actionable brand differentiators. It encourages discovering signature problem-solving styles, unique voices, and innovative approaches that make the brand memorable.

Advantage: Creative expression becomes a competitive edge. Women learn to leverage their originality, turning unconventional ideas into strategic opportunities that set their brand apart.

Citrine (Solar Plexus Chakra) – Belief: The Core Differentiator Citrine™

Problem: Many capable women struggle to articulate what makes their product or service truly unique. Even with exceptional skills and knowledge, they find it difficult to craft a compelling value proposition or package their offerings in a way that stands out in a crowded market. Self-doubt and imposter syndrome often amplify this challenge, making it hard to claim authority and show the world why they matter.

Challenges: Women may have a wealth of expertise but hesitate to define a signature methodology or approach. Fear of being "too visible," uncertainty about differentiation, and lack of confidence in promoting their unique strengths can prevent them from creating an irresistible offer that attracts clients, collaborators, or leadership opportunities.

Consequences: Without a clear, differentiated offering, their expertise can go unnoticed. Opportunities are missed, and even highly skilled women may be overlooked or undervalued. Their brand and impact remain underdeveloped, limiting growth and influence.

Solution: Citrine helps women step into their power by clarifying what sets them apart. It guides them to define a unique point of view, craft a distinctive methodology, and package their offerings in a way that is compelling and irresistible. By addressing imposter syndrome and building confidence and self-belief, women can sustain visibility, communicate authority, and stand out in their field.

Advantage: A strong, differentiated brand naturally attracts attention. Confidence and clarity turn expertise into recognised thought leadership, drawing clients, collaborators, and opportunities while establishing a powerful market presence.

Emerald (Heart Chakra) – Bond: The Evergreen Relationship Emerald™

Problem: Women are not purely transactional; they naturally seek meaningful, human connections. However, this strength can sometimes blur the boundaries between personal and professional relationships, making it harder to Make objective, impactful business decisions.

They deeply value empathy in business but often struggle to channel it in a way that nurtures sustainable, balanced relationships.

Challenges: Difficulty balancing self-interest with others' needs, challenges in fostering trust, and lack of community-building skills.

Consequences: Relationships feel shallow or short-lived, limiting referral opportunities, client loyalty, and long-term business growth. The brand may be seen as cold or impersonal.

Solution: Emerald guides women to Grow Sustainably Through Relationship Building and Community. It teaches how to convert empathy into a strategic advantage, building authentic connections aligned with shared values rather than temporary gains.

Advantage: Strong relational networks increase brand loyalty, referrals, and long-term opportunities. Empathy-driven marketing makes the brand magnetic and human-centered.

Sapphire (Throat Chakra) – Brightness: The Signature Message Sapphire™
Problem: Many women struggle to communicate their value effectively. Messaging can feel inconsistent, diluted, or disconnected from personal authenticity.

Challenges: Difficulty finding a confident voice, lack of storytelling techniques, and fear of being misunderstood or judged.

Consequences: Weak communication diminishes credibility, lowers engagement, and prevents a brand from being recognised in the marketplace. Potential clients may fail to grasp the brand's unique value.

Solution: Sapphire focuses on Confident Communication. It coordinates inner truth with outer expression, helping women develop signature phrases, storytelling methods, and communication frameworks, along with presentation skills for different media, that amplify authenticity.

Changemakers

Advantage: A clear, consistent voice elevates brand recognition, builds trust, and ensures messaging resonates with the right audience. Communication becomes a powerful tool to attract and inspire.

Amethyst (Third Eye Chakra) – Balance: The Amplified Authority Voice Amethyst™
Problem: Many women have valuable expertise and insights but struggle to share their message consistently and effectively. Even when they know their vision, translating it into content that reaches the right audience across multiple platforms - audio, video, blogs, podcasts, books - can feel overwhelming.

Challenges: Difficulty in defining a signature voice, uncertainty about which channels to use, and lack of confidence in producing or distributing content strategically. Women may also feel scattered, unsure how to package their ideas into formats that attract and engage their target audience.

Consequences: Without a clear multi-channel content strategy, their expertise can go unnoticed. Messages may be inconsistent, reach may be limited, and opportunities for influence, leadership, and growth may be missed.

Solution: Amethyst guides women to amplify their authority by helping them publish content strategically across formats that resonate with their audience. From blogs to podcasts, videos, and books, women learn to package their insights into engaging, accessible, and compelling content, ensuring their message reaches the right people in the right way.

Advantage: By aligning their content strategy with their unique voice and expertise, women build visibility, credibility, and influence. Their message is heard, recognised, and remembered - transforming knowledge into authority and creating lasting impact across multiple channels.

Diamond (Crown Chakra) – Brilliance: The Durable Partnerships Diamond™

This stage in the GemsCraft Journey represents the **tip of the diamond** - the visible brilliance built on all the work done in the previous steps (other "gems"). It focuses on **creating partnerships that are strong, reliable, and long-lasting,** turning your unique expertise and authority into enduring influence. It reflects not only stability but also the capacity of your network, collaborations, and alliances to withstand challenges while amplifying your impact over time.

Problem: Many women have developed their personal brand, content, and authority, yet struggle to translate this into **sustainable, high-value relationships.** Partnerships may be short-lived, opportunistic, or misaligned, limiting reach and impact.

Challenges:

- Identifying collaborators or partners who align with their values, vision, and unique offering.
- Sustaining relationships in competitive or fast-changing environments.
- Converting visibility and thought leadership into meaningful, long-term influence.

Consequences: Without durable partnerships, even highly capable women risk fragmented influence, missed opportunities, and diluted authority. Their expertise may be recognised in the short term but fail to generate lasting impact or legacy.

Solution: The Durable Partnerships Diamond™ guides women to strategically identify, build, and nurture collaborations that are aligned with their mission and strengths. It teaches how to transform connections into enduring alliances that amplify visibility, credibility, and influence. Women learn to operate at the tip of the diamond, where their accumulated work - skills, methodologies, and personal brand - shines most powerfully.

Advantage: By creating durable, high-value partnerships, women consolidate their authority, expand reach, and enhance long-term impact. These strategic collaborations magnify their value, inspire others, and ensure that their legacy endures, transforming individual brilliance into collective influence.

The Transformation: From Chasing to Attracting
The framework is a true journey of gem discovery and craftsmanship. I have experienced it myself, and I've seen it work for women in business. As you move through the process, you uncover and polish all seven gems, which together give you an integrated strategy.

When women complete this seven-gem journey, magic happens. They stop chasing clients and start attracting them. Internal alignment creates external magnetism. Confidence becomes unshakeable. Their story becomes their strategy, and premium positioning happens naturally.

When it comes to positioning your personal brand and standing out in the marketplace, you don't need to showcase all seven gems at once. This journey will help you **discover and focus on the few that shine brightest for you** - the ones most aligned with your true essence. By refining your energy and attention, your personal brand will become **clear, magnetic, and irresistibly authentic.**

Here are three transformational stories of women who discovered the Personal Brand Gems Framework and unlocked their unique brilliance.

Changemakers

Real Women, Real Transformations: The Gems Revealed

Indre's Transformation:

Indre, Wealth Coach, London & Milan.
When Indre first called me, her voice carried the weight of someone living a split life.

"I'm successful in banking, but I feel like I'm only addressing half of what women really need," she confessed. "I see them making smart financial investments while completely neglecting their health."

Her Ruby work revealed the hidden gem of her mother's wisdom, financial and physical health are inseparable. "What good is money in the bank if you're too sick to enjoy it?"

Her Carnelian spark came when she embraced her "crazy" idea of combining wealth coaching with wellness. What seemed impractical became her creative differentiator.

Her Citrine breakthrough arrived when she finally claimed her authority in this new integrated niche. She stepped into her power as a thought leader, pioneering a model that others now adopt.

Sara's Transformation:
Sara, London & Italy

"I'm whispering in a crowded room," Sara told me, describing her decade of feeling invisible despite transforming women's lives through style. Competing with Instagram-perfect stylists had nearly silenced her.

Her Emerald revelation was rediscovering her nonna's wisdom, style as quality, longevity, and care. This empathy-driven heritage became the foundation for her authentic connection with clients.

Changemakers

Her Sapphire turning point came when she found her voice. No longer whispering, she developed a confident, recognisable message becoming a Style Interpreter who communicates fashion as conscious life expression.

Marinella's Transformation:
Marinella, European Funds Consultant, Naples & Italy

"I feel trapped in this small box when I know I could be helping companies transform completely," Marinella admitted. Being labelled as "just a funding consultant" was suffocating.

Her Amethyst insight came when she realised her long-term vision, business was never just about funds but about guiding transformation with clarity and resilience.

Her Diamond moment was the integration of all her gems. She embraced her authentic brilliance as a Business Concierge, no longer boxed in, but recognised as a beacon, inspiring ambitious entrepreneurs. Today, she shines with influence, building legacy through her authentic worth.

The Thread That Connects: Pressure Creates Gems
Notice the pattern? Each woman's transformation didn't come from avoiding pressure, it came from understanding it as the force that reveals and polishes their authentic gems.

Most women never stop to discover their gems. They see only the rough stone. They forget the brilliance inside. This is why many lose themselves, buried beneath expectations, running in circles, polishing an image instead of uncovering their essence.

Indre's split between finance and wellness created the integration that revolutionised an industry. Sara's struggle with fast-fashion culture polished her into a sustainability pioneer.

Marinella's frustration with being "boxed in" shaped her into the Business Concierge, a role she now excels in.

And me? Sensitivity wasn't a weakness, it was a Ruby foundation. The so-called "crazy" ideas weren't flaws, they were Carnelian creativity. Together, they formed the Diamond brilliance waiting to shine. My own journey revealed how these hidden gems could be harnessed. Today, this insight shapes my work as a Human Personal Brand Creator, helping women uncover and polish their unique gems, transforming what makes them different into a personal brand that shines, resonates, and delivers tangible results, turning authenticity into influence, visibility, and business success.

Your Moment of Choice: The Gem Within You
Right now, as you read this, you stand at a crossroads. You can keep believing your sensitivity makes you weak, your creative ideas "crazy," your humanity unprofessional.

Or you can choose differently.

Every dismissal, every "you're too much," every "you're just crazy," every pressure you've carried has been shaping the precious gem that is authentically you.

The world doesn't need another manufactured personal brand. It needs your exact blend of sensitivity and strength, creativity and wisdom, humanity and authority. It needs the gem that only your unique pressures could create.

Being human makes you powerful. That teacher who tried to diminish my humanity? She unknowingly revealed my first gem, the Ruby of deep empathy and authentic connection.

Being "crazy" and creative makes you distinct. That partner who dismissed my ideas as nonsense? He applied the very pressure that shaped my Carnelian, purposeful, unapologetic innovation.

Changemakers

Every dismissal was actually discovery. Each crack revealed the raw materials that polished over time, became my authentic brand.

And here's the truth, *"in a marketplace of manufactured personas that profit from your insecurity, authenticity has become the rarest, and most valuable currency."*

The "Brilliance" Question.
The girl who felt too deeply. The woman with "wild" ideas. The professional who insisted humanity belongs in business. She wasn't broken, she was in formation, learning to carry the weight of her brilliance.

Your sensitivity. Your creativity. Your complexity. None of these are flaws. They are proof of your authenticity. The pressures you've endured haven't diminished you, they've been shaping you.

The world doesn't need another template brand. It needs you, your story, your essence, your worth. Don't let it stay hidden. So, I'll leave you with the question I ask every woman who begins this journey:

What if the qualities you've hidden to 'fit in' are raw, unpolished gems—the fire within you that can build a robust personal brand and transform lives?

The most precious things reveal their value only when they are brought into the light.

Your uniqueness awaits discovery. Your brilliance awaits expression. Your brand awaits creation, ready to shine.

Scan the QR code now to build a brand that shines like a diamond reflecting your worth and attracting the opportunities you deserve.

Marianna Penna
CEO & Founder, WOW Women of Worth London, PRCA London

Marianna Penna is the CEO & Founder of **WOW Women of Worth London,** Human Personal Brand Creator, Podcaster, Public Speaker, Event Organiser, and **G100 Italy Chair for Brand Creation & Marketing.** Born in Naples, Italy, with a degree in Economics, she has built a career across Italy and the UK, becoming a reference in authentic marketing and personal brand creation, helping women transform from invisible to irresistible, making them shine from the inside out.

Her career began in 2001 with major experience in finance as a controller for an American multinational in Italy, before moving into PR and marketing, managing international campaigns in food, fashion, and lifestyle. Later, as Marketing Director and Managing Partner at LEXeFISCAL LLP in London, she brought creativity and female leadership into the legal and fiscal sector.

In 2021, she founded WOW Women of Worth London to empower women entrepreneurs and professionals through a **holistic, human-centred marketing approach.** Her innovative frameworks guide women step by step: the **Marketing SPA concept** helps ground and balance their strategy; the **Natural Marketing Cycle Guide** translates this into an actionable roadmap; and the **Brand YOU GemsCraft Journey™** crystallises their unique identity into a distinctive, thriving personal brand.

Through WOW, her annual Marketing Festival "Walk The Talk" in London & Italy, her podcast Entrepreneurial Pulse, and live series WOW Voices Speak Volumes, and the last launched signature campaign and series of events promoting "AuthentiCITY" starting from the city of Naples in Italy, Marianna amplifies women's voices globally. With 25 years of international experience, she inspires women to align identity and business, creating brands that not only thrive, but leave legacies

Scan the QR code for More!

CHAPTER 8
FREEDOM FORGED IN FIRE

HOW BETRAYAL, LOSS, AND PURPOSE BUILT MY PATH TO FREEDOM

> *Purpose turns
> pain into power*
>
> - David Ravenscroft
>
> ...

It was the 28th of May 1999, and I was in my business partner George's office when he said,

"Hey Dave, you know that deal we've been discussing, the £10 million sale?"

"Yes," I replied.

"Well, we need to bring in a third party to help with the transaction. It'll take some time to close, but if you like, I'll buy your shares off you now, so you don't have to wait. How does that sound?"

"That's brilliant!" I said enthusiastically. "Thanks, mate. How will that work?"
"I'll get the lawyers to draw it up. It'll take a few weeks, and now we've agreed, you don't need to come into the office anymore. You'll still get paid and keep your Lotus Esprit Turbo company car until everything's signed."

"Ok mate, nice one."

We shook hands, and I walked out, relieved and optimistic.

Betrayal

The summer of '99 rolled on, but weeks dragged into months as the lawyers disappeared on holiday.

By Sunday, 29th August, I was in Tunisia at the Marhaba Palace Hotel, sat at the pool bar after a day at the beach. I'd just ordered a Tibérine and Coke, a local liqueur that goes down far too easily.

I picked up the phone to nudge George about the deal and to check on my dividend payment. Three months had passed, and things were dragging.

Changemakers

"Hiya George, are we any nearer to getting the deal done?" I asked.
"I'm working on it, Dave," he said.

"Ok mate, how about some dividends?"

"We don't have the spare funds at the moment."

"Oh… I thought you'd just bought another Ferrari?" I asked.

"Don't get f***ing clever, Dave!" he snapped.

"I'm not being clever, George, I'm only asking for what I'm due."
"That's it!" he shouted and hung up.

The next morning, I flew home. Waiting for me was a letter from HR. "You've been summarily dismissed for gross misconduct. Your salary and phone will be terminated. Your car and laptop will be picked up on Friday 3rd September."

I was in shock. George wasn't just a partner; he was someone I trusted like a brother. I had poured seven years of hard work into that company. When I joined, they were turning over a few hundred thousand and keeping records on 6x9 index cards. I computerised the systems, built processes, and helped push us toward £10 million in revenue. But in all of it, I'd neglected my own protection.

The news spread locally like wildfire. Some people relished my downfall. "You f***ed up there, didn't you?" one sneered.

"He's f***ed up," I shot back.

"Well, it doesn't look like it from where I'm sitting!" came the retort. And I couldn't argue with that.

The reasons for my dismissal were manufactured, the most ridiculous being that I hadn't been in the office for three months, though George himself had told me not to come in.

I went to see a lawyer. With no share certificates, no contract of employment, and no shareholder agreement, my only chance was an unfair dismissal claim. It was going to be long, expensive, and draining. So, I sought advice from a friend, the CEO of a PLC. After hearing me out, he said,

"Dave, you're not the first person to get kicked out of a company you helped build, and you won't be the last. Why don't you set up again, but do it right this time? Get your shareholders' agreements and contracts in place."

That advice was the turning point.

Starting Again

I set up a new company with three partners. The first two years were tough, still battling George's lawyers. On the day of the court hearing, they called with offers. At first it was insulting, my old car and a Rolex. I told them exactly where they could shove it.

Thirty minutes before court, I accepted a six-figure cash settlement. Nowhere near the £10 million once on the table, but it gave me closure and space to start fresh.

Within twelve months, we'd landed a major contract worth millions. Soon after, Australia Post signed on, and suddenly, we were international. By 2007, the company was flying. My partners and I stepped back from day-to-day operations. We still owned the business, but we now had time and financial freedom.

Changemakers

I became an offshore yacht master, bought a penthouse in Mallorca, and a yacht. I invested in property, renovated homes, and even bought my mum a house.

Life was good.

Cayman Life & Shakara

By 2010, with tax hikes in the UK, I moved to the Cayman Islands. Sunshine, health, freedom, I was living the dream.

I met Shakara in late 2009, and she joined me in Cayman. She was the love of my life. We built a beautiful future together.

But on 30th May 2013, tragedy struck. A call came from the Cayman police,

"Do you have a white pickup truck?"

"Yes."

"Was your fiancée driving it?"

"Yes, has she had an accident?"

"She's been involved in an incident. She's dead."

My world collapsed in that moment. The woman I loved was gone.

The days that followed were a blur. Friends and family supported me, but grief was overwhelming. My mate Steve, who'd lost his own wife, said, "I threw myself into work, Dave."

So that's what I did.

Rebuilding

I grew my UK property portfolio, launched a lettings agency, and invested heavily. I travelled the world, searching for meaning.

In Thailand, I met Gift, who helped me settle in. Through her, I met someone special, and love found me again when I least expected it.

In 2015, problems arose in Australia with our marketing company. A failed software rollout nearly destroyed us. We faced either shutting down or risking a $20 million fine. I came out of retirement to fix it. Within twelve months, we negotiated with the ACCC, paid a six-figure fine, and sold the Australian division for an eight-figure payout.

By 2016, I had seen the pattern clearly: partnerships, purpose, systems, and resilience.

The Blueprint

Every chapter of my life, success, betrayal, loss, rebuilding, taught me the same truth: business freedom isn't about the money. It's about building value, having systems, choosing the right people, and being prepared.

That's why I created The Business Freedom Blueprint, a framework to help entrepreneurs design businesses that run smoothly, scale effectively, and are always sale-ready.

Because if there's one thing I know for sure, it's this, freedom isn't given, it's built.

The reason I've shared these stories is there's a theme that runs through my life. All my businesses have been with partners. There has always been a purpose to my life and that is still true today. I love nothing more

Changemakers

than working with purpose driven business owners and entrepreneurs, helping and guiding them to create value in their businesses by hiring the right people and putting the correct systems and process in place. This increases the value of their business and makes it sale ready at any time, so they have the opportunity to fulfil their destiny.

That's why I developed The Business Freedom Blueprint.

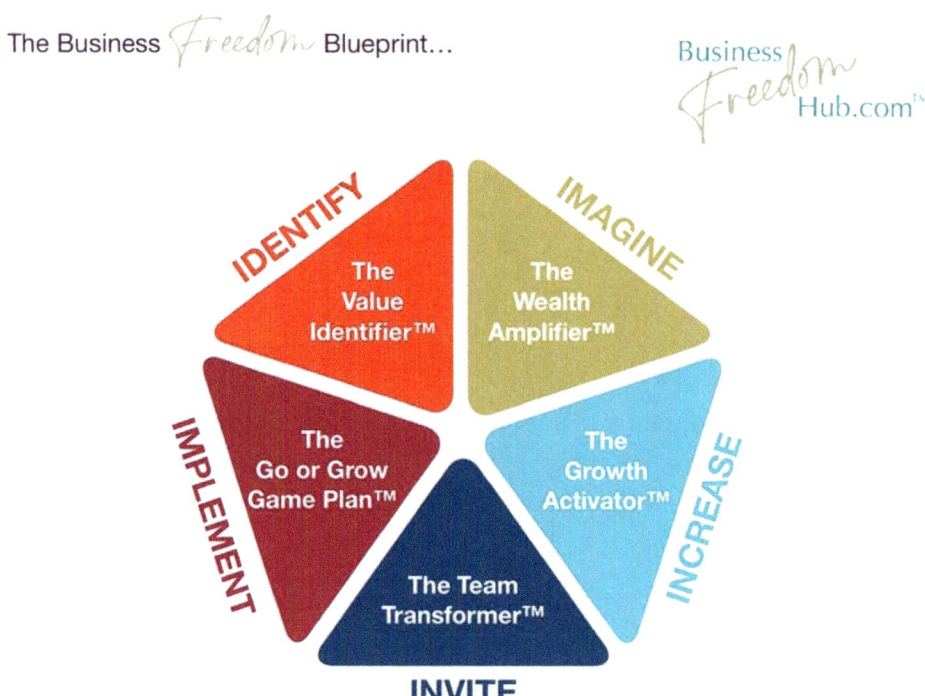

Here's a picture of The Business Freedom Blueprint.

1. IDENTIFY – The Value Identifier

The first step is to identify the true value of your business not the figure in your head, but what an investor or buyer would pay today.

Most owners don't know that number. They confuse revenue with value, or assume profit multiples will apply directly. But years of tax-minimisation strategies and personal expenses through the business often make accounts look weak, even if the business is strong.

The result? Disappointment at the negotiating table, false expectations, and deals that fall apart.
Even when sales happen, they often come with long "earn-outs" to justify a higher price keeping owners tied to a business they thought they'd left behind.

That's why the Blueprint begins with the Value Identifier. By stripping away noise and calculating true EBITDA, then understanding how multiples apply, business owners see clarity and opportunity.
This is the foundation: knowing what the business is really worth, and what it could be worth.

2. IMAGINE – The Wealth Amplifier

The second pillar is Imagine, building a compelling personal and financial vision for life after business.

Many owners think they're ready to sell, until they face the reality of life without their "money-making machine." Doubts creep in: Do I really have enough? Partners or family members raise late-stage concerns, sometimes halting deals entirely.

The net effect of not preparing personally is hesitation, regret, or underselling. Instead of freedom, owners risk ongoing uncertainty and even stepping back into the business they wanted to leave.

The Wealth Amplifier fixes this. Through structured questions, analysis, and planning, business owners map out exactly what they'll need, income, lump sums, lifestyle goals. The result is clarity in black and white, giving confidence to proceed when the right offer arrives.

3. INCREASE – The Growth Activator

The third pillar is Increase, activating smart, sustainable growth that drives value higher.

Flatlining businesses quickly lose their appeal. Buyers want to see momentum, systems, and
structure. Yet many owners chase short-term profit rather than building long-term stability.

The outcome is often chaos: over-reliance on one major client, weak margins, or growth that makes the business harder, not easier, to run. Value is capped or even reduced.

The Growth Activator reverses this. By professionalising operations, strengthening systems, and diversifying revenue, the business becomes more scalable, more resilient, and far more attractive to buyers.

4. INVITE – The Team Transformer

The fourth pillar is Invite, bringing in the right external professionals. Not operational staff, but advisors who protect the business and position it for sale.

The mistake? Relying on an end-of-year accountant who's never seen an M&A deal. Or trusting an online broker promising free valuations. Or, worse, having professionals who never coordinate, leaving the owner lost between conflicting advice.

This leads to false expectations, wasted time, collapsed deals, or exposure to risk from poor structuring and lack of protection.

With the Team Transformer, owners surround themselves with the right accountant, lawyer, tax expert, financial advisor, and broker or banker (when needed), all aligned and working together. The business is now operating at a professional level, with a team ready to act when the moment comes.

5. IMPLEMENT – The Go or Grow Game Plan

The final pillar is Implement. This is where strategy becomes execution, using the Go or Grow Game Plan. Every 90 days, the business owner and their advisor decide, grow the business further, or prepare it for sale.

Most owners drift. They chase sales, mistake activity for progress, or try to "fix everything" at once. Instead of clarity, they create a bigger, riskier version of the same problems.

The effect? Growth feels like firefighting and exit becomes rushed and reactive. They sell for less, or stay trapped for longer.

With the Go or Grow Game Plan, every quarter has focus. If the goal is growth, the focus is on strengthening systems, diversifying revenue, or professionalising operations. If the goal is sale, the focus shifts to tightening costs, protecting profits, and crucially identifying but not acting on future opportunities, so they can be presented to the buyer as upside. Either way, the business owner stays in control, compounding value while always being ready.

Because, in the end, it's not the businesses we build or the deals we close that define us, it's the purpose that drives us forward, giving meaning to everything we create and legacy that outlives us.

Never lose sight of your purpose!

Changemakers

What's Next?

If you're a business owner who wants to make your company more valuable and achieve true business freedom, I've created a presentation specifically for you.

Simply scan the QR code below, and you'll be taken straight to a page where you can watch it immediately.

And here's the best part, if what you see resonates, and you'd like to explore working with me personally, there's a link at the end of that presentation where you can complete a short questionnaire. From there, if it looks like a good fit for both of us, we can arrange a private conversation about your business.

David Ravenscroft is a serial entrepreneur and has spent more than 40 years building businesses across five continents learning firsthand the highs, lows, and life-changing lessons of entrepreneurship. Over the years, he has successfully exited companies three times, with deals ranging from six to eight figures. But ask him what he's most proud of, and he'll tell you it's not the numbers, it's the people, the adventures, and the purpose behind it all.

From boardrooms to building sites, courtrooms to tropical coastlines, David has always followed his instinct for opportunity and his belief that business should create freedom not stress. Today, that freedom looks like life in Thailand with his wife and two children, where he continues investing in and supporting entrepreneurs who want their business to serve their life, not consume it.

At his core, David is driven by one thing: helping purpose-driven founders build businesses they can one day step back from knowing they've created something that truly matters.

I'd love you to take that step. Here's the QR code I hope that I get to meet you.

CHANGE MAKERS

ENTREPRENEURS WITH A MISSION
VOICES WITH A MESSAGE

THE PROFESSIONAL SPEAKERS ACADEMY UNLEASHING 17 VOICES, 17 JOURNEYS.

ONE RIPPLE EFFECT THAT WILL TRANSFORM YOUR LIFE & BUSINESS.

CHAPTER 9
LIFE LESSONS FROM THE BIG C

> "It's when we are challenged, that we truly discover our inner strength."
>
> - Kevin Wright

"Mr Wright, you have a big problem. You have Non-Hodgkin's Lymphoma" With those words, my consultant delivered the diagnosis that I had cancer. Cancer, just the word sends shivers down your spine, doesn't it? According to Cancer Research UK, the statistics for survival for all non-Hodgkin lymphomas (NHL) in England are:

- Around 80 out of every 100 people (around 80%) survive their cancer for 1 year or more after they are diagnosed.

- Around 65 out of every 100 people (around 65%) survive their cancer for 5 years or more after diagnosis.

- It is predicted that 55 out of every 100 people (55%) will survive their cancer for 10 years or more after they are diagnosed.

Looking at this from the outside, this sounds hopeful, but when you are diagnosed, you are likely to have a very different viewpoint. Nobody wants to be in the 45% that don't survive for 10 years after diagnosis. I determined that I would be in the survivors, or better still conquerors category.

Why is this important?

This is not just about dealing with cancer, but how to manage your mind-set to achieve whatever you decide you want.

I've applied it to my business as well as my personal life, and I teach my property Ninjas Investors (mentees) how to harness a millionaire mind-set to achieve their portfolio building goals.

I set about applying the same techniques to dealing with my diagnosis. I call this approach:

Changemakers

The V.I.T.A.L. Conqueror Blueprint

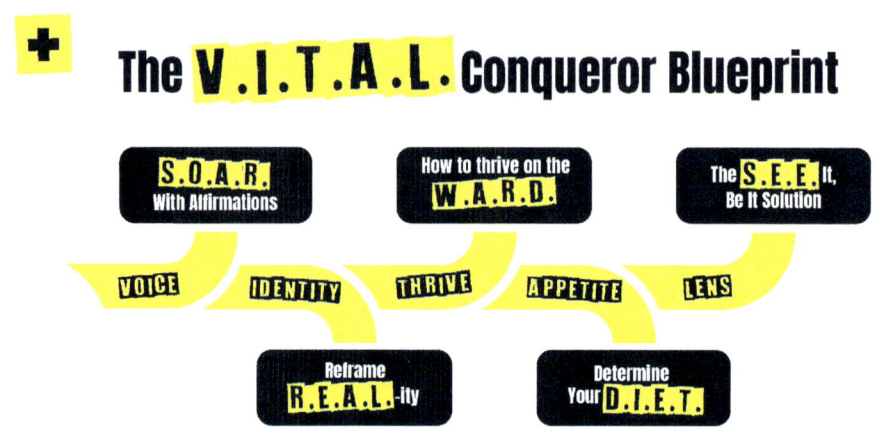

From my early thirties, I developed a thirst for knowledge about personal development, acquiring a library of self-development books. These formulated beliefs underpin the way I prepare for, react to and live life in general.

When it came to dealing with my diagnosis, I determined this was going to be a three-pronged attack :

The mental approach – using the power of my mind.

The research approach – learning as much as I could so my decisions were informed.

The medical approach – chemotherapy.

For decades, people, just ordinary people like me, have been using the infinite power of their mind, often unwittingly, to help heal their body of a variety of ailments.

V - Voice

I've actively practised Neuro Linguistic Programming (NLP) since the late 1990s, working with an NLP Master Practitioner. While I continue to use this skill informally, my diagnosis meant that I knew I was going to need support to keep my mind-set on track.

NLP taught me that I have the ability to re-frame any circumstance, any situation and determine my own meaning to it.

I looked for a local NLP Master Practitioner and having found one I felt was a good fit, we set about installing affirmations and creating visualisations.

If you're thinking 'but I don't have that health situation to deal with, so what has this to do with me?' These techniques can be applied to any challenge you want to overcome.

The first step for me was to install the right mindset and teach my internal voice to run the positive affirmations that would help me achieve a positive outcome.

I reasoned that allowing myself to think negative thoughts was detrimental to my mental state. If you believe that what goes on in your mind can greatly influence what goes on in your body, then each negative thought I allowed myself to have would be harming my body, and my body needed all the help my mind could possibly give it.

Not just thoughts though, words too, dialogue both internal and external. To get the best result, I had to be the guardian of both thoughts and words, and sentry duty was a 24 hour a day responsibility.

I discovered a quote some years ago that greatly helped me to position how to organise and control my thoughts and the grave risks of not doing so.

Changemakers

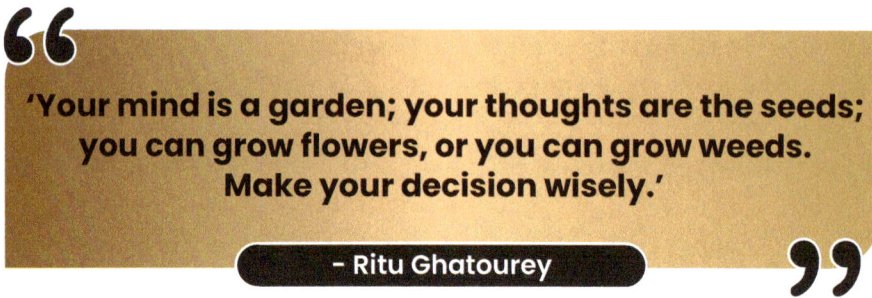

> 'Your mind is a garden; your thoughts are the seeds; you can grow flowers, or you can grow weeds. Make your decision wisely.'
> — Ritu Ghatourey

Weeds equal negative thoughts and words, and flowers (positive intentions, thoughts and deeds) are the positive counterbalance.
In a garden left unattended, naturally weeds will grow, no effort is required. For flowers to grow and flourish in a garden, it takes both time and effort.

The great news here is that the conscious mind cannot hold both a negative and positive thought simultaneously. Knowing that means that we can knowingly block out a negative thought with a positive one. This takes some practice, but it does get easier the more we do it.

I determined, almost from diagnosis, to introduce a phrase into my daily life…

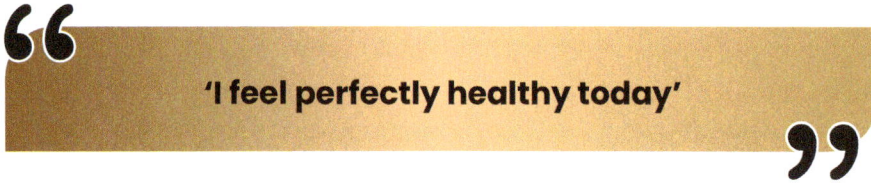

> 'I feel perfectly healthy today'

My intention being to use it as an affirmation, dropped into as many conversations as I can, both written and verbal as well as internally to myself. This was the precise message I wanted to send to my unconscious mind.

Some years previously I found this old Native American Cherokee legend, told through the generations of The Two Wolves.

An old Cherokee is teaching his grandson about life. "A fight is going on inside me" he said to the boy.

> "It is a terrible fight, and it is between two wolves. One is evil – he is anger, envy, sorrow, regret, greed, arrogance, self-pity, guilt, resentment, inferiority, lies, false pride, superiority and ego."
>
> He continued "The other is good – he is joy, peace, love, hope, serenity, humility, kindness, benevolence, empathy, generosity, truth, compassion and faith. The same fight is going on inside you – and inside every other person too."
>
> The grandson thought about this for a minute and then asked his grandfather "Which wolf will win?"
>
> The old Cherokee simply replied "The one you feed"

I found a simplicity and honesty in this that had a profound effect on the way I was determined to think in the future. It was a no-brainer to resolve that my evil wolf would die of starvation; I would feed my good wolf until he was full, every day.

We chatter to ourselves continually, usually internally, it's that voice in your head that you hold entire conversations with. Unfortunately, left to its own devices, that chatter can be completely negative which is the last thing you need when you are experiencing cancer – or facing any other challenge.

When I'm working with people who are looking at either starting out in property, or taking a leap to bigger and more profitable deals, there's a lot of this negative internal chatter going on in their heads,

"Everyone knows that property investing is risky, I could lose my savings."

"How will I know which deals are good and which are going to wipe me out?"

Changemakers

"It's a big step, maybe I should be satisfied with the way things are."

Whether it's property investment or any other career, the same kind of negative thoughts echo through our minds. There's a risk, and fear can have two effects, it will either persuade you to play safe and not take action, or it will give you the adrenaline to take BIG action and do everything you can think of to ensure you succeed. Your internal conversations need to be trained to help rather than hinder.

Your unconscious mind is mostly unjudgmental, whatever we believe or tell ourselves, it will accept as our truth. It doesn't matter if these thoughts are negative or positive, the unconscious will accept either. Human beings have absolute control over the material that reaches their unconscious mind through the five senses, although few regularly exercise this control.

The human brain is an incredibly powerful personal computer that is capable of providing the power to achieve your goals, if you treat it in the right way to gain the most benefit.

Your friends, family and business colleagues may not share your beliefs, and almost certainly, someone will try to persuade you that this course of action is not for you.

The secret is persistence, repetition and determination.

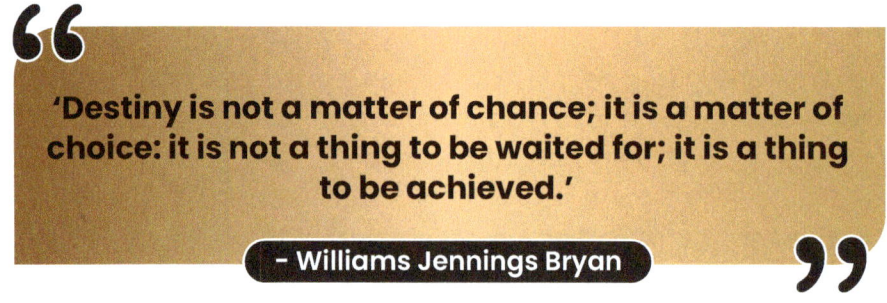

'Destiny is not a matter of chance; it is a matter of choice: it is not a thing to be waited for; it is a thing to be achieved.'

- Williams Jennings Bryan

I – Identity

One of the ten NLP presuppositions is,

'The map is not the territory'

In other words, we interpret the world, not as it is in reality, but how we see it based on our own belief systems. We generalise, delete and distort true reality to fit how we perceive things to be, our view of the world. For example, two unconnected people attend the same party. One found it a drab affair, the people were unfriendly, he spoke to almost no-one, hung around in the kitchen and left early. The other said that it was a fantastic party, the people were great, he made some new friends, he drank and danced and was one of the last to leave. It was the same party, but these two people experienced it completely differently.

Cognitive Reframing is understanding that how I see the world is my own free choice. My reframe in this case was to view my cancer diagnosis as that reframe fundamentally changed the way I reacted to the whole experience I had ahead of me.

> **'A wonderful opportunity to conduct a real-life experiment to find out to what degree I can use my mind to control what happens in my body'**

This applies to any challenge you may be facing. You choose how you perceive it.

Reframing provides the means to take any given situation or experience, and by placing a different frame around it, change its meaning, either directly or by placing it in an alternative context in which it means something else.

Changemakers

As Eleanor Roosevelt once pointed out,

"No-one can insult you unless you choose to be insulted."

You have a choice in how you respond to events in your life. If there is one thing in life no one else can control, it's our thoughts, we have the power to choose these.

Meaning influences behaviour. Change the meaning and you can modify your behaviour, so you respond in different ways.

Someone new to this form of thinking may find this to be a tall order but, although I have the advantage of years of familiarisation, that doesn't mean that someone new to this framework cannot understand and implement this thought process. My advice is to find an NLP Master Practitioner in your locality to help you become more effective.

Asking better questions is a method often used to elicit a different thought process. A simple example is the difference between the thoughts:

1. 'I can't do this'
2. 'I don't think I can do this'
3. 'How can I do this?'

The first is a statement of your negative belief, a certainty. The second is less negative but displays uncertainty. The third is a search for the answer and it also engages the help of the unconscious mind to find the solution, and it will.

T – Thrive

Letting things happen to you is not a good recipe for success in any field or situation. To succeed you need to take charge of your situation. Personally facing a serious health challenge meant finding out about the medical process, what to expect, what was expected of me and where there was room for me to push the parameters beyond those expectations.

To thrive I needed to be well-informed, but not just to accept that everything must follow other people's expectations. I'm not talking about rocking the boat and being difficult, after all, I needed the medical people on my side, but I'm referring to where I could apply my own approach.

This turned chemo treatments into a double-edged sword. The chemicals attacked the cancer cells, while at the same time I was using visualisation and meditation to mentally zap the cells, watching them die and shrivel away.

Everyone else in the chemo treatment room was reading, watching TV or scrolling on their phones. In fact, most of the nurses just assumed I was asleep, but I was mentally active internally to ensure my body thrived. Regardless of the situation in which you find yourself, it's important to understand all the elements before you start taking steps to shape things to how you want them to be.

A – Appetite

I was surprised to discover that the consultant had very little advice about diet, so I set about finding out about what might help me to combat those pesky cancer cells.

My first decision was to eliminate sugar. The PET scan used glucose to make the cancer cells active and visible. I definitely didn't want to feed them that. But then I looked into what else I could do and found an excellent book, listing the foods to avoid and, better still, what I could add to my diet.

Changemakers

This wasn't a weight reduction diet; it was a life affirming eating plan. I did drop a few pounds, but the main focus was to feed my system with the foods that would make my body a more difficult environment for cancer to thrive in.

This strategy fed my appetite for health. If you're not fighting a health condition, you may wonder what this has to do with achieving your goals. In my view, it's simple. You need to be fit for the future – that's the future you're choosing.

Whether you need to eat better, exercise more, or get more replenishing sleep, if you don't look after yourself, you won't have the reserves to take those essential steps forward.

It was interesting to note that while everyone was warning me of the dramatic energy drain chemo would have, I never experienced these. In fact, in the days following my chemo treatment I found I was more alert than usual and actually needed fewer hours of sleep.

I haven't researched the impact of an alkaline diet on energy levels, but the major change to my diet and mental approach definitely kept me in good shape while I fought the condition.

L – Lens

When we are in a mindset of fear, we inevitably create 'disaster movies' in our heads, the last thing we need to be doing when dealing with a cancer diagnosis. It is much better to create 'happy ending' movies. You choose the lens through which you view your situation.

Visualisation is one of the most powerful mindset techniques at our disposal. Elite athletes have used this technique in recent decades, creating very powerful visualisations of positive outcomes that they program into their unconscious minds.

We experience bodily changes when out of our comfort zone, shallower breathing, faster heartrate, sweatier palms, all classic 'fight or flight' responses. We exhibit these when it's a real-life situation, but also when we are just imagining doing something we are not comfortable with or have never done before.

The unconscious mind can misinterpret these feelings as a threat, remember its primary purpose is our survival. When we are imagining something out of our comfort zone or experience, displaying those 'fight or flight' symptoms, it's easy for the unconscious mind to trigger negative outcomes in an attempt to get us back in our comfort zone. It is not serving us to create the results we want. The resolution to this is to use our conscious mind to override negative images and create the positive outcomes we want.

You are in charge of your future.

Within NLP, Modelling is the process of recreating excellence. If one person can do something, it is possible to model it and teach it to others. In this way everyone can learn to get better results in their own way.

What you have read so far can be a template, the model that you copy to achieve your own result. But let's look at probably one of the best-known examples of modelling. People don't generally think of it as modelling, but, when you drill down a bit deeper, that's exactly what it is.

> It was on 6th May 1954 that Roger Bannister became the first man in history to run a mile in under four minutes. Decades later, the momentousness of such an achievement is probably dimmed somewhat, but, back then, it was big. In fact, it was bigger than big; it was HUGE.
>
> The world record for the mile back then had been stuck at 4:01:4 for some time. Medical opinion was divided on whether it was physically possible for man to run a mile in under four minutes.

Changemakers

> *John Landy, an Australian and competitor of Bannister in the previous Olympic Games, was the poster boy of the time, pushing himself closer to the magic four-minute mile. But he was quoted as saying "The four-minute mile is a brick wall, and I shan't attempt it again."*
>
> *Then something happened. Medical student, Roger Bannister, took to the Iffley Road track in Oxford, on 6th May 1954, and ran 3:59:4.*
>
> *The barrier is conquered, the wall was broken, and lo-and-behold, John Landy, the man who failed six times, ran 3:58.0 six weeks later!*
>
> *From then more and more athletes achieved the 'impossible', they ran a mile in under four minutes.*
>
> *How did Landy suddenly mirror what Bannister achieved only weeks later when previously he had continually come up short? He changed his process, he modelled Bannister, he copied what Bannister did using pacesetters, having previously run alone. When Landy eventually broke four minutes with his 3.58, he not only had pacesetters, but competitors who pushed him all the way through to the bell.*
>
> *He also changed location, to Finland, where they had better quality track surfaces, similar to those Bannister used in England.*

The real point is that if someone else has proved it's possible, 'impossible' is no longer a valid reason.

Become your own film director.

Make your own mind movies visualising success, make them engaging, make them empowering, and make them triumphant. Get clarity on what the best result you could have is, then create your movie around that. What would it look, sound, smell, and feel like? Use those sub-modalities we learned earlier to make it compelling.

And replay it constantly, many times daily. Tweak it, edit it if you uncover ways to make it even more empowering.

Strategies for success

Manage your attitude
A positive attitude is not an act; it must be genuine. When things are going well, a positive attitude becomes self-perpetuating and easy to maintain.

Changemakers

It doesn't matter how many times you fall down. It's the number of times that you get back up that counts.

Henry Ford is credited with this gem of wisdom, but there is a much older Japanese proverb that states this:

'Fall down 7 times, get up 8'

A positive attitude is a state of mind which can be maintained only through conscious effort.

Train your mind

The unconscious is trainable; you train it with certain thoughts and principles and beliefs. Once these are set in your mind it becomes difficult to change them – but not impossible. While you try and change a habit you've learned, your unconscious is constantly resisting. The only way to beat it is to keep persisting until it believes in the new idea/course. Once it has belief and faith in that route it will start protecting the new path and follow it just as fervently as the original route.
With this in mind you can understand why we all have great ideas, even make promises (New Year's resolutions) to ourselves and somehow never follow them through.

The unconscious mind is very clever when it stops us, it not only tells us to stop, but it also comes up with lots of rational reasons why we should maintain the existing situation. You've probably had conversations with yourself in these situations.

> 'Eating salads in January isn't good, the produce isn't as good quality as in the summer and my body needs fuel to combat the cold temperatures.'

> 'Going for a run in the dark is dangerous, it would be better to wait until the mornings/evenings are lighter.'

'It isn't a good time to start prospecting for new clients, I'll wait until the beginning of the new financial year, when people have the budget to spend.'

Remember when you are rationalising you are telling yourself Rational Lies.

> **'Faced with the choice between changing one's mind and proving there is no need to do so, almost everyone gets busy on the proof.'**
>
> **- John Kenneth Galbraith**

Listen to your internal voice and argue back when it starts coming up with negative language. Reposition that thought in a positive way and keep doing that until the new way becomes a habit.

It takes approximately 30 days to change a habit or route. Don't give up; if you persist you can achieve anything.

So, what's your big challenge?
What can you do to help your mindset focus on success?

The next step
If you or someone you care about would like to dig deeper into my strategies for conquering cancer, I've written a not-for-profit book and created an equally not-for-profit video programme that details my V.I.T.A.L. Conqueror Blueprint approach. You can find out more about both here: www.thinkpositivelyaboutcancer.com

Changemakers

If the above isn't you at this time but you'd like to explore the Millionaire Mindset, there is a video programme exploring how to apply this here: www.recycleyourcash.co.uk/store

> **Postscript:** If you're wondering how my strategies worked in relation to my health. I had fewer chemo treatments than originally prescribed, my second PET scan showed a 99% reduction in cancer cells, and I had virtually no symptoms or after-effects from the chemo, other than some hair loss. I continued to work as normal throughout. I proved these techniques work, not just for health, but in my business too.

Kevin Wright is a property trainer with a difference – he doesn't just teach what to do, but shows people how to do it, step-by-step. He also encourages his delegates to adopt a millionaire mindset to help them achieve their goals.

He runs regular training sessions including online workshops, 1 and 3-day experiences as well as his in-depth Ninja Investor Programme and both a mentoring programme and a mastermind group. He has established one of the fastest growing property networks in the UK - Recycle Your Cash Property Chats. This is different from any other property networking group, no fees, no speakers and no BS, just pure property networking.

Scan the QR code for More!

CHAPTER 10
MOVES OF THE INFINITE PLAYER IN THIS GAME CALLED LIFE

> "A belief is a thought that you continue to think, and your thoughts are the mental architects that create your future, choose them both wisely."

- Donna Marie Costello

It's Monday October 17th, 2022, 3.30am and I am rudely awakened by the harsh siren sound of my alarm. As I walk half asleep to my bathroom to commence my morning routine, I gaze in the mirror and think to myself "there has to be more to life than this." The ungratefulness of a secure position as the Director of a fencing retail yard, within a long-standing established family fencing erection business was starting to overwhelm me.

I was starting to feel like my days were equivalent to a wild animal caged up for the purpose of human entertainment, albeit I was trapped in a portal cabin for 12-14 hours per day, 5 days per week. Every day was Groundhog day, arise early, go to work, come home, microwave meal and bed.

However, little did I know that today was going to be the day that I experience a spiritual awakening.

As I arrive at work and get out of my car, I feel a chill as the cool autumnal breeze flows through me. First things first "a coffee" to warm up the cockles and awaken my senses, I say to myself.

6am and our first customer arrives. I greet him with a smile, and we exchange pleasantries, I ask him if he had a good weekend and he proceeds to tell me all about it. It certainly sounded fun filled as I listened with a look of enthusiasm, but deep down inside, I was feeling resentful. I think back to the days when I looked forward to Friday night's as they always kickstarted the weekends social gatherings.

However, over the past couple of years I had been declining social invitations as the long hours during the week were taking their toll on me. I much preferred to stay in and relax with a movie. A far cry from the social butterfly that I used to be.

With my customer's order placed, I take payment and he departs out into the yard to have his van loaded.

Changemakers

As I return to my desk and sit down to enjoy a now lukewarm mug of coffee, a voice arose inside of me, a voice that was gentle yet meaningful saying "it's time to go,
it's time to leave".

I have always had a strong intuition but my experience of it has always been a feeling rather than the voice that I just heard. I sat with it for a moment, but shortly after, I heard it again as clear as day, and this time the voice was stronger "it is time to go, it is time to leave".

My first reaction to it was to question "but what will I do?" then I thought to myself "I haven't been happy in a long time." Over the past 14 years I had successfully achieved getting the next division of the company off the ground even when at first it appeared the odds were stacked against me. I was a woman in a man's world and had little knowledge about fencing. However, I successfully secured our place on the map alongside the 2 main long standing fencing retailers within 3 years. Throughout the next 11 years the business continued to soar, but my passion had diminished. My intuition was right; it was time to leave. For ease of tying everything up in the business, I set my departure date for the 30th of June 2023, to allow my departure to coincide with the end of the financial year.

Once I had spoken my decision out loud, I knew for sure I had made the right one as an overwhelming sense of peace rose up within me. It was like the lioness was set free from her cage to roam free in the wilderness.

A couple of months prior to leaving I still hadn't decided what the "right next move" was. I knew a definite change was required. I wanted to experience a new enthusiasm for life. I wanted to find a career that I was passionate about. I wanted to wake up every morning with a spring in my step grateful for the opportunity to experience another great day. With these desires in mind, I stepped out of my comfort zone and invested in myself for the first time ever with a spiritual mentor to teach me personal development and growth.

Investing in myself was the greatest decision I have ever made. Learning about the truth of this universe, its energy, the gifts we hold inside and how to work in harmony with universal laws completely changed my life, but more importantly understanding my soul's purpose and elevating my consciousness completely transformed me as a person.

From my early 20's I suffered with anxiety, a state that I learnt to hide from the outside world. The feeling of unease within my body was a daily occurrence, brought on by an underlying programme in my subconscious mind that I was not good enough where friendships or romantic relationships were concerned. A lack of self-worth conditioned me to have the disease to please, to overcompensate the emotions I was feeling, but this often led to the being betrayed by others or being taken advantage of.

My personal life appeared to be a never-ending ride on a merry-go-round, the same situations kept arising just with different people playing different characters.

My pity parties were starting to become more frequent as I sat and thought to myself, "why does life keep throwing me curve balls when all I do is try to do my best for others?"

The answer was made clear to me; we are all spiritual beings having a human existence, and these were beliefs within my consciousness and an opportunity to expand my soul. The scenarios that I experienced were an opportunity to eradicate my soul's baggage and heal from the belief's that I was unworthy, that I needed validation from others to make me feel whole and that love was attained from the outside.

In order for my soul to correct these beliefs, I had to change my perspective and look at the challenges as an opportunity for my soul to grow. Understanding that lasting change can only come from transforming my internal state from feeling unworthy to worthy, the need for validation to an understanding that I am already whole, and the need to seek love from external things to love myself first and then love others without fear.

Through the correction of my soul, I could feel my connection to source energy strengthen, my intuition was getting a lot stronger, and a sense of protection surrounded me. I was also elevating my consciousness to new levels of awareness, and this gave the experiences a new sense of purpose. Every time I responded to life instead of reacting to it, I was filling my cup of wholeness up and gaining credits towards this game of life.

Consciousness is the one and only creator, and I kept recreating the same scenarios in my personal life because I was creating from my memories, whereas in business, my consciousness was focused on a vision.

Understanding that life is just a mirror to our thoughts, memories, feelings, and beliefs, and these things are what makes up our consciousness, made it easy to comprehend why I was successful in my career and unsuccessful in my personal life.

However, I am pleased to say that the corrections I have made with my consciousness using the tools given to me by my mentor have accelerated my experiences in life in a way that I can only describe as magical. In the past year, I have manifested the love of my life, a new home in a new county, a book deal and the opportunity to be a participant and tell my story alongside other powerful change makers within this book.

In relation to my body, expanding my soul and my consciousness to understand the truth of this universe and the truth of who I am, resulted in the anxiety to completely dissolve. For the first time in 30 years, my emotional state is one filled with peace and tranquillity.

As for my career, well that was easy, I was so inspired by the wisdom that I had embodied that changed my life, I decided to become a spiritual mentor and help others to heal their souls and elevate their consciousness. My niche is one with business owners, entrepreneurs, sole traders and managers.

We have all been taught that to be successful, you have to hustle and grind, and yes working the hours I did, I believed that too. However, there is an easier way, the effortless way and that is breaking away from the ego and working from the soul's perspective in conjunction with source energy.

Changemakers

Through my programmes I firstly...

EDUCATE my clients on the truth of who they are, how the universe operates, and bring awareness to the universal laws. I shed light on the universal energy and the importance of aligning with this energy. I also incorporate the teachings of our inner sight, mindfulness and the importance of having an empowered identity.

ELIMINATE the release of all negative self-talk, old beliefs, any guilt & shame, perfectionism, the past, comparison to others, the need for approval and judgement towards themselves and others.

ENVISAGE creating the right consciousness, how to use the imagination correctly, the power of meditation, the embodiment of this material in contrast to just gaining knowledge, the importance of aligning thoughts, feelings, beliefs and actions. Acting from the place that your desires have already been received and feeling the feelings of gratitude for them in the present moment are all necessary attributes to manifesting a life by design.

EXCHANGE all old patterns for the creation of new habits, beliefs, attitude, behaviours, assumptions, self-love and a new lifestyle.

ENHANCE the importance of having a spiritual practice to keep you connected to source energy for the continued expansion of your soul, together with self growth, self-talk, self-belief, self-discipline, self-approval and self-responsibility.

ELEVATE, now it is time to transform as you will have complete certainty. Knowing that you are limitless, that your level of awareness is now elevated, you will recognise guidance from source energy through your intuition, you will radiate a new profound confidence that will be an authentic version of yourself that is a magnet for miracles.

Changemakers

It is Monday 8th September 2025, it's 3.30am... and I am sound asleep! Long gone are the days that I am rudely awakened by the harsh siren sound of my alarm to signify another 12-14-hour day in a portal cabin.

Instead, I rise at 5am with a spring in my step grateful for the opportunity to experience another great day, one filled with enthusiasm for my new life and passion for the opportunity to assist other beautiful souls with their own transformations.

I chuckle to myself as a thought enters my mind, "Life is just a game".

Are you ready to play?

Donna Marie Costello is a passionate spiritual mentor for entrepreneurs, business owners and managers seeking to unlock their fullest potential through the power of manifestation. With a vivid imagination and a gift for seeing possibility where others see limitation, she helps business owners align their consciousness, expand their soul, and act with certainty to create extraordinary results. Donna Marie believes all success starts with transforming yourself first from within and then the world will match your transformation. With her knowledge of universal laws and spiritual wisdom, she's living proof that imagination, intention, and belief can take you on the most magical journey of your life.

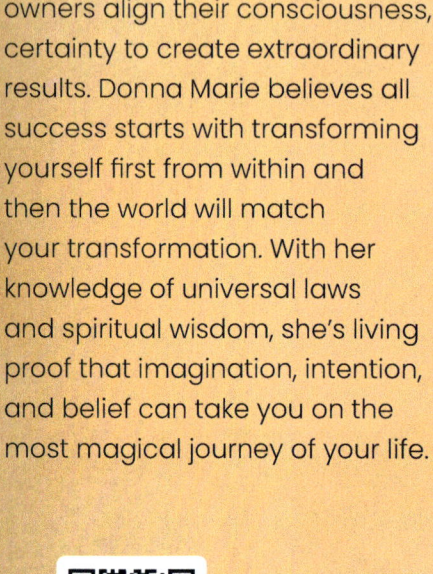

Scan the QR code for More!

CHAPTER 11
UNLOCKING THE MAGIC OF IRISH TRADITIONAL MUSIC

> *None of us came out of the womb knowing anything!*
>
> – Tara Connaghan

I open my eyes, suddenly aware of the sweet chocolate notes of stout wafting from the nearby tables. I realise I've been in a trance, one that music frequently induces in me when I'm bouncing my music off the musicians around me. It brings me to an utterly higher level, a place that I cannot reach while doing any other task or activity. A place where I play my best music, and I am totally in flow. And it is addictive, my drug of choice.

This connection with something greater than me, greater than my music or any one person's music, is what drives and motivates me. I can sense and feel that it motivates others too. Not just the musicians in an Irish traditional music session, but those listening as well. That's when the room bounces, and everyone feels the sparks of magic in the air. It is an unreal feeling, like we are connecting somewhere in the ether, somewhere outside the realm and constraints of the room, somewhere outside reality.

Have you ever witnessed people connecting and building rapport? Or a couple in that first flush of romance – and you felt the energy ripple outwards? The honeymoon phase where the magic happens? With the right ingredients, a session transcends routine, and we can all be elevated to that honeymoon phase. Yet it doesn't stop when the session or music becomes overly familiar. We can continue to be elevated to an even deeper level where everything just seems to fall into place, and we play better than we've ever played before. I mean, how could that not be addictive?

This is the feeling so many musicians crave, and yet too few realise exists.

In pursuit of my curiosity to dissect the ingredients of a magical session and partially inspired by probing questions from my group of adult students, I have chatted with many musicians, from beginner to advanced and as much of the in-between as possible. Some of these conversations have found their way onto my podcast (and indeed are the reason I started the podcast) 'In Tune with Tradition - Perspectives on Session Etiquette in Irish Traditional Music.' I want to share those conversations so that every musician has the potential to experience true feelings of belonging and connectedness in sessions.

Irish music sessions are social gatherings and where there are social gatherings, etiquette follows. When we drive on the road, we find road etiquette, where we work, we find work those who breach etiquette. The word etiquette originates in France from the "ticket" or "label" which historically referred to rules for court behaviour. It is defined as "Customs or rules governing behaviour regarded as correct or acceptable in social or official life" and "Established customs or unwritten code of practice followed by members of certain professions or groups."

The unwritten nature of these behavioural codes is what people find most difficult to grasp, primarily musicians on their learning journey or musicians crossing over from other musical genres. Not knowing these customs or codes or even being totally unaware that existing customs are in place, can cause anxiety for those unknowingly in breach of customs and also for those striving to maintain an inclusive session. And it shouldn't be something that 'breachees' should feel embarrassed about. None of us came out of the womb knowing anything. We all had to spend time learning behaviours in different environments as and when we engaged in them. Irish music sessions are no different.

At a festival around the year 2000, I acutely remember feeling the struggle of not knowing what to say to a musician who joined a session I was playing in. I tried ignoring his insensitive behaviour until it reached unbearable levels. I then tried the compliment-sandwich method of addressing his behaviour, but I ended up receiving a fist threat to my face, so I retreated and suffered in silence for years. Many advanced and experienced musicians harbour this pain because they don't want to offend or discourage learner musicians or new faces.

The result? High quality private sessions behind closed doors away from learners or newcomers and also shielded from the spontaneous magic that can enhance sessions held in public spaces (frequently held in pubs) where you can physically see the excitement radiating on everyone around you. Ironically, it's newcomers and learners who could benefit most from experiencing this, if only the etiquette could be demystified.

I also remember feeling anxiety in my first year in university in the mid 1990s where I felt like an imposter, like I was participating in something way over my head and I received the feedback that maybe I should 'learn some more tunes' before I should join a session. Have you ever felt inadequate, like the weakest link? It hurts. And it can leave scars that our future selves try to protect us from.

But it also presents us with a decision. Am I going to do something about it - an 'action' that means I will address my shortcoming? Or will I keep experiencing this hurt and blame others - the 'inaction' of doing nothing? Or will I give up and move on to something else - a 'distraction' where I do something else to pretend the hurt is not there?

I chose action. I built up my repertoire over time and joined sessions without dread, but I went so far down the gathering repertoire path that I almost lost sight of my passion for experiencing the joy of the music, until a night in 2011 with the master Donegal fiddle player, Danny Meehan. Danny is a larger than life character with fingers the size of three of my fingers, having paved the streets of London for years, it's said he could carry two large paving slabs in each hand, but yet he plays the most sweet, delicate and agile music on the fiddle that you have ever heard. That night while sitting and playing beside Danny, he nudged me (almost off my seat!) to pass on the wisdom of his observation "Tara, don't you think it's time you started to enjoy the music that you play?"

His words unsettled me, and I had to hide that I had taken offence. The seeds of doubt lingered and grew more pervasive, eventually coming to the forefront of my mind at the next session. I wondered defensively and maybe a little resentfully "What did he mean??? Did he think I wasn't good enough? Of course, I enjoy the music I play!". But the pit of my stomach said otherwise. Deep down I realised that I was lying to myself.

Changemakers

I had been playing for other's approval, compensating for the hurt of not knowing enough tunes and of feeling inadequate. I had played what I thought I should, for those I thought were judging me. Not for myself. A bit like a musical "keeping up with the Jones's".

Have you ever found yourself overcompensating for past hurts or inadequacies? Or even for current hurts for that matter? We all do it, more frequently than we care to admit.

Maybe you attended a session in Ireland and felt like such an outsider that when you went home you stuck rigidly to the format of the Irish sessions you attended. "If I stick to the exact tunes and the exact chords, with the tunes in the exact order that I heard in Ireland, no one can say I am an imposter or that my session is not traditional enough. And I will make sure that everyone who attends the session will stick to these rules because this is what happened at a good session I attended in Ireland" with the result that creativity is stifled and smothered and visiting musicians feel anxious about joining or upsetting the current flow (or lack of flow). The fun and excitement are missing, and you don't feel the same magic you felt at that session in Ireland, even if you hide that fact from yourself and others.

Or perhaps you are worried about being the 'session wrecker', if you unknowingly have broken an unwritten rule at sessions on your learning journey. You ask about the rules but only receive vague answers leaving you more confused than you started and even more anxious. Your hands tremble as you fumble to start a tune. Is it the right time to start a tune? Are you allowed to start a tune? Should you wait to be asked? The anxiety is causing more anxious behaviour. Have you ever noticed that anxiety seems to feed itself? This can manifest in defensive behaviour, even if you know deep down that you are not a naturally defensive person. Sometimes sessions can feel more like a test than a celebration because you seem to be second guessing every movement.

Let's look at a scenario:

Changemakers

Imagine you arrive at an Irish traditional music session that you haven't been to before. Musically, you are fairly confident that you know a few tunes and can play along. Physically, the room is comfortable and safe. You look around and notice the musicians are chatting amongst themselves and it seems they know each other well. You don't know any of them. They don't immediately invite you in.

A small but significant sense of a lack of belonging makes you feel hesitant. You feel a slight tightness in your chest, the start of anxiety. You start questioning whether you belong "Maybe I'm not welcome, maybe I wouldn't fit in, maybe they don't want me to join but are too polite to say."

You decide to join despite your unease. You pick up your instrument and try to follow along. You catch a few notes, but the tempo and the rhythm seem different to what you're used to. You feel like you're losing your place in the tune and your anxiety intensifies. Then your fingers start to fumble and the tunes you knew well at home seem to evaporate into thin air and you're worried that others will notice your mistakes. Your palms start sweating and you can't even hold your instrument comfortably. You feel both invisible and painfully exposed all at the same time. You hear a lull in the session and think it's a good time to start a set of tunes. But you are so nervous you speed up until it's beyond your ability and you are not able to keep pace with yourself.
What's worse? No one joins in so you are left vulnerable and exposed. Your discomfort feeds itself and you expect failure and rejection. You focus on your mistakes and they start compounding, one mistake and uncertainty on top of each other, confirming your fears and deepening your feeling of being an outsider. So, you start to withdraw physically and emotionally, retreating into yourself. Ultimately questioning whether you would ever start a tune again, and you may begin to question if you should come back or even continue playing this music.

Changemakers

I frequently see musicians struggle with this snowballing anxiety and that's why I created The Session Etiquette Explorer - a system to transform anxious beliefs into empowering habits, providing a framework where musicians can thrive, contribute and fully enjoy the magic of Irish music sessions.

So, let's see if we can change the scenario above with small interjections from ourselves and others:

Imagine you arrive at the same session. The musicians are chatting amongst themselves but one of them notices you have an instrument case. They nod and give you a warm smile [Interjection from session member]. You notice their body language is open [self-interjection]. Your heart rate slows, and you feel a subtle relief.

You walk over to the session and ask if the session is open to visitors [self-interjection], they reply that it is, and they seem to genuinely appreciate that you asked. This opens up space for more conversation and some banter between you and the musicians which you engage in and you tell them your name and mention where you are from, how long you have been learning and that you are open to learning more and receiving feedback if they think it's appropriate [self-interjection]. You start to feel like there is a connection and that there is good energy in the room. You join in with the music, your fingers naturally find the notes, even the unfamiliar tunes seem to start developing patterns in your head. The rhythm is becoming hypnotic, and you feel like you're playing better than ever. You are included in conversation with musicians between tunes while your music is being invited and respected as part of the group musical conversation. One of the musicians asks, "Have you got a tune?" [Interjection from session member] and you intuitively understand that you will be supported in playing that tune. You recognise it is not a test to 'lead' the session where you would feel under pressure, it is an offer of further camaraderie and support. You open yourself to connection and appreciation and this allows you to experience the musical highs of the session [self-interjection].

Changemakers

Everyone in the room seems to be feeding off the positive energy in the session. And even if you find yourself making a mistake, it is not a big deal, it is greeted with empathy not criticism. It feels like the musicians want to help you on your learning journey. Your chest swells with excitement and pride. Your self-esteem and confidence grow with every note. You feel like you really belong and you realise that it isn't just a session of music, you feel a deeper connection to the music and to the people, you have found your tribe. A tribe that nurtures, nourishes and challenges. You go home eager to practice and learn more, informed by the inclusive conversations you had with the musicians, and you are hungry for more.

As you can see, some small self-interjections and interjections from established members of a session, can transform a session and be the difference between a musician giving up or beaming from ear to ear. So how can you move from suffering the anxious state of the first scenario to enjoying the bliss of the second scenario?

I believe when you master the subtle art of decoding the unspoken rules of interaction, every session becomes an opportunity for magic. The Session Etiquette Explorer is an easy-to-use framework with 5 key areas to help people demystify sessions, using the acronym S.H.A.R.E. Sharing is caring. And Irish music is all about sharing the music and sharing the session space.

Changemakers

S **Scene**
Understanding the session scene, types and functions of different sessions

H **Handbook**
Practical tips and helpful suggestions

A **Awareness**
Understanding our own strengths and limitations

R **Relations**
Dealing with challenging situations

E **Excellence**
The next steps

Decades of playing Irish music in sessions, stages, recordings, and teaching and mentoring have taught me this: the best sessions aren't built purely on flawless technique or encyclopaedic knowledge of the repertoire. They are crafted on understanding the social language, customs and values that have been passed on from generation to generation, that underpin all types of communities.

As experienced musicians, it is selfish to withhold wisdom. But learners must come with a willingness to grow so that the experienced musicians can facilitate and nurture their journey. When Irish traditional music practitioners help each other achieve greatness, we can all experience musical highs. The session can be a sacred space to SHARE our music, which is how this practice lives and grows.

If you sometimes feel anxious or you crave greater joy in an Irish music session, I invite you to listen to the podcast 'In Tune with Tradition, Perspectives on Session Etiquette in Irish Traditional Music', visit www.sessionetiquette.com or simply scan the QR code below to take a short self-assessment to discover your strengths, identify areas for growth and unlock resources to ignite your journey.

Tara Connaghan is a highly regarded fiddle player and podcaster from Glenties, Co. Donegal, in the Northwest of Ireland. She has been an active performer in the traditional music scene for over 30 years and is widely respected for both her artistry and her work in promoting Irish culture.

Tara is a founding member of the all-female, 13-strong Donegal fiddle collective SíFiddlers, which includes renowned musicians such as Mairéad Ní Mhaonaigh, Liz Doherty, Bríd Harper, Róisín Harrigan and Clare Friel and have attracted front-page national media coverage for their headlining concerts.

In 2025, Tara took on the bold task of examining the often-controversial topic of session etiquette. She launched the podcast In Tune with Tradition – Perspectives on Session Etiquette in Irish Traditional Music, which quickly established itself as an important platform for open conversation within the traditional music community.

Her contribution to Irish traditional music was recognised in 2024, when she was honoured as the Festival Guest of Honour at the Cup of Tae Festival in Ardara. That same weekend, Cairdeas na bhFidiléirí, of which Tara is a board member, received the Outstanding Contribution Award at the TG4 Gradam Ceoil Awards. She has also released the well-received album The Far Side of the Glen with fellow Donegal fiddler Derek McGinley, appeared on multiple recordings, and featured in over 40 television programmes, including presenting TG4's Geantraí. Tara studied music at University College Cork and completed the inaugural Masters in Irish Traditional Music Performance at the University of Limerick. She also holds a Postgraduate Diploma in Arts Administration and undertook a three-year programme with Na Píobairí Uilleann, learning the craft of uilleann pipe making.

Beyond performance, Tara has worked extensively in arts management and advocacy. She has served as Festival Director of Carlow Arts Festival, worked as a Traditional Arts Specialist with Clare County Council Arts Office, and as a Deis Advisor with the Arts Council of Ireland. With a broad curiosity across artforms, she is especially interested in the creative thought processes that connect music and other disciplines.

Following the death of her father in 2014, Tara took over her family's construction business, becoming the only woman in Ireland at the time to head such a company. Under her leadership, the firm specialised almost exclusively in large-scale civil projects for ESB Networks, building electrical substations nationwide. Despite these demanding responsibilities, she continued to perform and teach in a limited capacity. In June 2022, she began transitioning out of the construction industry to devote herself fully once more to her lifelong passion for music, cultural engagement, and creative legacy.

Scan here to begin your Session Assessment and unlock resources.

CHAPTER 12
A JOURNEY TO FREEDOM

> "Freedom begins the moment your company no longer needs you and thrives because your people can carry it forward together."
>
> - Patrick Neudorfer

Changemakers

How do you design a business that grows stronger the less it depends on you? How might that set you free? How would it reshape your time and energy? And how would you use that new potential?

When I joined waldner partner in 2015 as a project manager, I didn't see it coming. I wasn't thinking about succession. I wasn't planning to take over a business. All I wanted was to deliver excellent work and grow as a professional. That was it. But once inside the organisation, I began to sense the weight our founder was carrying. The day-to-day decisions consumed him and the client relationships that lived in his head after working hours. I started to feel what it meant having a business depending on one person. Then came a moment that changed everything. Not only for me, but for the company as whole. I didn't inherit a business; I helped rebuild it from the inside out.

This is a story about stepping up, not stepping back. About a transformation, that took place through the courage of letting go, and ability to create space for others to rise up to the occasion. It's a guide to empowerment and for any business owner who suspects their greatest act of leadership might be to make themselves less dispensable.

Maybe you've built your own thriving business through years of hard work and commitment. However, if you're honest, your company might thrive only because you're an indispensable part of it. You are the one seeing the whole chessboard while others only see their own square. The tasks you delegate to your team boomerang half-done back to you, not because of a lack of talent, but because of a lack of perspective. That's why you might stay late at work to rework the other people's tasks. That's how you potentially miss a dinner you promised you wouldn't miss. You tell yourself it's just a season. And seasons have a way of turning into years.

Perhaps you are emotionally bound to what you've built. Undoubtably, you might have put your savings, and your reputation into it. So, when you whisper questions to yourself: "What's left if I step away? And what comes next?", consider it wisdom, not a weakness.

Changemakers

The question is whether you'll take deliberate action to find answers in due course to shape your freedom intentionally, rather than have circumstances dictate its terms to you.

Zurich. November 2015.
It's late afternoon in an office building in the centre of Zürich. The space is exactly what you'd expect from a firm that lives and breathes architecture: bright, minimal, transparent. The space is airy. Clean lines. Honest materials. It feels like clarity. But in a meeting room behind a closed door, something messy is unfolding. A man in his mid-to-late 50s with short grey hair exudes an aura of calm authority. He is a doer and a decision-maker. A builder in every sense and the mastermind behind the company he built. Dany Waldner is having a meeting with one of the employees considered for succession. A long-timer. A safe pair of hands. The conversation is meant to be the next step towards a carefully designed handover.

After an hour of tense deliberations, the colleague says at last, "Dany, I'm afraid I can't do this anymore. It's too much for me. The pressure, the expectations. I thought I could step into your shoes, but unfortunately, I can't. I'm stepping away. I'm out." The room falls quiet. The future that had seemed within reach suddenly feels fragile, almost imaginary. Dany's plan to gradually hand over his business, his baby evaporates in a single sentence and with it, the company's best-laid assumptions. His face changes. Shoulders that always carried certainty now carry disappointment. This is the moment Dany realises, there is no Plan B.

That evening, Dany goes home with questions no founder ever wants to face "What happens to my company if no one is willing to carry it forward? What happens to the people who depend on it? What happens to everything I've built?

Zürich, September 2016.
Nine months later, the questions turn into a decision. It's a warm late summer day. Lake Zürich is a blue sheen beyond the windows. The air carries the scents of warm stone and early autumn.

Inside a conference room, 30 colleagues sit in a circle. Dany stands in the front, speaking with the calm of someone who has wrestled with hard truths and made his choice.

"I want the company to continue without me," he says. "Handing it over to the family is not an option. I also don't want to sell to outsiders. The people who shaped this place until this point, should also be able to shape its future. By 2020, you will have the chance to own this company." The words land heavily. Silence. Doubt. Curiosity. Some look startled; others sceptical. What once seemed like a straightforward succession is now an invitation to create something entirely new.

For Dany, this is the moment of letting go. Not of the company, not yet, but of the idea that one designated successor will carry it all. He is opening the door to another solution.

By that point, Dany Waldner AG was a well-known player in trade fair construction, general planning, and project management, with 35 employees across two locations in Zürich and Basel.

And me?
I'm sitting there as an employee, listening to Dany's words.
This is my turning point, the moment Dany's decision becomes my responsibility.

Could we, as a team, really own and lead this company together? Could we prove that a business needn't depend on a single figure at the top? Could decision power be shared without impeding our progress?
At this moment something lights up inside me. I don't have the answers, but I know I want to try. In the days that follow, I talk to colleagues, I listen, I ask questions.

I dig into books and get absorbed by case studies on employee ownership, co-operatives, sociocracy, holacracy, and self-managing teams. On my quest for clarity, I hunt for tools and systems that help me understand how organisations are structured.

Changemakers

The more I learn, the clearer it becomes that traditional leadership systems are outdated. They serve founders, not futures. I begin to understand that we need something else. Something built on shared responsibility and empowerment, not on inherited positions. So, I start sketching organisational structures. Eventually, I step forward. That is the moment I choose to stop watching from the sidelines and start designing the future. Not just mine, ours. So with a team of first movers, we pitch this idea to Dany. Dany is convinced that ownership is not just about shares, it is about stewardship. He sees that real continuity comes not from appointing a single successor, but from distributing responsibility across many shoulders. Empowered by Dany's trust, we moved forward, shaping what would become a new organisational model.

Zürich, 2017-2020
In all honesty the next years weren't always easy.

People left. Some didn't want the responsibility that ownership implies. Others didn't trust the model without a boss at the top. At times, even I questioned whether we were on the right path. We made mistakes. We over-consulted on some decisions and under-communicated on others. But most importantly, we learned.

In the meantime, critics didn't hold back:
"Employee-owners? You'll regret it."
"Who makes the hard calls when it's ugly?"
"Fine in theory, impossible in practice."

And yet, quietly, something shifted. People began stepping up. They asked better questions. Not just about their tasks, but about intended outcomes, priorities, and delivered value. The company grew stronger because more people started pulling their weight.

And Dany? Still on board, not as the central node, but as a vital contributor, mentor, and peer in a shared system. That alone is a radical act of leadership. It takes courage to trade control for legacy.

On 1st July 2020, we officially became the co-operative waldner partner. Today, we run a healthy, and successful business.

But the real hallmark of achievement is our resilience. During the pandemic we encountered our greatest test to date. Many companies went into survival mode. We did something counter-intuitive, we launched a new business unit. That decision didn't come from a heroic founder's hunch. It came from a system where many people felt empowered to keep the finger on the pulse, propose new initiatives, and take responsibility. The lesson I learned is, in a crisis, distributed ownership breeds resilience.

That's why today we are successfully steering the company. Together. And the best part? Since the beginning of our journey, our transformation has been featured in various articles and podcasts and even documented in a case-study book. In 2022, our successful transformation was even recognised with the Swiss HR Award in Culture & Change.

That's the reason why today, my inbox bursts with e-mails containing the same question: How did you do this so successfully?

This transformation became a conviction and that conviction crystallised into a framework I now teach, the Successful Successor System. It helps owners design their own journey to freedom while elevating their people to carry the business beyond them. It's not a theory; it's a concrete blueprint of what worked, what didn't, and what I would do again.

Over the years, it has become unmistakably clear for me. The key to a successful business is building a company that doesn't depend on any single individual.

And the way to do that? Employee empowerment that is real, structured, and cultural.

Changemakers

The Successful Successor System™

The Successful Successor System is a four-part progression. I tell my clients that they can start at any of the four segments, however if you want momentum that lasts, I suggest moving along the system in order.

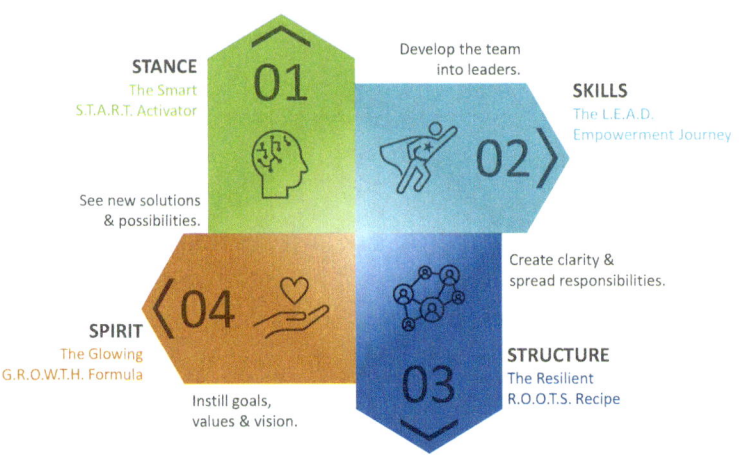

1 STANCE
Shift the beliefs that keep you trapped.

Why it matters. STANCE is your posture towards the business. It's the unspoken rules I hear when I work with business owners: "If I'm not involved, quality suffers." "Clients expect me."
"They aren't ready." These beliefs make sense; they're also the ceiling of your freedom. Change the stance, and the ceiling will move.

Where owners get stuck. When succession starts to feel real, many oscillate between over-involvement and frustrated delegation. I notice that this is especially common at the start of succession planning. Business owners feel the need to act differently but don't know how. Without clarity, they're frozen in place.

What changes. I usually tell my clients: "Your business can only grow as much as you do." The Smart S.T.A.R.T Activator is the framework I use with my clients to work on those beliefs and break old patterns. It shifts perspective from doubt to possibility.

Outcome. As one client put it: "My role isn't to protect the business. It's to prepare it for life without me." After the Next-Generation Successor Summit that we organise, leaders shed doubts and start seeing opportunities and solutions they had never imagined.

2 SKILLS
Build capability at every level, not just the top.

Why it matters. SKILLS turn potential into performance. Owners often assume others "should know by now," forgetting it took them years to acquire their instincts. SKILLS is the bridge between your embodied know-how and your team's emerging capability.

Where owners get stuck. Unrealistic expectations. When a gap emerges, trust drains on both sides. Employees feel tested rather than developed. Owners feel reaffirmed in their suspicion: "I knew it. They're not ready." The cycle feeds itself.

What changes. To help build SKILLS at every level, I assist my clients with the roll out of the L.E.A.D. Empowerment Journey across the organisation. It is not just for managers; it is for everyone. It combines on-the-job challenges with mentoring, coaching, and peer learning. Crucially, it's tied to real decisions and value creation, not abstract workshops. People are taught to think like owners. How does this create value? What's the cost of delay? Who decides? What's the smallest safe step?

Outcome. Initiative-taking replaces approval-seeking. Meetings shorten and decisions crystallise because capability rises to meet responsibility. In our own transition, a project lead who never handled pricing strategy

Changemakers

took it on through mentoring. The first iteration wasn't perfect. The second won margin we had been leaving on the table. The key wasn't talent; it was space to practise and a structure to learn.

3 STRUCTURE
Remove bottlenecks;
make ownership operational.

Why it matters. STRUCTURE is how authority, information, and workflows move. Without it, empowerment collapses under ambiguity. With it, founder-centric heroics are replaced by distributed, aligned action.

Where owners get stuck. The bottleneck syndrome. Everything critical routes through the owner "just to be safe". It feels prudent; it is actually expensive. Opportunity slows. People hover. The owner burns out.

What changes. My clients implement the Resilient R.O.O.T.S Booster. A practical redesign that spreads responsibility, clarifies roles, and formalises decision rights. We identify single points of failure. We define what gets decided where, by whom, and with what input. We introduce lightweight, consent-based decisions to move fast without risking the company.

Outcome. The first time a proposal passes by consent, "not perfect but safe enough to try", you can feel the company breathe out. Small, reversible decisions stop clogging your calendar. Big, consequential ones get the airtime they deserve. That's how my clients move from "Ask the owner" to "Follow the map". Clients stop noticing who answered because the answer is consistent. You regain headspace for strategy, product, or simply, life.

SPIRIT
Embed a culture where values aren't posters; they're behaviour.

Why it matters. SPIRIT is the lived culture: values, rituals, and norms that make behaviour predictable and relationships strong. In succession, culture is either your greatest asset or your hidden saboteur. I usually tell my clients, "The values that founded the business aren't necessarily the values that will make it future proof."

Where owners get stuck. Many succession plans ignore culture or treat it as aftercare. Misalignment then shows up as friction, politics, and passive resistance. Transitions fail not because the plan was wrong, but because the culture couldn't carry it.

What changes. My clients run Culture Design Labs using the Glowing G.R.O.W.T.H Formula. Teams co-create value codes (how we behave when it's hard), feedback formats (how we tell the truth with care), conflict resolution (how we handle conflicts with care and clarity), and celebration rituals (how we recognise progress). We make culture operational, embedded in hiring, promotion, decision-making, and client experience.

Outcome. My clients' organisations become flexible where they should be and distinctive where it matters. Values stop being posters and start being practices.

Together, these pillars turn businesses into self-sufficient ecosystems and owners into free agents of impact. We weren't just building a system; we were building successors.

The paradox of succession is that the more you try to hold on to control, the tighter the trap of rigidity. The more you share ownership with clarity, the freer you - and your company - become.

Changemakers

Looking back, the transformation of waldner partner, and of my clients, is not just about structures or legal forms. It is about people: how they grow, what they need, and what they give when they are trusted. Along the way, a handful of insights proved essential.

Insights that matter

Emotions
Change is emotional before it is structural. It takes time, energy, and patience, because people rarely shift at the pace of strategy.

Trust – Trust – Trust
At the heart of any change lies trust, built, maintained, renewed, again and again. Without it, nothing holds. With it, everything becomes possible.

Transparency
The more people are included, the stronger the system becomes. Transparency draws others in, creates alignment, and allows the company to carry more than one person ever could.

Courage
Waiting for perfection is paralysing. Progress requires courage: the courage to try, to learn, to adjust. "Good enough to try" is how transformation stays alive.

The "Why"
Purpose is the compass. When everyone is clear on why the business exists, decisions align and momentum follows. Without it, structures wobble and culture drifts.

Inner Work
The deepest shifts are inside us. Owners and employees alike must do the inner work: challenging beliefs, releasing control, and choosing a stance that serves the future, not just the past.

These insights are not theory; they are lived experience. They enable a business to move from dependence on one to the strength of many. They allow a founder to step back with confidence, and a successor to step forward with hope. Above all, they prove one truth: freedom begins the moment your company no longer needs you and thrives because your people can carry it forward together.

What we built and what you can build

A company without a single foreman sounded radical in 2016. Today, it's my everyday experience. We're a co-operative by design, not ideology, we chose the structure that best aligned with our intent-shared responsibility, shared reward, and shared future.

I started this journey as an employee who watched a succession plan dissolve in one sentence. Unexpectedly but with a clear intent I became a successor myself by choosing to design a company that didn't depend on me, nor on any one of us. The prize wasn't a title. It was freedom within a successful and thriving company, the freedom to be essential without being indispensable; the freedom to lead without being the bottleneck; the freedom to leave one day, knowing the business will go on.

If you're an owner, your greatest legacy may not be what you built while you were there. It may be what continues to live on and evolve when you're gone. Aim for that, and your freedom will come early.

You don't have to become a co-operative to achieve that. Ownership can remain with a family, a trust, or a partner group. What matters is that operational ownership, decision rights, accountability, capability and know-how are distributed, not concentrated with a handful of key people. The legal structure of the company can support the philosophy, but it does not replace it.

Changemakers

If you are an owner contemplating your next chapter, here are some uncomfortable truths intended as an invitation to reflect:

- You cannot delegate responsibility while hoarding authority.
- You cannot empower people with lofty speeches; you must redesign the system.
- You cannot create successors if your business model requires a hero.

The path is learnable. It starts with STANCE, becomes visible through SKILLS, becomes sustainable through STRUCTURE, and becomes unstoppable through SPIRIT.

My invitation to you: Do not just plan your succession. Design it! Create a company that grows stronger the less it depends on you. Build an organisation that secures both your legacy and your freedom, while unlocking new value and growth for the people who carry it forward. If this speaks to you, let's talk. I'll share what I've learned and together we will explore what your path could look like.

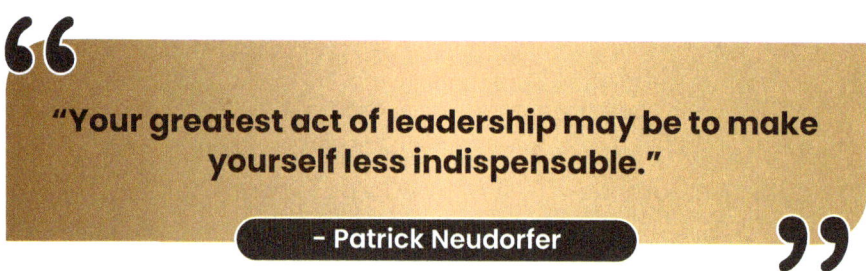

"Your greatest act of leadership may be to make yourself less indispensable."

– Patrick Neudorfer

Patrick Neudorfer born 1983 is an architect, entrepreneur, business adviser, and change-maker. He has always been drawn to change, not out of desire to stem the tide, but driven to make sense of it, connect the dots, and guide through uncertainty with passion, clarity, and poise.

His career began as an architect, with professional experience in Austria, China, and now Switzerland. Over the years, Patrick has spearheaded numerous large and complex construction projects, skilfully aligning diverse interests and navigating complexity with steadiness. He quickly realised that every building project, at its core, is a change project. That's why he believes real progress doesn't stem from rigid plans, but flows from deep listening, alignment, and empathetic leadership. His strength lies in reading the room, understanding the needs, and helping teams move forward, together.

But his work didn't stop at commercial real estate. These same strengths became invaluable when he played the leading role in a business transformation. Starting as an employee and eventually becoming successor and co-owner of the employee-owned co-operative waldner partner in 2020.

This unique journey of transformation was recognised by the Swiss HR Award 2022 in the category Culture & Change. It revealed something greater than Patrick had imagined.

Inspired by this experience and leveraging his deeper understanding of leadership, ownership, and legacy, Patrick developed the Successful Successor System. A framework that helps business owners shape the future, empower their people, and build organisations that thrive beyond themselves. Today, he supports entrepreneurs navigating succession, and implementing structural, and cultural change.

He believes the best positioned companies for the future are the ones that empower driven individuals to take ownership, combining real leadership with resilient structures to create lasting impact, not just for today, but for the generations to come.

Scan the QR code for More!

CHAPTER 13
BUILT TO RUN WITHOUT YOU

"

> Real freedom in business begins the moment you stop being its engine and start being its architect.
>
> — Andy Hooper

"

It's past midnight again.

The glow of my laptop screen is the only light in the room, my wife asleep upstairs. I'm on Google, typing the same phrases I've typed countless times before:

"How to be a CEO."

"How to get out of the daily grind."

"How to work on the business, not in it."

Click. Read. Disappointed. There's nothing real out there, nothing complete, practical, or proven. Just vague advice, motivational soundbites, and overpromises. No actual framework that could help me escape the trap I'd built for myself.

Because that's the truth, I built the trap.

Like so many owners, I believed I had to be involved in every decision, every day. I started my business for freedom yet chained myself to it. My phone never stopped. Every question, every approval, every fire to put out, it all came through me. I wasn't running a company; I was babysitting one.

And here's the kicker: it became my comfort zone. I knew how to work in the business. I'd never learned how to lead it without being inside it. Holidays weren't a relief, they were stressful missions. I'd sit on a beach with my phone in one hand, scanning emails for disaster, while Becki read a novel beside me. Even when I was "away," I was always there. Burnout doesn't always look like 90-hour weeks. Sometimes it's quieter, it's when you dread showing up. When you feel short-tempered, flat, and disconnected from the thing you built. You're not leading anymore; you're enduring.

Changemakers

One night, staring at the ceiling, it hit me, nobody's coming to fix this. If I wanted out, I'd have to create my own way out. That was the birth of **STEMS®,** a framework built in the trenches, not in a classroom. Five gears that, when working together, transform a business from owner-dependent to owner-free,

Scale. Structure. Systems. Stability. Synchronise.

Gear 1: Shift

Most owners think scaling means bigger teams, more sales, new markets. But scaling starts with you, the owner, not the company.

In April 2017, I was in the worst shape of my life, drinking too much, smoking too much, and carrying weight I didn't want. I didn't have the energy or focus to lead anything. So, I made a choice, up at 6:00 a.m., gym every morning for an hour. I listened to audiobooks and podcasts while training, what Tony Robbins calls NET time (No Extra Time).

That one decision changed everything. I gained discipline, energy, and mental clarity. And I made it a rule, if I wasn't healthy and sharp, the business couldn't be either.

The second part of Scale was alignment. In 2018, Becki and I sat at the kitchen table and mapped out a 10-year plan together. We agreed exactly where we wanted to be, financially, personally, as a family, by the time I turned 50. That alignment meant no more friction between home and business. If I needed to travel for work, she knew why. If she wanted more time for her horse, I encouraged it. We supported each other's goals while chasing shared ones.

From that point, my businesses exploded in growth, £100,000 to £500,000, then £1m, £2m, £4m, £8m+. And it all started with personal health, learning, and relationship alignment.

Gear 2: Structure

Structure is the foundation of a scalable business. Without it, you are the bottleneck. Every decision waits for you. Every small issue becomes your problem. That's why most businesses stall somewhere between £750k and £2m, they can't grow without exhausting the owner.

Structure means clarity: a vision, a mission, values, and a plan & budget that allow the team to act without you. When those four are in place, the business no longer depends on your constant presence.

When we invested in a warehousing business, the owner was burnt out, and the company was sliding backwards. We put in the Four Ps:

Product – make sure it was right for the audience.
Polaris – set a clear North Star (vision).
People – right people in the right seats.
Plan – a detailed roadmap to hit targets

Within 12 months, the business doubled, and the owner got his freedom back.

Gear 3: Systems

Systems turn your wins into repeatable processes. Without them, you're on the "good month, bad month" rollercoaster, some months booming, others scrambling to plug holes.

I break the systems into four stages:

1. **Awareness** – generating consistent leads.
2. **Close** – converting them into customers.
3. **Delivery** – fulfilling exactly what you promised.
4. **Consistency** – doing it at the same high standard every time.

We documented every process in the business, refined it, and trained the team until they could deliver without me. Systems stopped the leaks, stabilised revenue, and made growth sustainable.

Gear 4: Stability

Stability means profitability and cash flow strong enough to fund growth and reward you as the owner. Without it, you're always on the edge, scrambling for payroll, late on supplier payments, stuck in survival mode.

I use S.C.A.R:

Systems & Software – track and automate finances.
Cash Flow Forecast – predict inflows/outflows.
Actuals – know the real numbers.
Reporting – act fast when things slip.

In one acquisition, we paused unnecessary payments, renegotiated terms, reduced debtor days, and increased prices. Two months later, £300k extra profit was in the bank, and the valuation jumped nearly £1m in a year.

Gear 5: Soar

Synchronise is the bird's-eye view, seeing exactly what's happening across the business in real time.

Forget 3,000 metrics. You need six, tracked weekly:

1. Satisfaction/NPS.
2. Leads.
3. Conversion rate.
4. On-time/in-full delivery.
5. Churn.
6. Margin.

Colour code them: red, amber, green. If it's red, fix it now. If it's amber, monitor. If it's green, keep going.

Once all five gears turn together, the transformation is undeniable. When we bought Expandly in 2023, a software company doing £250k a year and losing £10k a month, we ran **STEMS®** through it. In 12 months, it hit £2.5m turnover with a 16% profit margin.

When we invested in a warehouse fulfilment company doing £600k, it jumped to £1.3m in nine months.

The formula works because it was built in the trenches, tested on my own companies before being applied to others.

Extraction changes everything.

From an investor's perspective, a business that runs without its owner is worth far more. If a company does £1m turnover and £200k profit with no owner involvement, the owner's salary is added back into profit. On a 4× multiple, that's a £1.2m valuation.

But if you're still inside it, a buyer has to replace you, lowering the multiple and slashing the value, sometimes by hundreds of thousands. Even if you never plan to sell, extraction gives you what you started for: freedom, choice, and the ability to build wealth without burning out.

STEMS® is that gearbox. If one gear jams, the engine struggles. But when all five turn smoothly, the business runs faster, cleaner, and gets you where you want to go without breaking you in the process.

I built **STEMS®** to save myself. Now, it's the framework I use to save others from the same trap.

You don't have to live in your business. You can lead it from above. You just need the right gears turning.

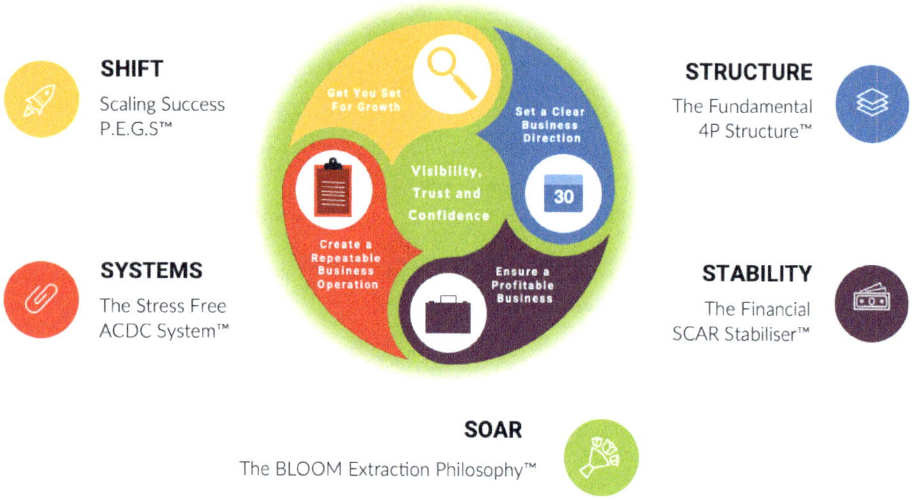
SHIFT
Scaling Success P.E.G.S™
SYSTEMS
The Stress Free ACDC System™
Get You Set For Growth
Set a Clear Business Direction
Visibility, Trust and Confidence
30
Create a Repeatable Business Operation
Ensure a Profitable Business
STRUCTURE
The Fundamental 4P Structure™
STABILITY
The Financial SCAR Stabiliser™
SOAR
The BLOOM Extraction Philosophy™

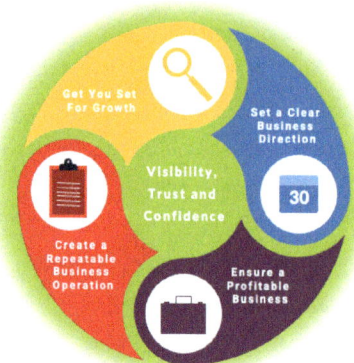

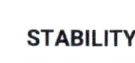

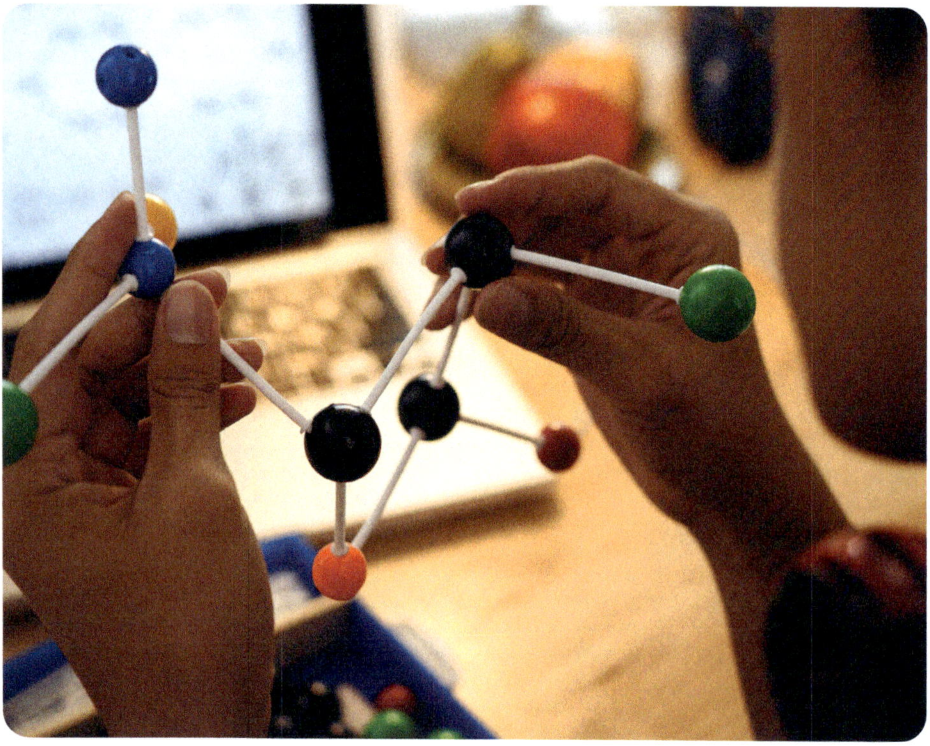

Andy Hooper – Investor, Entrepreneur & Global Expansion Strategist

Andy Hooper is an accomplished investor, entrepreneur, and international speaker, specialising in scaling e-commerce businesses and service providers into globally successful enterprises. With nearly two decades of experience in business development, consultancy, and coaching, he has built a reputation for turning ambitious ideas into scalable, sustainable, and internationally competitive companies.

As CEO of **Expandly,** Andy is on a mission to make international expansion simple and frictionless for e-commerce brands. Many entrepreneurs hit a ceiling when scaling globally, facing compliance hurdles, fragmented service providers, and limited infrastructure. Expandly removes these barriers by delivering the software, systems, and expertise needed to expand at the click of a button, guided by Andy's proprietary **Global Expansion Pathway®.**

Through GEE Capital, Andy also acquires and invests in e-commerce service providers and B2B businesses, building the ecosystem that supports global growth. By strategically combining technology, infrastructure, and specialist services, GEE Capital enables brands to scale confidently across borders.

Andy is the creator of the **STEMS®** framework, a proven methodology for building businesses that grow sustainably, attract investment, and allow founders to step back from daily operations without risk. Alongside **STEMS®,** his **OATS™** and **GEP™** models provide practical, results-driven tools for entrepreneurs looking to scale, systemise, and succeed internationally. These frameworks underpin both his acquisitions and Expandly's growth programmes.

For more than a decade, Andy has also inspired audiences as a motivational speaker. His talks blend personal development principles with real-world business experience, empowering individuals and teams to set bold goals and achieve their full potential. His approach is practical, outcome-focused, and rooted in the belief that the right mindset and strategy unlock limitless growth.

Passionate about supporting SMEs and emerging brands, Andy is dedicated to helping entrepreneurs break through barriers and access new opportunities. Whether guiding a founder through global market entry, designing operations for scalability, or preparing a business for acquisition, his focus is always on creating long-term success.

Outside of business, Andy is an avid adventurer on the water, sailing, windsurfing, or wing foiling, channelling the same energy and determination that fuel his professional journey.
Speaking Engagements:

Andy is a regular speaker at events including The Harbour Club, Hampshire Business Show, White Label Expo, and Payoneer Global (China), among others.

Scan the QR code for More!

CHAPTER 14
THE COST OF SOMEONE ELSE'S DREAM

> "I dance where I was once caged – turning pain into fire, and fire into freedom"
>
> - Krasimira Raykova

Childhood in Grey

What happens when someone tells you how to live?

And what does it cost you...when you listen?

I am eight years old, standing barefoot on the parquet floor in my bedroom in Pazardzhik, Bulgaria. The buildings around are concrete, square, one of many stamped across the town like copy-paste boxes from a ruler's plan. The stairwell smells of damp wool and boiled cabbage, voices always low, cautious, as though words themselves might be dangerous if spoken too loudly.

Outside, winter hangs heavy. Coal smoke snakes through the cracked window, clinging to the curtains. Everything is grey - the streets, the sky, the buildings, the silence.

But inside me? Inside me, there is colour.

I tie a sheet around my waist, spin in front of the cracked mirror, and imagine myself on stage under a blaze of light. In my mind, my skirt isn't white cotton but molten fire, reds, golds, oranges. My bare feet strike rhythms the walls of this country cannot contain.

From the kitchen, my mother's voice pierces the fantasy: "Krasimira! Don't be late for school!" I twirl once more, pretending not to hear. For a few stolen minutes, I can be free.

The music I imagine isn't mine; it's the music my father plays when the curtains are drawn tight. In secret, in shadows. My parents are the best dancing couple in town. When they move together, the air itself seems to pause and watch. My father's hand firm on my mother's back, her smile radiant as he spins her, her laughter light enough to melt the frost from the windows.

Changemakers

One evening, I sit cross-legged on the floor, watching them practice. I blurt out: "When I grow up, I want to dance just like you."

My father kneels, presses his forehead to mine, and whispers, "Better than us, princess. You'll be free."

But here, in communist Bulgaria, freedom is dangerous.

The Knock

The danger arrives one spring morning. The sound is not a knock but fists – relentless, pounding, rattling the door in its frame. My stomach plunges.

My mother freezes mid-step, then quickly masks her fear. She opens the door to two men in long dark coats. Their presence sucks the warmth from the hallway.

"You're coming with us," one says.

"For what?" my father asks. His voice is steady, but his jaw tightens.

The answer is delivered without emotion, as though read from stone, "Dancing to American music. Wearing Western clothes."

They lead him away.

I press my face against the cold glass of the window, watching the car disappear. My mother's trembling hand grips my shoulder as though to hold both of us upright.

Eight months later, he returns thinner, quieter, his eyes shadowed. The music in our house becomes no more than a whisper.
And the rules change.

"Don't dream too much, it only makes life harder" my mother warns while folding laundry.

"Be strong. Be useful" my father adds, staring into his tea.

And then, the sharpest cut of all, "Never trust a man. All men are the same."

I nod, obedient. But inside, the little girl who wanted to dance curls up and hides. From that day on, I become the girl who excels at school, who never causes trouble, who is useful. Even when I turned sixteen our married neighbour pretends to be one of my father's best friends and tried to rape me…I defended myself and kept it quiet….but I still remember that corner in my bedroom and his smelly breath of cigarettes and alcohol.

At nineteen, I marry at a ridiculously young age, not out of love, but out of duty. "That's what good girls do" my mother insists, and I so desperately wanted to be good.

I begin to pour myself into duty, into survival, into proving I'm enough.

Libya: A Cinematic Fear

This was a time when my hunger for survival almost cost me my freedom. At twenty-seven, working abroad to support my family, sending money home across borders, often through jobs that blurred the lines of legality. My son was only 6 months old when I began work illegally in Cyprus, behind a bar. Hearing the word "Police" I had two choices, to hide in the toilet or run out through the back door.

Then Tripoli, Libya. "Sukra Private Hospital" as a register nurse. My days are long, wrapped in long sleeves and skirts, adapting to a culture so far from my own. My passport locked with the Manager of the Hospital. Then one afternoon, a limousine with tinted windows pulls up outside. A man and woman step out and point directly at me.

"Come."

Changemakers

"Why?" I ask, my heart already hammering.

The woman replies softly: "We are taking you to a special hospital." But when the gates open, I realise where I am, the palace. Tanks. Rifles. Soldiers.

We are searched by towering female bodyguards, then ushered into a cold, sterile room. Seven women. Waiting. Knowing.

And then, he enters. Muammar Gaddafi.

Tall. Slim. In a tracksuit. Eyes like black ice. He stops in front of me. "What is your name?"

Then, without pause, "You will work for me and my family as a nurse." I shiver, but my voice stays steady. "That is impossible. My son is with me here."

He moves on, but later the conditions arrive like shackles, "If you work for me, you cannot go to parties. You cannot speak of what you see. If I call at one in the morning, you must be ready within thirty minutes. Can you imagine? Me, wild, untamed, aching to dance, caged in a palace of control.

That day, we were fed and sent back to the hospital as if nothing had happened. But everything had.

Two months later, after my son's school year ended, we returned to Bulgaria, and I quickly divorced my husband. He took half of my money, the rest I gave to my parents. Because sometimes the most powerful thing a woman can do is say no to control, and yes to freedom. I packed a suitcase, a few clothes, some photographs, and guilt so heavy my hands shake. With £80 in my pocket, I board a plane to the UK.

Survival in a New World

"Start over. Work hard. Don't look back," I whisper to myself as the plane descends.

The first year's blur into exhaustion. Double shifts in hospitals until my feet swell, my back aches, my bones hum with fatigue. My English is clumsy, so I scribble words on scraps of paper between patients.

I am nobody here. Invisible. But invisibility has its advantages, it teaches you to watch, to listen, to learn.

Slowly, brick by brick, I build. I study property contracts late into the night, risk what little I have, and reinvest.

Twenty-three years later, I own properties across the UK and Europe, all mortgage-free. I have money, status, independence.

And yet, inside, I am starving.

The Silent Weight of Motherhood

There is one truth I have carried like a stone in my chest; heavier than all the suitcases I dragged from country to country. My son from my first marriage, a gentle boy with eyes like mine and the only child I have.

When I left his father, I also left the only version of motherhood I knew. Not because I didn't love him, my God, I loved him, but because I had nothing left to give.

His father, wounded and bitter, sharpened his pain into lies: "Your mother abandoned you. She doesn't love you. You don't need her." My son never repeated these words to me, but I saw them written across his face. In the way he averted his eyes. In the distance that grew between us like a wall I couldn't climb.

Changemakers

At night, lying alone, the questions pressed down like stones. Am I a bad mother? Will he ever understand? Did I destroy the one thing that mattered most?

And yet, another voice whispered softly: You cannot mother from emptiness. You had to leave to save yourself. One day, he will see that.

Still, guilt became my constant companion. No matter how much success I built, it curled up beside me in the dark.

A Mirror That Looked Like a Stranger

By the time my second marriage ended, my heart was already weary. Malcolm and I hadn't fought in any dramatic way, we had simply drifted, the space between us widening until it felt unbridgeable.

One night, I poured a glass of wine and stared at my reflection in the darkened window. The woman staring back was strong. Independent. Successful. And yet her eyes were strangers to me.

"What if this isn't freedom?" I whispered to the glass. "What if I have built another cage, only prettier this time?"

I had money, properties, independence. But joy? Connection? Love? They were as absent as the music my father once played in secret.

The Call of the Dance

It happened on an ordinary night, scrolling without purpose, that I saw it, FEMININITY RETREAT – MALDIVES.

The words pulled at me like a tide. Before my mind could argue, my finger clicked Book Now.

When I stepped off the plane weeks later, the air wrapped around me like silk. The ocean shimmered in impossible shades of blue, the sun spilling gold over everything it touched.

For the first time in years, I felt the possibility of warmth not just on my skin, but inside me.

The women who greeted me didn't ask, "What do you do?" Instead, they asked, "How do you feel?" The question caught in my throat. I didn't know how to answer.

That night, we gathered barefoot under the stars. No mirrors. No phones. Just the pulse of waves and the heartbeat of a drum.

The facilitator's voice washed over us: "Let your hips tell the truth your voice has silenced. Let your body become your home again. It is safe now. You don't have to perform. You just have to feel."

At first, my movements were awkward, my steps small. But then, something loosened. My hips began to sway. My arms rose. My feet pressed into the earth with a rhythm my mind had long forgotten.

And then the tears came. Hot. Unstoppable.

I cried for the little girl in Bulgaria who was told not to dream.

I cried for the mother who left to survive.

I cried for the woman who mistook hardness for strength.

Through tantra rituals, kundalini awakenings, and sacred dance, I shed layer after layer of armour. Each movement was a reclamation. Each breath a return.

"You don't have to be hard to be strong," the facilitator whispered. "Your softness is your superpower."

For the first time in my life, I believed it. I wasn't just healing.
I was being reborn.

Love, Revisited

When I returned home, I felt different in my very bones. The guilt that had always sat on my chest had shifted, lighter now, like smoke instead of stone.

On impulse, I picked up the phone.

"Malcolm," I said, "would you like to meet?"

We sat across from one another at a small café. For a moment, neither of us spoke. Then our eyes met, and in that instant, I knew, the love had never truly left. It had simply been buried under the weight of all I hadn't yet healed.

"I don't need to fix you," I told him, voice trembling but steady. "I only need to feel myself. I'm not here to lead. I'm here to love. And I finally love myself enough to be loved."

We began again. Not from need, not from duty, but from alignment. Our love is deeper now. Not perfect, but real.

Claiming My Fire

Today, I am no longer the woman I once was. I am not the frightened child hiding her dreams, nor the woman numbing herself with endless work, nor the stranger staring back from a window's reflection.

I am a certiffied life coach. A kundalini activation facilitator. A guide for women who are ready to return to themselves.

I created my authentic program 'The Radiant Feminine Awakening system.'- a journey designed to awaken sensuality, softness, magnetism, and power. Through sacred dance, tantra rituals, and embodiment practices, I help women lay down their armour, break destructive patterns, and reignite the fire that was never lost, only buried. These six principles are not theory; they are the practices and truths that helped me reclaim my softness, my magnetism, and my joy.

BELIEFS – Rewiring the Feminine Mind

What I see again and again in high-performing women is a familiar pattern: achievement without fulfilment. They are constantly checking boxes and hitting goals, yet still feeling empty, disconnected, and secretly dissatisfied.

In "The Radiant Feminine Awakening" System, I guide them through a ritual tool I call the Purposeful Passion Activator. This practice helps them rewire old mental and emotional patterns, shifting from harsh self-criticism to magnetic confidence, from burnout to joyful discipline. Most importantly, it reconnects them to their inner feminine fire, the source of self-belief and radiance that achievement alone can never give.

BALANCE – Finding Harmony Through Breathwork & Kundalini Activation

The modern businesswoman lives in constant "go, go, go." Cortisol and adrenaline pump through her body for years at a time, creating chronic stress.

In a safe, sacred space, I guide women through The Inner C.A.L.M. Creator, a combination of breathwork and kundalini activation that helps release trauma from childhood and dissolve negative emotions that no longer serve. What emerges is balance, clarity of mind, steadiness of heart, and a nervous system finally allowed to rest.

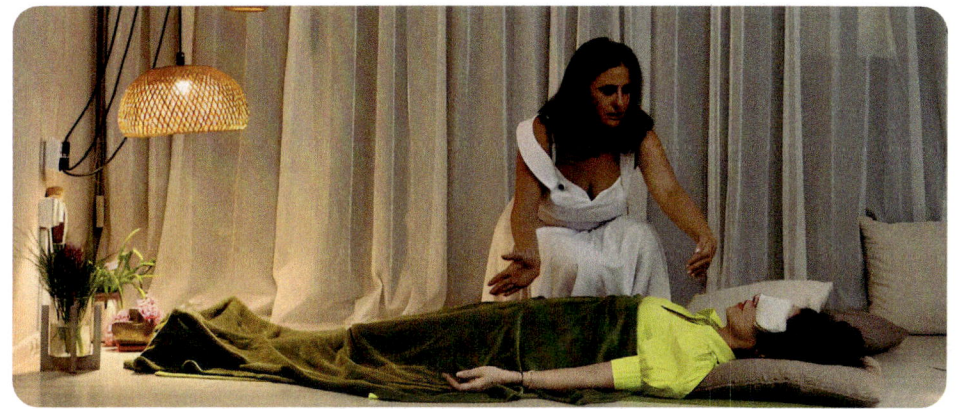

Changemakers

BONDING – Nurturing the Feminine Spirit Through Creativity
Let's be honest, many responsible, high-achieving women have no hobbies outside of their phones and their work. Their lives are efficient, but their spirits are starved.

That's why I created The Magnetic M.U.S.E. Activator. In my retreats, women tap into their creativity in surprising, delightful ways. Whether through painting, writing, crafting, or simple play, they unlock the joy of creating without pressure. Feminine energy is creative energy, and when it flows, a woman becomes magnetic.

BEYOND – Rediscovering Sexuality
Intimacy is one of our deepest human desires, and yet it is also where many women carry the most shame.

Ambitious women often live in logic and responsibility, pushing sensuality aside. Their bodies tighten, their pleasure is suppressed, their libido fades. Through my sacred A.P.H.R.O.D.I.T.E. Attractor Method, I help women release shame around desire and sexuality. With rituals, exercises, and sacred feminine teachings, they awaken pleasure and reclaim confidence in their bodies. They learn that their sensuality is not a weakness, but a divine power.

BEAUTY – Radiance as Success
So many women know how to succeed by doing more, but the next level of success comes not from effort, it comes from radiance.

In The Cleopatra Secrets Code, I teach women to nourish their bodies, embrace ancient beauty rituals, and unlock their natural glow. When they lead from their radiance instead of just their résumé, they become unforgettable. Their presence influences more than their words ever could.

BELOVED – The Mystery of Relationships and Magnetic Communication

Masculine energy often serves women well in business, but in relationships, it can create imbalance. They either attract emotionally unavailable men or find themselves over-giving, over-controlling, and quietly resentful.

In my program, The P.E.R.F.E.C.T. Partnership Protector, women learn how to communicate from their feminine essence and how to choose partners who honour their hearts, not just their achievements. They discover that love flourishes not in competition, but in polarity, when they allow themselves to receive as much as they give.
This is the journey of **The Radiant Feminine Awakening System™,** I know what it feels like to lose yourself. And I know what it takes to find her again.

For me, the cost of living by other people's expectations was devastating. I lost my joy, my softness, my body's wisdom, and the intimacy I craved.

But I also know this, those chains that once silenced my dance became the very fire that set me free.

A Word to You

If you are reading this and you feel exhausted from proving your worth...
If you have been strong for so long that you no longer remember what softness feels like...
If you are starving for love, for freedom, for joy.
Hear me.
You are not broken.
You are simply being called home.

Home to your body.
Home to your rhythm.
Home to your truth.
Home to your feminine fire.

Changemakers

And when you are ready, I will be here.
With open arms.
And a drumbeat to guide your dance home.

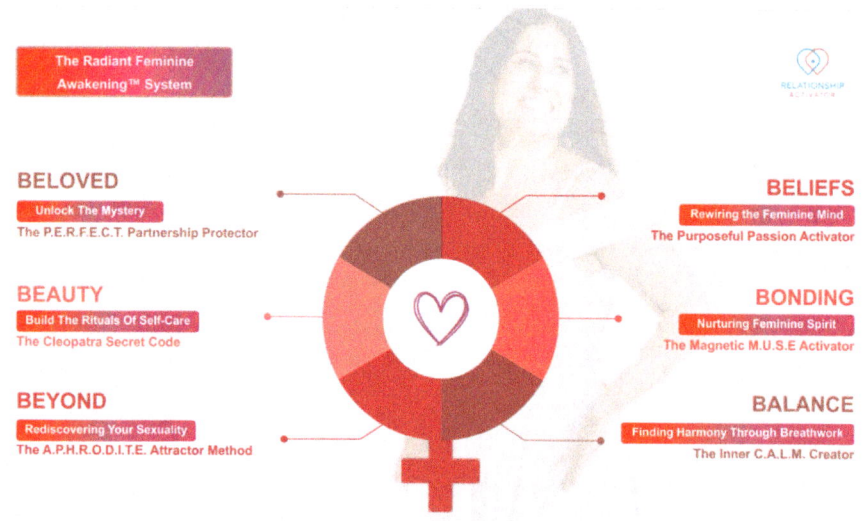

Krasimira Raykova is an author, speaker, coach, family therapist, registered nurse, and the CEO and founder of **The Radiant Feminine Awakening™ System.** Her mission is to guide ambitious women in releasing the armour of achievement and awaken their softness, radiance, and magnetic feminine power through retreats, workshops, and coaching. With extensive experience, including 70-hour weeks on the COVID frontline and managing successful property businesses in the UK and Bulgaria, she blends deep care with strength and vision. Her own awakening began at a retreat in the Maldives.

Krasimira enjoys traveling, dancing, sun-soaked days by the sea, and soulful connections in nature, and is also a loving wife and mother.

Scan the QR code for More!

CHANGE MAKERS

ENTREPRENEURS WITH A MISSION
VOICES WITH A MESSAGE

THE PROFESSIONAL SPEAKERS ACADEMY UNLEASHING 17 VOICES, 17 JOURNEYS.

ONE RIPPLE EFFECT THAT WILL TRANSFORM YOUR LIFE & BUSINESS.

CHAPTER 15
A JOURNEY INTO WHOLENESS

STEPPING FORWARD WITH GRIT, GRATITUDE, AND GRACE

> "It all begins with a single choice: to choose yourself and keep going, one step at a time."
>
> - Sheetal Radia

"You have Multiple Sclerosis."

Four words that change my life forever.

Have you ever felt like your world has been turned upside down? Just like that. No obvious warning. And you know that when the pieces are put back together life will never be same.

That was me. June 2004. Walking out of Clementine Churchill Hospital. Blindsided. Speechless. A blameless clear blue sky sailing above. The air hanging heavy with a myriad of unanswerable questions for what lay ahead.

I know exactly what MS is. It has taken a close friend into a wheelchair overnight.
"What is it going to do to me? How is it going it affect my family? What about my children, what are their chances of getting it in the future? Will I be able to continue working? How long will I be able to walk?"

The gift of being diagnosed with an incurable neurological disease that is progressively disabling. One that affects the brain and myelin sheath, the covering which protects nerves along the spinal cord. No exact causes. No definite remedies. And no way of knowing exactly what will happen in between. A game of waiting and watching. Living with uncertainty is one of the hardest things to do. Living with threatening uncertainty is even harder.

Disease Modifying Drugs are offered with the caveat that at best they lengthen the time between relapses; aren't effective for everyone; the body acclimatises to them after which another is sought, and they all come with inherent side effects. For me, it seems like Russian roulette. Too many unknowns along a downhill slope.

For the next few months, I'm not ready to tell anyone; my friends, my family, my parents. I don't want to worry them; I don't want to be labelled, and I don't want to be treated differently. I want things to stay the same. Except on the inside, everything has changed.

Changemakers

My children are young. The one thing I do know is 'waiting and watching' isn't my game.

So, I hit the internet, and I am led to a book, MS a self-help guide by Judy Graham and in it I find Dr Kingsley. A GP well ahead of his time who has helped thousands of patients with MS, cancer and numerous chronic conditions recover with his holistic approach of treating the person not the illness. His advice being 'take away the bad things, add the good things and keep life in balance.' So that's what I do. Eat well, sleep well and travel to him for monthly intravenous infusions of vitamins and minerals. It works, the symptoms subside but here's the problem, a couple of years in he retires and I fall out of the routine of really taking care of myself. With a few dietary modifications I brazenly continue with my life. The times I overdo it I feel the repercussions. I rest and do nothing until they pass. My approach is working, or so I think.

I dive into my professional role as an architect and seize an exciting project. For six whole months I live, breathe and sleep it and to be honest it takes me away from keeping any balance in my life. I love what I am doing. My body does not. The signs are not outwardly apparent; they are simmering underneath.

It is August 2016. The project is complete with fantastic results, and I am flying high. I've booked a fancy lunch to celebrate with my family and as we walk towards the restaurant my left leg starts doing this strange puppet swing. With each step my foot starts to scuff the ground and just like that I nose-dive down to a super low. All over again.

This is downward progression. Not something I can ignore and if I do, I will be making my way into a wheelchair. My choices are clear, continue and let my mobility decline or I can do whatever it takes to keep on walking.

Denial, delay and distraction carry a heavy price tag when living with a chronic health issue.

It is 10pm in the evening. Everyone has gone to bed. The house is silent. I sit in my lounge in the dark. My heart heavy with fear. An endless stream of calculations whirring through my fragile mind. I know I have to dig deep. I have two beautiful teenagers. If not for me, I must do everything in my power to stay well for them. I want to dance at their celebrations.

I scroll endlessly on my phone searching for solutions and flickers of light start to appear.

Like striking a match in a dark place, hope springs up from books. In 'Recovering from MS' by George Jelinek and Karen Law. I find real life stories of hope and inspiration of others who, with the same condition at a similar stage, have ventured beyond the beliefs and boundaries of the Western medical model to recover some, if not all, of their health.

If they can do it, then so can I.

Time to go back to the drawing board; to live breathe and sleep the model of Holistic Health; this time to empower myself with courage and consistency.

Have you ever considered what empowerment really is? Is it something you are born with? Or is it something you develop over time?

Changemakers

And what is the model of Holistic Health?

Traditionally associated with Eastern philosophy, it works on the principle of salutogenesis; building on our capacity to move beyond disease focus and cultivate human flourishing. By exploring the underlying causes not the symptoms; by treating the whole person instead of individual parts. In contrast, the Western model of healthcare is pathogenesis; the focus on managing disease symptoms, fixing parts and pieces of the system relying on pharmaceutical or surgical interventions.

Should you give your power away or hold it, nurture it and use it to change your life?

I chose to do the latter and the more sustained work of peeling back my layers began.

I surrounded myself with those on the same mission as me and became a mentor on a Recover from MS Naturally group, a community of people determined not to hand their health over to chance. We shared knowledge and celebrated every little win along the way; a collection of ordinary people quietly doing extraordinary things.

I trained to become a Scaravelli inspired yoga teacher. The focus being on working with the body and not against it; working through it rather than imposing preconceived ideal positions on to it. I am inspired to teach yoga as a way into the body; to guide my students to become aware of their ability to undo habits, remap movement patterns and empower themselves with inner awareness to respond to rather than react to life situations.

My real love is in exploring what lies beneath the surface to understand the connections between mind, body and spirit. So, my training went further and deeper to qualify as a professional yoga therapist. Yoga therapy is an emerging modality in the field of lifestyle medicine. Its focus is on a bio-psycho-social-spiritual model; on the basis that individuals are composed of different energetic layers – physical, mental, emotional, and spiritual, living together in community. It is a personalised therapeutic somatic process. A session is co-creative in nature, and its intention is to bring more coherence to the individual's energetic field by releasing restrictions held within and integrating any arising wisdom into their lives.

We are bound by layers of conditioning influenced by the culture we are born into, families who bring us up, our peers and the environment we inhabit. Our stories are woven into the fabric of our tissues. Our bodies are our biographies. The issues are held in this weave. Everything we put into our system affects us, whether it is food, drugs, relationships, thoughts, love or fear. Every choice we make has a consequence. There is no escaping that truth.

Disengaging from running on autopilot is a challenge for most people. It is easier to respond to the external stimuli picked up with our five senses. If we listen and pay close attention to the emotions, feelings and sensations that arise within us, we will find that our bodies are always talking to us. Issues arise when what may start as a whisper, ignored enough times turns into a roar, by which time the person is usually in a crisis and cannot ignore what their body has been trying to alert them to.

Our bodies are the containers. The breath is the medium between inner and outer worlds. As we enter the world, the first inhalation animates us. The last exhalation carries us away. And in between our lives consist of a series of breaths. A series of choices. A series of subsequent experiences. Every single day.

Alongside my thirst for knowledge, my daily efforts to recover continue. I have read countless books and have engaged in varied alternative therapies from homeopathy to hyperbaric oxygen; made changes in diet and have supplemented with high doses of Vitamin D; made lifestyle shifts from body brushing to brisk walks in the dawn light, chiropractic adjustments to cold water showers, resting and releasing toxic relationships, lots of meditation and movement daily whilst tracking my steps like a Fit Bit Ninja.

Every action and interaction has played its part in being where I am today. But here's the thing, nothing changes until you change. To truly recover and heal I have had to change from the inside out; rewire new circuits and shed layers of old patterning to shine my own light, whilst having complete faith in the innate intelligence that weaves in and around us. Every single breath of the way.

It has been an undulating path interspersed with extreme highs and lows. Light filled days when you witness an inch of progress; those extreme moments of joy when you feel like nothing is impossible. And dark days of despair that are an uphill journey. Times when the ascent feels so steep that all you want to do is stay stationary and do nothing. But when it's the hardest, it matters the most. That's the time to go in, to go slow and gather the reserves. To wake up the next day and start all over again in putting up a good effort to rebalance all that is out of kilter.

At times like this, surrounding myself with a kindred community has been an essential source of support. I have participated in numerous powerful workshops and retreats both in the UK and abroad. Time spent in these has been priceless. Whilst teachers have shared their evolved wisdom, the magic has come from the shared connection in community. When like-minded people retreat from their everyday routines and environment to come together with an intention of being rooted in deeper presence with each other, something truly mystical happens. People change people. We are doing it all the time.

There is a continual energetic crossing not only between the boundaries of our own internal layers but also those of others. Our energetic bodies are always talking to each other without even saying a word.

We are all the same, yet everyone is different with unique challenges and obstacles in their path. We are all journeying together, emitting individual ripples out into the world. Each affecting the other, yet evolving at our own pace. In this way we can influence but we cannot change the other. The work of inner change can only be undertaken by oneself.

In the final count, you are the only one living with yourself twenty-four hours a day, every single day. Nobody is coming to save you; nobody really has the power. Except yourself.

It all begins with a single choice: to choose yourself and keep going one step at a time.

Or in my case 3300 steps.

It is October 2023. 5am on my birthday.
We are some 3210 km above sea level.

2 days, 3300 stone steps and 25km later, I am standing ridiculously happy at the top of Poon Hill in Nepal. My children, adults now, are beaming at me with pride. My husband is radiating relief we all made it safely to the top. Trekking together along undulating peaks and valleys through sun, wind and rain hasn't been easy but every step taking us higher and higher has been completely worth it.

It is dark. The air is crisp. A crack appears in the clouds and golden light pours through to reveal the majestic Himalayan mountains. I am on top of the world, inside and out. In that humbling breathtaking moment, I am filled with nothing but love, joy and gratitude for being alive. I am also shown that ANYTHING is possible if you make a CHOICE to reach for it.

This is my journey of how little by little, through non-conventional routes, I am rebalancing my health and have achieved goals not thought possible. My walking challenges are not over, and neither is my persistence to overcome them. I am proud to share that I am not in a wheelchair. Instead, I have climbed mountains. Real and imagined.

Changemakers

Now I am passionate about helping people climb their own mountains. Whether literal or metaphorical, each one of us has a summit to reach.

We all have the potential to heal and outlive expectations if we are willing to become proactive experts and participants in our own health. To this end, it is with joy and purpose I share **The Intelligent Holistic Health Blueprint ™,** my compilation of six key areas to empower, change and evolve from the inside out. For professionals, business owners and executives, this programme, a combination of knowledge and practice, has been created for you to enhance your chronic health recovery and unravel the layers wrapped around yourselves to reveal your true brilliance.

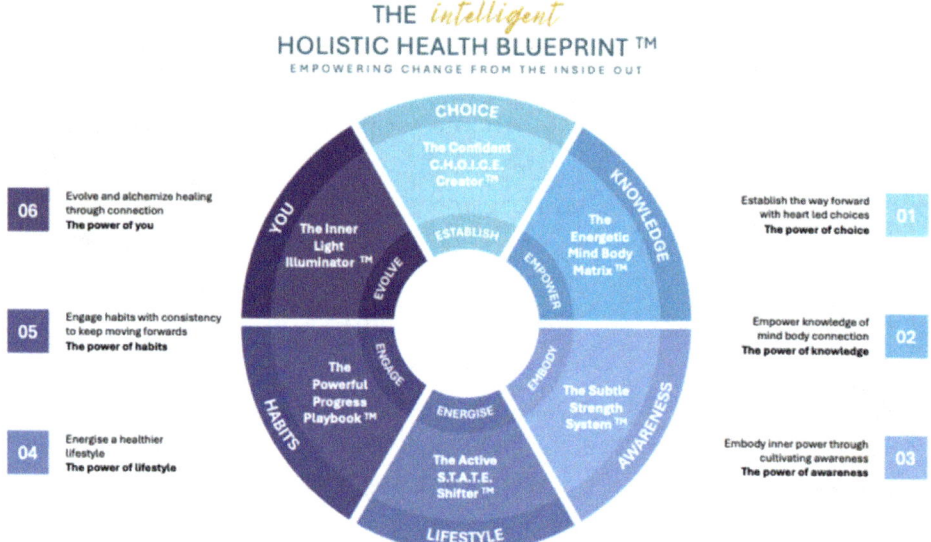

i. The power of choice

The fundamental starting point is understanding the power of choice. The Confident Choice Creator establishes the foundation and direction going forward with heart led choices.

ii. The power of knowledge
The Energetic Mind Body Matrix provides an understanding of the mind-body connections. Being empowered with this knowledge enables us to make full use of the resources within and increases motivation to apply action.

iii. The power of awareness
Awareness is the greatest catalyst for change. The Subtle Strength System provides key insights and practices to tune in to the body and make shifts within the internal landscape, to rebalance power and embody inner strength, rebalancing the nervous system.

iv, The power of lifestyle
The Active State Shifter gives an understanding of what is happening in the body in 5 key lifestyle areas. It provides information on changes which will energise lifestyle to take health forward in a positive direction.

v. The power of habits
The Powerful Progress Playbook provides tools to evaluate and engage consistently to keep moving forward. Consistency is the key to long lasting change. Once habits are rewired and the benefits become evident then motivation kicks in, sustaining momentum to propel us on our path of evolving and healing.

vi. The power of you
The focus of this final key area is on the social and spiritual aspects that make us whole. The Inner Light Illuminator provides key steps and practices for individuals to evolve and connect with themselves, with others and with the loving intelligence weaving in and around us. At the heart of it, it is this connection that is our true superpower and the alchemy to healing.

We are in constant relationship. With ourselves. With others. And with something beyond.

Changemakers

So why is now the right time to become a proactive expert in your own health?

Never has there been a time when information has been so rapidly available to us at the touch of a button. This knowledge is revealing to us that the world behind our eyes and under our skin is where our real power lies. So, it would be prudent to learn how the brain works, how the body functions, and how ultimately you can positively influence your own health journey.

Given what is happening in relation to the rise of chronic health conditions, the emerging model of holistic and lifestyle medicine has never been so important. Current data from the World Health Organisation indicates that chronic diseases are the major cause of death accounting for 75% of all deaths worldwide. That's a staggering 7 out of 10 people and the projections are rising. It is incredibly important to act now and do what you can to help yourself not get swept into this tide of statistics.

The old way of doing things is no longer working. There are growing communities worldwide who are engaging in holistic ways of rebalancing their health. Who are realising there is another way. It is no longer hippie or trendy. And alongside it, there is a growing body of scientific theory and evidence that is recognising that we are more than a system of parts. We are whole. It is a pivotal time in history where Western knowledge is merging with centuries of Eastern traditions and wisdom; where science is meeting spirituality. We are in the privileged position of being able to use the fusion of this knowledge, take action to put the wheels in motion and empower ourselves to become the pro-active expert engines in our lives to drive our own health forward.

Why is taking action now crucial? **If not now, when?**

Sheetal Radia is a yoga teacher (BWY), yoga therapist (B-CYT) and creator of **The Intelligent Holistic Health Blueprint.™**

As a Holistic Health and Transformation Coach, she empowers professionals, business owners and executives with chronic health issues to create change from the inside out. The knowledge and service she offers comes through her personal journey of transformation. After a diagnosis of Multiple Sclerosis in 2004, she has kept her health in balance holistically and has achieved goals not thought possible. Her story is a testament of hope, faith and resilience.

Sheetal is a proud mother of two and lives in the UK with a beautiful network of family and friends.

Scan the QR code for More!

CHAPTER 16
THE ART OF SIMPLIFIED SCALING

HOW TO TURN A GOOD BUSINESS INTO A GREAT ONE: SCALABLE, VALUABLE, AND READY FOR THE FUTURE YOU WANT TO CREATE.

> "On the brink of collapse, I discovered a system that saved my business— and my life. And has since helped thousands of entrepreneurs build stronger, lighter, more valuable companies."
>
> — Sander Klos

The one and only question

The city fell silent around us. It was a late spring evening in Amsterdam, years before the word 'scaling' became fashionable, the air still carrying a trace of chill before summer arrived. I sat across from Brian Tracy on a low boat drifting through the canals. Evening light spilled molten over the surface, burnishing it gold. Glasses chimed; bicycles rattled on distant bridges. The tall houses leaned in, crooked and curious, as if the city itself strained to overhear.

I looked at him. A man whose books had sold millions, whose voice had filled conference halls across the globe. Now just the two of us, with one chance for a question. The question weighed like a coin in my palm. "Brian", I asked, careful not to waste the moment, "what is the number one source of happiness?"

His answer came with the calm of a man who had lived his words. He leaned back, eyes steady, and said softly, "That is an easy question. Of all the things people chase, only one prevails, peace of mind."

The words landed with surprising force. Perhaps because I was trained as a computer scientist, taught to reduce the world to logic, to debug reality as if life were a faulty code. Yet here was something no algorithm could fix. Peace of mind. I almost smiled at the disarming simplicity of it. Later, as I spoke with entrepreneurs across industries and continents, I began to see what he meant. Different challenges, different ambitions – yet beneath it all, the same restlessness. Not the lack of money. Not even the lack of growth. But the absence of peace of mind. The gnawing sense that the business owned them, not the other way around.
So let me turn to you directly. You have built something with your own hands. Hustled through long nights. Carried the weight of responsibility. You should be proud.

But does it give you peace of mind?

Because success is not working yourself raw while your family eats dinner without you. It is not being chained to a desk while life goes on elsewhere. Success is freedom. Impact. Legacy. A business that works harder than you do, so you can live on your own terms.

And if you are honest. Is that not what you truly want? A company that fuels you instead of draining you. A business that grows, scales, thrives, yet still leaves you time to breathe, to love, to live.

One path to that peace is Simplified Scaling, embodied in the 5FortyFive Growth System. Because happiness is not a destination. It is the silence between two sentences. The breath you take without needing to prove you matter. Because you already do.

And if peace of mind is the true measure of success, then it is worth asking, "where are you now?"

Carrying silent weight

Maybe you wake in a house you built yourself and instead of pride you feel the walls closing in. The rooms echo with unfinished tasks. The very thing meant to set you free now keeps you bound from dawn until long after midnight.

Cash flow pulls like a riptide, silent until it drags you under. Invoices stall, margins thin, and each new month feels like a gamble played with your sleep.

But worse than the numbers is the fog. Without a clear plan, every decision feels improvised. You move forward, but some part of you suspects the road is folding back on itself. You wake wondering if you are circling the same ground.

And then there is the sting of comparison. Competitors in the same market lift off like kites in a summer breeze, their growth seemingly effortless, while you drag a piano uphill in the rain. You wonder if they know a path you somehow missed.

Changemakers

Now picture something else. A business that runs like clockwork, breathing on its own. Calm at the centre because everything flows. A company no longer tethered to your pulse, moving to its own rhythm, delivering results you can trust.

See a client base that not only stays but thrives. Customers who praise your work, who speak of you with pride, who know you create real impact.

Watch profits steady and reserves grow. Cash no longer evaporating in thin margins but gathering into choices. Choices to invest in real estate, to protect your family, to scale on your terms.

And imagine the hidden dividend. The day you decide to sell. Not because you must, but because you can. Because you have built something that stands without you. A business lighter to lead and worth more precisely because it breathes on its own.

Beyond the numbers lies something deeper. Peace of mind. The certainty that your business lives even when you step away. That you can lead without being needed, rest without guilt, and live without chasing every detail.

Changemakers

Do not build on effort. Build on a system. Lay structure beneath what is now instinct, your customer journey, your profit model, your team, your brand. That is where breathing space begins. To accelerate what works and to complete what is missing. That is what the 5FortyFive Growth System makes possible.

I know the weight because I have carried it myself. And one spring morning, it nearly ended me.

He studied me with professional detachment. "Stop, and maybe you live. Refuse, and you die." Then he turned and left, as if my life were a file to be closed.

The doctor's words pressed down without mercy, heavy and shapeless. For a moment the room seemed to tilt, as if the bed and I were sliding toward an edge. Not panic. Something quieter. Shame. A muted guilt, like being caught cheating on a test you wrote yourself. I had just made a big investment. Twelve people on payroll. A launch ahead. Everything lined up. And suddenly I realised, I was not the hero anymore.
I was the liability.

Walks by the Amstel. Books I picked up and put down. Podcasts I did not hear. The laptop stayed close, like a dog I did not trust off the leash. Silent. Watching. Like me.

One morning I met Oswald. Linen shirt, sunglasses, glass of wine as if time itself were optional. A serial exit entrepreneur, informal board advisor, early investor in IENS, and by then a good friend. He studied me as if weighing how much of me was still left.

"You need to do something", he said at last. Not advice. A mirror.
So, I called Jay Abraham, the marketing genius. Not for growth. For air. For survival. His voice over the phone was calm, almost casual, as if quoting a menu. "Twenty-five thousand dollars a month. Plus twenty-five percent of the profit increase." One sheet of paper. A lifeline disguised as a contract.

Together we stripped everything back. Not masterplans, just the basics. A clear client journey, plain and repeatable, something alive that could move even when I could not.

The team resisted. Too American. Too rigid. "Our business is different. Our clients are special." Yet slowly it worked. Clients renewed. Processes aligned. By month seven, sales equalled the first six months combined. Shareholders nodded. One of them said, "How many sales and marketing people fit in the office? Hire them. Scale. Push."

And then one morning I walked in and saw it. The business breathing on its own. A team humming. A rhythm set. No heroics. Just breath. Better than anything I had seen before.

What felt like collapse became the glimpse of something larger, the outline of a system that could carry more than just me.

From doubt to design

That morning by the Amstel was more than recovery. It was the glimpse of a system. A way for a company to breathe without draining its founder.

At first, the idea was dismissed. "Growth is chaos," some said. "You can't box it in." Others smiled politely and shifted the conversation back to hiring or product tweaks. A few laughed. "Systems are theory. Business is blood and sweat."

I knew those voices, they had once been mine. I too believed a growth system could never work. Convinced it would collapse in practice, I tested it on my own business, step by step, determined to expose the flaws. But it held. More than that, it worked better than anything I had seen before. Clients renewed. Processes aligned.
The business began to breathe.

Even academia resisted. A professor once withdrew an internship, insisting a universal, easy-to-apply growth system was theoretically impossible. The ridicule reminded me of Copernicus, scorned for saying the earth moved around the sun. Theory said it was impossible. Practice proved otherwise.

That scepticism taught me something, resistance is not proof you are wrong. It is proof you are onto something that matters.

So, in 2016 I began testing the idea beyond my own walls. One entrepreneur at a time. No grand promises, just the question, would it work for them too? The first results were cautious but real. A consultancy owner who swore municipalities never responded to marketing suddenly saw steady leads. A small retailer who thought he was "too small for structure" finally had his weekends back.

Demand grew. One company became several. Individual sessions turned into groups. And in those groups, I discovered something powerful, entrepreneurs learning as much from each other as from me. What I thought would be a compromise became a multiplier.

That was the birth of Systemising University. Not lectures, not theory, but four days of building, testing, refining, under pressure, with skin in the game.

The work kept evolving. With our members we created the Scaleup Tracker, a tool to project growth and valuation, making the invisible visible. Writing TurboProfit forced me to sharpen it further. Three years of work distilled into a field manual that gave entrepreneurs language for what they already felt: growth could be lighter, clearer, predictable. It became a bestseller and quickly sold out, leading to a second edition.

The simplified scaling system

What began as fragile outlines grew into five strategic movements, refined until they could hold under any pressure. That system became 5FortyFive, a universal growth system for founder-led SMEs that turns instinct into structure, so your company scales without you at the centre. We don't call them commandments or principles, though they hold things up as firmly as any Roman column. They are five strategic movements every business must master to grow with ease and sustain that growth under pressure. Miss one, and growth falters. Use all five, and the system compounds.

Magnetic Market Alignment
Find the market already waiting for you. No shouting. Just resonance.

Unique Brand Magnifier
Your brand is not your logo. It is the gut feeling people carry when you leave the room. This movement clarifies, aligns, and amplifies it.

Magical Marketing Maximiser
Marketing is not begging or noise. Done right, it is flow, the right people arriving at the right moment, ready.

Profitable Business Blueprint
Your model is your silent partner. Shaped well, the frontend pays for the backend and profit replaces stress.

Client Closing Curve
Sales is not manipulation. It is choreography. A calm process that guides clients to choose with confidence.

Together these movements connect to the six growth drivers of every business. As I showed in TurboProfit, raise each by just 10%, more leads, more clients, more sales per client, higher price per sale, more products per sale, longer client lifespan, and your company grows fivefold in three years. One movement helps. Five change the game.

No magic. Just mathematics.

The result is a system that does not rely on your energy, but on structure. A business that works even when you do not.

Systemise. Scale. Succeed. That is the order, and the promise.

Wise-Up!

Inge Willems ran WiseUp from a garden house behind her home. Three team members. Local government clients. Around €600,000 in revenue. The work was solid, but growth felt heavy. Every new hire was a risk, margins stayed thin, and sales dragged.

She had tried programmes before. None had stuck. Her team had grown wary: too theoretical, too commercial, too far from their reality.

Inge herself had a master's degree in Marketing. She knew the theory, yet real growth remained elusive. When I told her about the outcomes of the system, she paused and said, "Then there is only one explanation. This system must truly work." That conviction pulled her across the line. Her team doubted. "Municipalities don't respond to marketing."

"Our sector is different."

"Structure will kill our flexibility." Scaling systems, they agreed, belonged to another world.

But she started anyway. Quietly, step by step. Not with fireworks, but rhythm. Clear journey. Repeatable steps.

At first the doubts remained. But results came. Municipalities responded, not to campaigns, but to structure. Trust grew. Leads steadied. Projects flowed. Even the sceptical team began to lean in.

Next came the backend. Instead of one-off projects, WiseUp designed longer trajectories. Clients stayed for years instead of months. Margins grew. Value increased. What once felt "too commercial" now felt like clarity.

Today, WiseUp resides in a penthouse office. A team of over thirty senior managers and advisors. A client base covering much of the country. With their young professional concept, they built a key instrument for maximising front-end results. Multi-million buy-and-build strategies are now live options, with cash in the bank to fund the next move.

And yet in that penthouse, one meeting room still carries the name The Garden House. A reminder that pleasure and success are not distant dreams, but waiting for every entrepreneur.

When asked for the source of her success, Inge always replies, "I just follow the growth system as intended, without deviating from the roadmap. You don't start a debate with Google Maps when you want directions."

A step that could change everything
By this point you may be wondering how to bring the 5FortyFive Growth System into your own company. The truth is it is not a giant leap. For you, it is just one step. Small enough to take today, yet powerful enough to change the entire course of your company, your freedom, and your future.

And if you choose not to? Then nothing changes. The same late nights. The same uncertainty. The same questions without clear answers. You already know how that story feels, because you are living it now.

Changemakers

Not everything about growth can be learned from slides or theories. Some things you have to build, test, and feel in real time. That is why we created Systemising University. Not a seminar, but closer to a business hackathon where entrepreneurs step out of the noise and into focus. Four days fast paced. No endless PowerPoints, no passive note taking. Instead, live design, direct challenge, constant feedback that turns ideas into operating rhythm.

Muhammad Ali said, "Champions aren't made in the gym." He meant that real strength is forged in the ring. The same holds for entrepreneurs. Champions are not made in classrooms but by structuring and testing a business under real pressure. By the end, the noise has fallen away. What remains is clarity and a living blueprint you will actually use. Participants arrive for different reasons. Some are chasing profit, others calm. Some prepare their company for an exit, others for a legacy. Whatever the reason, the outcome is the same: a business that finally breathes on its own. If there is a challenge in this, it lies in the simplicity. Making something as complex as universal business growth feel as straightforward as assembling an IKEA cabinet is no small task. Hemingway once wrote that he did not have time to write a short letter. Years of testing and refinement went into making this feel light, while it holds firm when the pressure is on.

Simplified Scaling is not only about structure. It is also about leverage. Today that means using AI in ways most entrepreneurs never manage. Without a system, AI is just another experiment. With 5FortyFive, AI finds its place. Algorithms become assistants, data becomes decisions, and automation becomes freedom.

What we do not offer is fluff. No napkin strategies that vanish by Monday morning. We do growth that sticks. Systems that scale.
A business that breathes.

So, take the step. Join us, and the thousands of entrepreneurs who already have. Build the business you once dreamed of, lighter, stronger, finally free to breathe.

Changemakers

The future rarely knocks twice. Will you stand back politely, or walk through the open door into the future you desire?

The choice is yours. And from Amsterdam Airport, your next chapter is only a flight away.

Every entrepreneur dream of freedom:
A business that runs smoothly, scales with ease, and creates lasting value.

Not just more profit today, but the power to exit tomorrow on your own terms.

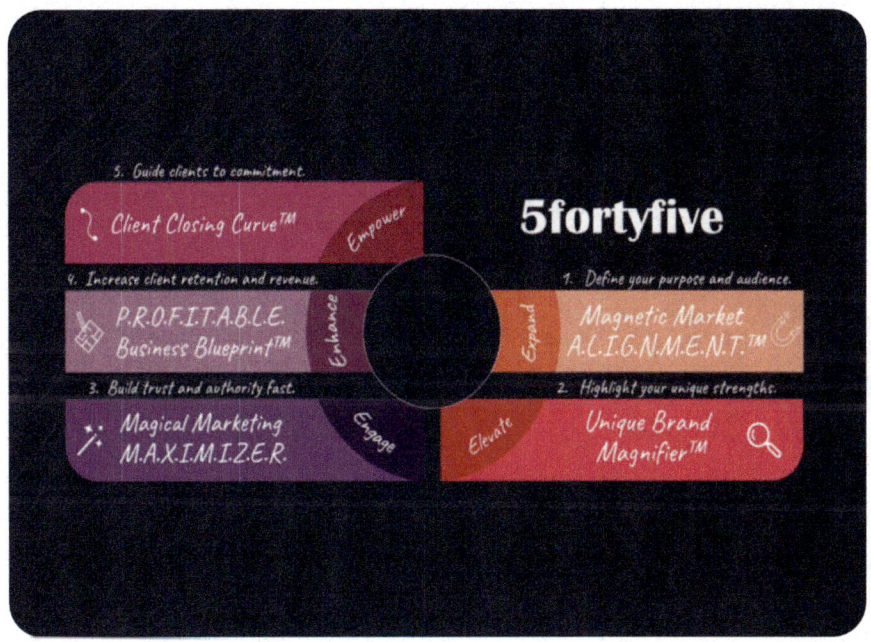

Sander Klos is an entrepreneur, strategist, and bestselling author. He has led companies through growth, scale, and sale. CEO of restaurant booking site IENS, later acquired by TripAdvisor. Part of the executive board that scaled fintech company Back base, now valued at over €2.5 billion. Founder of database specialist KRMG, sold to a London-listed firm.

As the founder of Business Accelerator and creator of the **5FortyFive Growth System,** he has worked with more than two thousand entrepreneurs to systemise their growth, their profits, and above all their peace of mind. His book TurboProfit became a bestseller and is now in its second edition.

He lives in Amsterdam, where the canals have often reminded him, that flow matters more than force. Those who work with him describe him as sharp, practical, and quietly reassuring. His own search for peace of mind has shaped the system he now teaches to others.

Scan the QR code for More!

CHAPTER 17
THE WHOLE SELF ADVANTAGE
FOR NEUROBRILLIANT SUCCESS

NEURODIVERGENT BRILLIANCE IN LIFE AND BUSINESS

> "You've never been 'too much' or 'not enough'! You are exactly who you're supposed to be! And you're exactly what the world needs.
>
> - Rebecca Mitchell Welsh
>
> ..."

Changemakers

Have you ever felt like you were built to think differently? And yet, you keep being handed instructions to life, that don't quite make sense?

And have you ever wondered how life and business might change if you finally had the secret manual in your hands – the one written for your exceptionally unique brain?

If so, you're not alone.

For so many ADHD, AuDHD, ASD, Dyslexic and Gifted entrepreneurs, professionals, and creative thinkers, the experience is the same, trying to succeed by following a manual that was never written with their unique brains in mind. It's following a neurotypical narrative, which doesn't include sidenotes or specific chapters for neurodivergent differences. It's no wonder everything can feel clunky, exhausting, or even impossible.

Maybe your brain feels like a browser with 274 tabs open – three of them playing audio, one about quantum physics, one with the latest health trend to come back to later... and another still holding a shopping cart from 2021. And the tab with your actual to-do list? Missing in action!

Or perhaps you sit down at your desk to work, ready to tackle something important... and somehow find yourself alphabetising your spice rack instead. That one urgent email still glares at you from the corner of your mind, but at least now you know exactly where the cumin lives.

Potentially it's not tasks but people. Getting out the magnifying glass and replaying every interaction like a detective: "Was I too blunt? Too much? Did I overshare again?" Picking up on feelings and vibes in a room is a skill like Detective Columbo, yet the overcompensating to lift everyone for peace is exhausting! Networking events feel like social escape rooms, and success looks reserved for super confident extroverts and polished social media influencers.

Changemakers

Possibly it's relationships. Misreading tone, forgetting birthdays, and needing 36 hours of solo recovery after one corporate meeting, kids' birthday party or a planned group dinner. It's either sending three paragraph texts at 3am or ghosting people for weeks. There is no middle ground. And then comes the guilt: I'm a bad friend.
A bad partner. A bad parent.

And let's not forget health. You know self-care matters - perhaps you've pinned 43 routines to follow, downloaded 5 meditation apps, and bought a yoga mat that now doubles as a laundry display stand. But when your nervous system is on high alert and your business and family life is pulling you in different directions, self-care becomes just another thing to fail at. Some weeks it's spirulina smoothies, journaling at dawn, and cold-water plunges. Other weeks? Toast for three meals and a cry in your dressing gown. There is no in-between.

What Does This Lead To?

- Unfinished projects.
- Missed opportunities.
- Businesses that lurch forward in chaotic bursts of brilliance… followed by mysterious silence.
- A constant background hum of guilt, shame, and imposter syndrome whispering, "Everyone else has their life together. Why can't you just do the thing?"

And that whisper? It grows louder.

But What If It Could Be Different?

Now imagine something else.

Picture your mind as a calm, creative studio - not a hurricane of papers, coffee cups and confetti. Ideas flow in, get captured, acted on, and completed. You know what matters today, not everything ever.

Decisions feel clearer. Your day has rhythm. Your brain isn't yelling "Do all the things!" anymore - it's saying, "We've got this."

Imagine starting tasks without the mythical beast of "Later" lurking over your shoulder. You break things down instinctively. They feel they will fit and support you! No more frantic all-nighters or inbox anxiety - just aligned action, at your pace, fuelled by clarity.

Picture yourself walking into a room - real or virtual - where you don't need to rehearse every word or decode every emoji. You feel seen, understood, not too much, not, not enough. You've found your people. You belong.

Envisage relationships that nourish you instead of draining you. Family dynamics that feel easier. Friendships where you don't need to shrink or over-give to be accepted. Conversations that don't end with you second-guessing yourself into the ground.

And finally, imagine health that isn't an afterthought. Rest isn't laziness, it's strategy. You wake with more energy, your nervous system isn't permanently in fight-or-flight, and you finally feel like you're not running on fumes. Your body is nourished and it's working for you!

So How Do You Get There?

I believe the answer lies in a Whole Self Strategy.

Because for neurodivergent people, success isn't just about mindset hacks, time-blocking, or working harder. It's about learning to work with your Brain, honour your Body, align your Business, and nurture your Bonds - instead of cutting parts of yourself off just to survive the day.

Changemakers

Taking a 'Whole Self' approach, enables all areas in life to complement each other in balance, and to thrive!

This is the work I do.

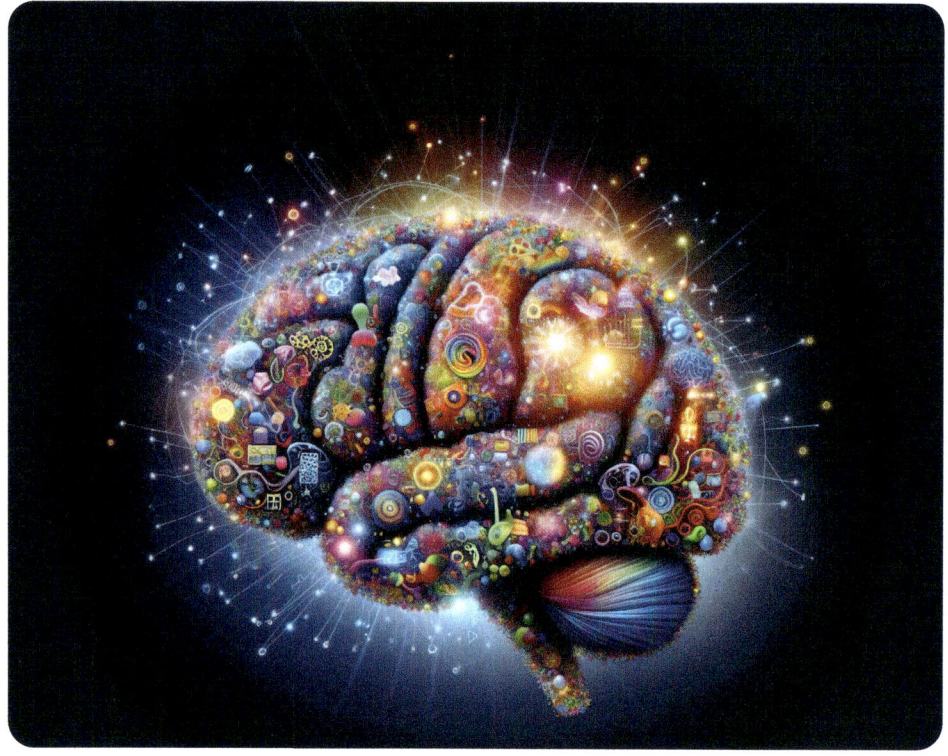

My own ADHD diagnosis arrived at age 42! And just like divorce... it's not an easy emotional road after the official stamp!

Navigating the "lost years", is a by-product of diagnosis - that's the grieving part - the realisation that I wasn't 'broken', and ruminating over the missed opportunities of years gone by and... 'what if' I had been diagnosed earlier...

I have vivid memories of little Rebecca ("Rebecca the Wrecker" no less, a whirlwind with an equally appropriate nickname as a toddler and young child), full of energy cartwheeling everywhere; growing up saying and doing the wrong things all the time it appeared, missing social cues with friends, learning to copy their behaviours and the start of people - pleasing; plus hyper focusing on collecting things, creative art projects and 'super stuff' - Dinosaurs, story writing and my football obsession are stand outs!

Teenage Rebecca was renowned for being late for school, forgetting homework and studying for exams at the last moment. Teachers said they were surprised I got the grades I did, and I felt shame for doing well. In the background, my sports obsession continued on the court and off, writing short stories evolved, and my own home projects became more important than homework of course!

University Rebecca managed to get a Journalism Degree, with hyper focus on certain modules and projects, but an avoidance for others. Everything was to deadline (in the days of lining up in the hallway at the Submissions Office at 3pm on a Friday...). And yet I had a high-achieving side quest as the enthusiastic, networking Sports Editor! Had all the time in the world for that...

Navigating my working life, I can see where there were struggles with day-to-day tasks and time management, yet as a creative and innovative person, this was superseded by areas where I exceeded targets, increased productivity and revenue, and was highly successful. Additionally, on the side quest subject, set up an online retail business, volunteered on the Local Authority Sports Council and joined a national 'Think Tank', to make positive political change...

Looking back I can see how I was always a very creative person, and I had a firm focus to make a difference! Did you know that neurodiverse people have a strong sense of justice? I was always doing something to support positive change, and yet I always felt it wasn't good enough. I wasn't good enough.

And then my relationships! My four incredible children! And then recovering from a narcissistic abusive marriage...

Changemakers

How did I end up here? I did a lot of work around this! I furiously researched, investigated and wrote, becoming a Narcissist Abuse Specialist and trained as a Trauma Coach. This led to becoming a number 1 Best Selling Author and developing "the Wellness Steps", a programme to support women recovering from trauma.

Following my ADHD diagnosis, I continued to research and write about neurodivergent people finding themselves in narcissistic and abusive relationships.

I became a Number 1 Bestseller again, in fiction this time!
I never gave up on my love of writing stories!

My side projects made sense, as I started to make positive change, volunteering locally, getting more girls into football, and growing our local Girls Football Club to over 100 members. As a coach, I gained my UEFA C License, Talent ID License and SFA Coach Educator Award, as well as joining the Professional Speakers Academy and training as an ACE Mentor. I found my voice! And I continued to serve and support others to make positive change!

And bit by bit, I started seeing the transformation of implementing changes into my life and my routine, with techniques gathered from all over, and this flourished.

This is the system I've built from combining research with lived experience. Bringing best practice together from training and coaching for over twenty years, and seeing how volunteering is a force for neurodiverse people! It is called:

The NeuroBrilliant Blueprint ™

This is a Whole Self Strategy, working with neurodivergent strengths, to overcome challenges, which enables living a quality and successful life, balancing all areas! The NeuroBrilliant Blueprint focuses on five distinct and essential areas that come together to provide the Whole Self Advantage!

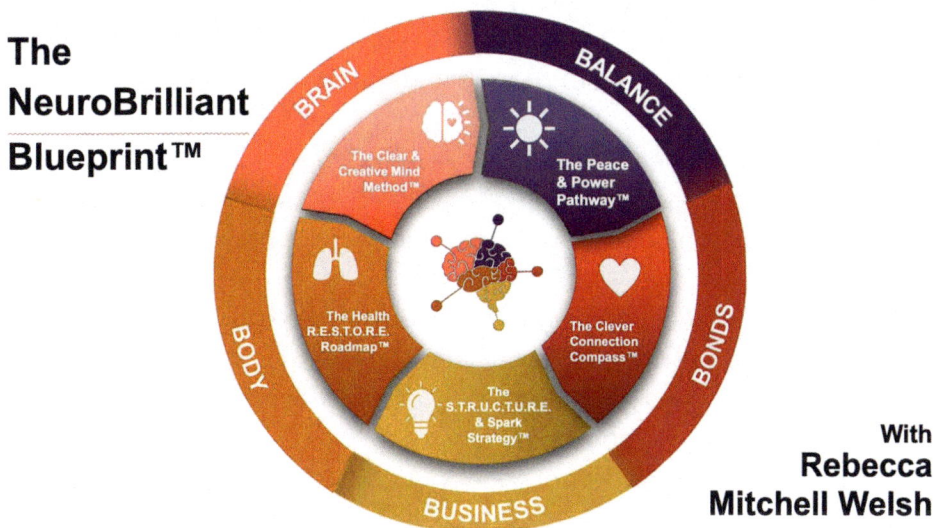

With
Rebecca Mitchell Welsh

1. BRAIN: The Clear & Creative Mind Method™
Understanding a mind alive with ideas, creativity and unique strengths

The incredible ADHD, AuDHD, ASD, Dyslexic and Gifted Brain is different indeed, and has many qualities, and therefore it is essential to understand how to manifest this difference for a better quality of life!

A problem I see is that some neurodiverse people enthusiastically want to make changes in their lives and have the best intentions – plus a nice, new, shiny notebook to get started – and yet there's no understanding of how their brain works. And this means when it comes to sticking to routines, and the new way of doing things, it all breaks down because there is no understanding, the 'Why?' and 'How?'. This can lead to the negative self-talk and the downward shame spiral!

I look at it like this, it's like a separate operating system, kind of like how Android is to Apple, and you've been given the instruction manual to the wrong one!

I believe it is essential to understand the differences and how neuroBrilliant brains work the way they do. Can you imagine the advantages when you start working with your creative brain, rather than using an operating system or manual that is not fit for purpose?

That is one area of the Clear & Creative Mind Method, and within the Five Steps here - Perceive, Process, Prioritise, Personalise and Pause - there is focus on self-talk, mindset, beliefs and values, and reframing.

Did you know that individuals with ADHD receive an estimated 20,000 more negative comments by the age of 10 than their neurotypical peers? Imagine the weight of that. It's probably fair to say that all neurodivergent people have experienced this. It's no wonder so many have grown up with an internal critic shouting louder than their natural creative voice.

The problem with this is that significant negative comments while growing up amounts to low self-esteem, shame, anxiety and a feeling of being 'different' or 'not fitting in' in adulthood.

There is also a heightened sensitivity to criticism and is known as 'Rejection Sensitive Dysphoria' (RSD), where individuals feel pain and overwhelming negative emotions in response to perceived rejection.

But here's the truth! Your brain isn't broken. It's brilliantly wired and has been using a neurotypical manual instead of enabling it to shine in its bright way! What needs shifting isn't your worth, you've always been enough just as you are, it's re-framing your thinking!

Cognitive reframing has been shown to reduce rumination and strengthen problem-solving (Beck, 2011), and it is a distinctive part of my Clear & Creative Mind Method. ™

Personally, I carried that inner critic with me for years. Every time I achieved something, it whispered, "Not enough. Not good enough." The shift came when I learned to pause and reframe. Instead of asking, "Why can't I do this?" I started asking, "What do I need in order to do this my way?" That single shift transformed my outlook, and my output.

Changing the frame changes the story. And when you change the story, you change the outcome.

2. BODY: The Health R.E.S.T.O.R.E. Roadmap™
Awakening energy and restoring health through nourishment, movement and nervous system care

Through media and advertising, we're told to push harder, fuel ourselves on easy processed foods and caffeine, spend money on the latest health gadgets and fads, and then pat ourselves on the back that we're now officially healthy!

But the reality is, it's a sticky plaster. Ignoring your body isn't resilience. It's sabotage. It's like expecting your phone to run all day on 1% battery, eventually, the screen goes black.

Burnout creeps in quietly. It can start with heavy eyelids and growing brain fog. Then it's the irritability, the sugar cravings, the late-night scrolling because your nervous system won't switch off. And yet it seems the world claps you on the back for "pushing through", right up until your system gives way. Have you heard of Autism or ADHD Burnout - and try AuDHD Burnout on for size too?

I see energy as the foundation of sustainable success. I see that neuroBrilliant people have an abundance of energy for a reason. Without it, creativity and clarity don't stand a chance!

Changemakers

One study found that even a single night of poor sleep can reduce working memory performance by up to 40% (Lim & Dinges, 2010). And notoriously, neurodiverse brains are not the best at getting a good night's sleep as it is - the internal playlist starts and the inner voice asking whether the door is locked, replaying a conversation from ten years ago and wondering what penguins would look like if they wore hats...

Understanding these unique challenges, I created the Health RESTORE Roadmap to ensure the body is energised, to support everyday life and to resist burnout.

You see, I believe that neuroBrillant people were born with incredible energy, more than average people, and thrive through movement! We're active in our minds, with creative thoughts running continuously like a waterfall, and then there's the movement in our body with fidgeting and stimming, let alone sports and exercise! Ensuring motion is part of the ADHD, AuDHD, ASD, Dyslexic and Giftedness routine is key to vitality!

Nothing changes without movement, after all!

The Health RESTORE Roadmap moves forward with Nutrition, Hydration Gut Health and the Gut-Brain Connection, Hormone Changes awareness, the Nervous System and Vagus Nerve understanding and exercises, as well as Movement and Meditation.

Why is this important? Well, there's so much to consider in the body! And therefore getting a firm grasp of neurodiverse differences and effects enables positive change and rapid results in productivity!

This is what happened to Rachel, an entrepreneur with ADHD and Dyslexia. When I met Rachel, she had been cycling through late-night laptop marathons and burnout crashes. She joked living on "coffee, crisps, and chaos." But armed with new knowledge from the Health RESTORE Roadmap, she was able to implement effective routines because this made sense to her specific challenges, and leaned into her strengths.

A reluctant cook yet Rachel found a hyper focus! Exploring the recommended herbs and spices, and understanding their benefits, was a key element of finding tastes she liked, replacing artificial flavourings, and as a result boosted her health and productivity. And rapidly, she was calmer and more focused, and laughs that her the biggest win wasn't her productivity, it was that people stopped saying, "You look tired."

Because here's the thing, heading for burnout isn't a badge of honour. It's a warning. And when understanding neurodiverse differences underpins action, and you restore your body, you don't just get through the day. You get to live it.

3. BUSINESS: The S.T.R.U.C.T.U.R.E. & Spark Strategy™
Aligning personal strengths to build sustainable systems and success

It is in plain sight, rigid planners and colour-coded spreadsheets are often sold as "the fix" with countless Apps, Processes and Platforms out there promising the magical solution! But for many of us, they collapse within a week. It's like trying to wear a smaller-sized shoe, ok to wear for a short while as a quick fix, to hobble along, but very sore indeed and not suitable for the long run.

However, systems should serve you, not shackle you. Flexible, visual systems harness creativity instead of crushing it. Research shows that externalising tasks visually improves engagement and completion for ADHD brains (Clear, 2018). Therefore, one of the key areas in The STRUCTURE and Spark Strategy, is setting up business and professional solutions that fit the neuroBrilliant brain - and work.

Changemakers

As a Business Strategist, I analysed how to support neurodiverse brains in business and I pulled the key areas for success into nine skills to master: Simplify, Time, Rebuild, Understand, Clarify, Tidy, Use Techniques, Reflect, Execute.

These became the important ingredients for succeeding!

You see, neurodiverse people can struggle with organisation and expectations, drowning in sticky notes and piled up papers on desks, trying to stay updated using several organisation Apps, and spreadsheets open over copious desktop tabs.

Yet some of the most incredible change makers are neurodiverse! Albert Einstein, Temple Grandin, Richard Branson and Greta Thurberg are all recognised for the poweful impact they've made in their fields. They established structures to work with their unique brains, enabling their passions, creations and ideas to come to life and make positive change!

Focusing on the skill from Use Techniques, in the STRUCTURE & Spark Strategy, it's about simplifying and finding that one way to stay on top and in control, that works for your brain.

Far too often I've seen organising strategies start and fizzle out because they are not working for the neuroBrilliant mind. Through a range of Techniques, it's about finding the right one that fits you.

It's essentially a tailored approach in Business, and not a one size fits all policy. From working personally with neuroBrilliant minds, structures that work for one, won't work with another client – and vice versa! Just like all neurodiverse change makers! Therefore it's about finding your own strengths, your own personality, your own systems that will work for you.

That's the power of structure. Not rigidity. Not restriction. But systems that flex with you and your neuroBrilliant mind, and spark your creativity and progress.

4. BONDS: The Clever Connection Compass™
Creating Connections shaped by compassion, integrity and belonging

'Masking' can feel like the safest way to belong, hiding quirks or struggles so people won't judge. For neurodivergent individuals, this started a long time ago, to fit in, and be liked. And sometimes it is hard to see where the mask stops, and the true self starts...

But masking is like wearing a big fancy-dress costume all day. You might get through the party, but it gets heavy and exhausting!

Research shows masking is strongly linked to anxiety, depression, and burnout (Hull, Petrides, & Mandy, 2017). Throw in RSD and it can be overwhelming in social situations, friendship groups, work settings, business meetings, family gatherings...

Ultimately though, belonging doesn't come from performance. It comes from honesty and care. It is essential to be surrounded by people who understand you, for being you, as you are incredible as you are, with no mask!

That's why the Clever Connection Compass became so important! And using a five-step process: Connect, Clear, Create, Community and Centre, enables connection with self, others, nature and source.

Connection is essential to human existence – even though neuroBrilliant people can find this really tough to navigate! Although it can feel like two opposing magnets trying to fit together, connection is important in our family lives and professional lives!

But did you know that one of the strongest connections are the bonds we form with the natural world? Research shows that when we give our brains and bodies space to breathe among trees, water, sky or even a patch of green, something shifts – our attention sharpens, the invisible pressure under our skin eases, and life feels more meaningful (Jimenez et al., 2021).

Changemakers

Furthermore, a 2024 study found that neurodiverse participants experienced improved sensory-motor regulation, emotional resilience and a greater sense of inclusion when immersed in nature-responsive environments (Finnigan et al., 2024).

So stepping outside the meeting room, or pausing mid-scroll to feel the wind, or sitting quietly beneath a tree, you're not just taking a break, you're reinforcing a bond. You're giving your system the nourishment it needs to think, create and connect in a whole new way.

The Clever Connection Compass is designed specifically for neurodiverse individuals to feel connection. To build bonds that last. That are deserved of you! And supported by the right human connection! Finding your tribe is life-changing!

5. BALANCE: The Peace & Power Pathway™
Living with peace, purpose and power every day

Some people believe balance means splitting equal time between every role: business owner, parent, partner, friend. But that's like trying to keep a dozen plates spinning at once. Exhausting. Destined to shatter.

The truth? Balance isn't equal time. Balance is integration. Research has shown that integration across life areas or domains offers a richer and more health-promoting perspective and helps future outcomes, rather than rigid management approaches (Kerksieck et al, 2024). This is very helpful for anyone who experiences the symptoms of 'time blindness'.

So, balance isn't plate-spinning at all. It's conducting an orchestra. Not every instrument requires equal volume all the time, you bring different sections forward depending on the music.

In the Peace & Power Pathway, there are five areas to support living in Balance. These are Awareness, Anchor, Align, Adjust and Advance.

All parts here are important, and focusing specifically on the first skill, Awareness, is about recognising "triggers". These are indicators specific to an individual, showing a slight decline, or the start of losing balance, and can be noted across business or personal life. Examples here are: noticing that you are ordering take away food more often, or pouring another glass of wine each night (or perhaps finishing the bottle...) or maybe starting to skip showers, or increasingly staying at home to be alone, or putting off replying to business emails regularly, or delaying the kids' bedtime story ritual more...and more...

When these triggers are caught early, and the root cause is addressed, everything stays in balance, alleviating the threat of the Downward Spiral, to remain in a positive and powerful state!

This Awareness method was used by Leila, a Business owner with AuDHD, who felt constantly torn between her business and family. Leila identified that she had invented a new 'doom scrolling' safety mechanism, which took her away from both! In fact, it had started to play out like an addiction, and all areas in her life were suffering, as she procrastinated and avoided the key problems.

By understanding her trigger, she was able to use the skills from the Peace & Power Pathway to reroute her energy. To integrate in her life, rather than feel pressure of letting everyone down. Laila was elated and energised and said that this had allowed her to intertwine both her work and home life, enabling her business to grow, and she became more present with her children.

Integration isn't about balance as in scales. It's about balance as in rhythm. And when your life finds its rhythm, everything changes.

Changemakers

The Ripple Effect

These Five Pillars of The NeuroBrilliant Blueprint are not abstract. They are lived, proven, and powerful. They support moving from browser-tab chaos and burnout spirals to clarity, energy, and impact. Moving on from surviving by someone else's manual - to thriving by writing your own.

And the ripple effect doesn't stop with you. I've seen entrepreneurs escape burnout and grow thriving businesses. Professionals silence their inner critic and step into leadership. Creatives complete pieces of work that changes lives!

When one person rewrites their manual, it doesn't just change their life. It transforms families. Teams. Communities.

It simply starts by using neurodivergent energy and movement, in the right places.

Why Now Is the Time to Act

NeuroBrilliant people have survived years of doing things the hard way, following a map that wasn't written in the right language, being misunderstood and mistreated as a result. And here's the truth, waiting doesn't make change easier. It makes the cost higher.

Women with ADHD are three times more likely to experience anxiety and depression (ADDitude, 2023). Up to 79% of autistic adults report autistic burnout, with women particularly vulnerable due to masking and late diagnosis (Raymaker et al., 2020).

This isn't just stress. It's survival mode. And survival isn't enough for the change-makers the world needs!

Now is the moment to move.
Now is the moment to choose yourself.
Now is the moment to write a new manual, one that finally works for you!

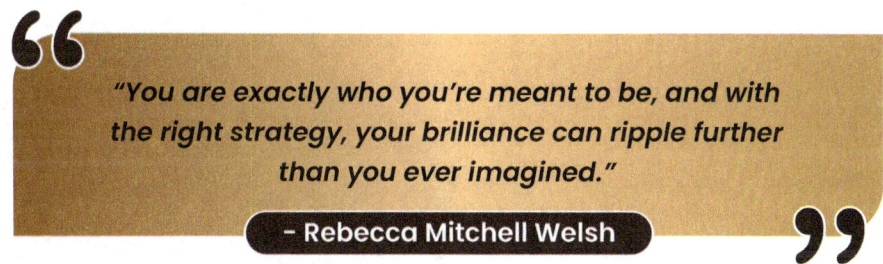

"You are exactly who you're meant to be, and with the right strategy, your brilliance can ripple further than you ever imagined."

— Rebecca Mitchell Welsh

Brain   Body   Business   Bonds   Balance

REBECCA MITCHELL WELSH

Rebecca is a Wellness and Business Strategist, actively blending her expertise as a number one best-selling author, professional speaker, ACE Mentor and licensed coach to create positive change.

With a specialisation in ADHD, AuDHD, ASD, Dyslexia and Giftedness, she provides tailored strategies that empower neurodiverse entrepreneurs, professionals and creative thinkers to unravel their unique obstacles and leverage their strengths for unparalleled success in professional and personal life.

Her trauma-informed approach and expertise in navigating narcissistic abuse ensure that clients are equipped to overcome personal hurdles and achieve their goals confidently and compassionately.

Rebecca lives on the west coast of Scotland, overlooking the Isle of Arran, and is a proud mum to four actively wonderful children. An advocate for volunteering for lasting impact, Rebecca coaches football locally as a qualified UEFA C Licensed Coach and Talent ID Scout.

Scan the QR code for More!

CONCLUSION

CONCLUSION

The Changemakers:
Entrepreneurs With a Mission, Voices With a Message

As we close this powerful anthology, one truth echoes through every page: **real change begins with one voice, but it never ends there.**

Each of the 17 changemakers you've met in this book began with a spark - a burden, a conviction, or a call for change that refused to be silenced. They faced resistance, fear, and failure, yet they rose and took action - not because the path was easy, but because their purpose was non-negotiable. In choosing to show up, speak up, and stand out, they proved that purpose-driven entrepreneurship is not about self-promotion - it's about transformation.

The Professional Speakers Academy has not merely shaped speakers; it has birthed leaders, reformers, and trailblazers who carry messages that awaken hearts and shift nations. These stories are living proof that when you align your voice with your mission, you create more than success you create significance.

But now, the baton passes to you.

Yes - you, the reader who felt that pull while turning these pages. You who have a message stirring in your spirit, an idea waiting for breath, a dream asking for discipline. This book was never meant to end with applause for others - it was written to activate the changemaker within you.

Because the world doesn't need more noise; it needs more truth.
It doesn't need more competition; it needs more conviction.
It doesn't need more followers; it needs more leaders who serve.
So, take what you've gleaned, guard it, grow it, and go do something with it. Start that business. Share that story. Step onto that stage.

Changemakers

Lead that movement. Become the ripple that someone else's breakthrough depends on. Remember this: you were never called to blend in; you were created to break through and stand out. The changemakers you've read about didn't wait for permission - they answered purpose's call. And now, it's your turn to rise, speak, and serve with the power and authenticity that only you can bring.

Because when one voice awakens, another finds its courage.

And when enough voices rise together - the world shifts.

The Changemakers aren't just in this book. They're in every one of us who dares to believe that our message matters.

Now go.

Be the change.

Your ripple starts here.

Seventeen voices. Seventeen journeys. Seventeen lives that dared to break the mold and say, "I will not settle for ordinary when I am called to extraordinary."

"The world doesn't shift when you dream — it shifts when you decide. Rise, act, and let your life become the evidence that change is possible."

Printed in Dunstable, United Kingdom